A TRANSFORMATIONAL GRAMMAR OF RUSSIAN ADJECTIVES

by

LEONARD HARVEY BABBY

Cornell University

1975

MOUTON

THE HAGUE · PARIS

LIBRARY OF CONGRESS CATALOG CARD NUMBER: 73-83929

Printed in The Netherlands by Mouton & Co., Printers, The Hague

ACKNOWLEDGMENT

I wish to thank Horace G. Lunt, who introduced me to Slavic linguistics, and Roman Jakobson, who inspired me to work in general as well as Slavic linguistics.

I would also like to thank Catherine Chvany, Richard Brecht, Wayles Browne, Robert Rothstein, Morris Halle, and John Bowers, whose work and advice on the application of the theory of transformational grammar to the Slavic languages has been invaluable.

Finally, I would like to express my gratitude to Henning Andersen, Charles Townsend, Omry Ronen, and Richard Leed for their advice and moral support. I am particularly grateful to my parents, Benjamin and Gertrude Babby, and to Margaret Troupin for their help and encouragement.

TABLE OF CONTENTS

INTRODUCTION

VERBAL PARTS OF SPEECH IN RUSSIAN

0.1 *A Transformational Grammar of Russian Adjectives* is primarily a practical application of the theory of transformational grammar to several unsolved problems of Russian syntax. At the center of this investigation is the syntactic relation between the long form (LF) and short form (SF) of adjectives and participles in modern literary Russian. Chapters 1 through 3 are devoted to demonstrating that the LF and SF are surface structure categories (or derived "parts of speech"): they both derive from the same deep structure category V (verbal).[1] In other words, the base phrase-structure rules do not generate LF or SF. It is shown that V, which is introduced by an expansion of VP (verb phrase) by the phrase-structure rules, will emerge from the transformational component as a SF if it receives the features of gender, number, and person by an agreement transformation. The category V will emerge in the surface structure as a LF if, in addition to these agreement features, it receives a CASE feature. To put it in slightly different terms, the LF is a SF that has acquired a case feature by virtue of its transformational introduction into the constituency of a NP (noun phrase). It must be stressed that "LF" and "SF" are abbreviations used in this study: they stand for "long form" and "short form", respectively, and are never employed as symbols in deep or surface phrase markers (cf. (3.10): the short form *pravy* 'right' is at no point in its derivation dominated by the lexical node "SF").

The manner adverb in *-o* (*gromko* 'loudly') is also analyzed in terms of acquisition (or non-acquisition) of syntactic features. Thus the surface structure opposition LF:SF:adverb in *-o* (*gromkaja*:*gromka*:*gromko*) is explained in terms of a single underlying category V and the features this V acquires in the transformational component.

[1] What is traditionally called "adjective" is V with the feature [+adj], and what is traditionally called "verb" is V with the feature [—adj]. For the purposes of the Introduction, we will simply use V for both "subcategories" with the understanding that in a more explicit discussion the feature [adj] must be specified.

The transformational analysis outlined above also provides an explanation for the following phenomena: the LF appears to function as the active participle of the SF (cf. §2.12): the passive participle has both a LF and a SF, i.e. behaves syntactically just like an adjective, while the active participle has only a LF; prenominal adjectives and participles in modern Russian must be in the LF; when the subject *vy* 'you (polite)' refers to one person, the predicate LF must be in the singular, and the SF must be in the plural (cf. §4.5.4).

The transformational analysis of adjectives and participles offered here necessitates the detailed discussion of a number of basic syntactic phenomena. Among them are: the passive transformation; Relative Clause Reduction and the formation of active participles; case and agreement in a transformational grammar of Russian; the deep and surface structure of the "copula" *byt'* 'to be'; infinitive formation; the "obligatory" predicate instrumental (§3.5.1); and *dalek (–a, –o)* 'far' and *daleko* 'far' in the predicate (§3.3.3). Chapter 4 deals with the classic problem of the semantic distinction between the LF and SF in the predicate.

0.2 *A Transformational Grammar of Russian Adjectives* was my doctoral dissertation (Harvard University), and was completed in January 1971, when I was an assistant professor at Princeton University. It is based primarily on the "Aspects Model" (cf. Chomsky, 1965) and the courses on transformational grammar that I attended at MIT (M. Halle and J. Ross) and Harvard (G. Lakoff). In recent years there have been significant changes in transformational theory (cf. J. Bowers, to appear, Chapter 1, for a summary), yet I have decided not to make major revisions in the main text. This would involve a long delay in the book's appearance and, more importantly, would obscure the fact that my major conclusions about the syntax of Russian adjectives have not been essentially affected by recent theoretical changes.

Implicit in my analysis of the LF and SF of adjectives and participles is a theory of "parts of speech in a transformational grammar". For the convenience of the reader, these ideas are made explicit below in §0.3. This discussion involves both new material (especially gerunds) and a considerable alteration of my original theory of parts of speech; it is based on the "Extended Aspects Model" (cf. Bowers, to appear). Paragraph 0.3 also contains two more arguments demonstrating that the LF is a deeper SF that has received a case feature, and thus also serves to strengthen our main hypothesis about the syntactic relation between the LF and SF in modern Russian.

0.3 PARTS OF SPEECH IN A TRANSFORMATIONAL GRAMMAR OF RUSSIAN

0.3.1 The following paragraphs (§§0.3.1 to 0.3.1.3) contain a summary of the theory of parts of speech implicit in *A Transformational Grammar of Russian Adjectives.*

The base phrase-structure rules introduce DEEP STRUCTURE CATEGORIES: V (verbal, i.e. adjective and verb), N (noun), P (preposition), etc....

0.3.1.1 In Russian, a deep structure category seldom appears in the surface structure unaltered (P is the notable exception). For instance, V will appear in the surface structure as either a LF , SF, or manner adverb in *–o* (or as a finite verb, active participle, infinitive, or gerund) depending on the features it has acquired as a result of the operation of the transformational rules. Accordingly, LF, SF, active participle, etc., are all derived, or surface structure categories (parts of speech), since they do not exist at the level of deep structure.[2] A deep structure category plus its syntactic features are "spelled out" as LF, SF, infinitive, etc., by the morphophonemic rules.[3]

0.3.1.2 It follows therefore that derived parts of speech are not dominated by nodes labelled "active participle", "LF", "infinitive", etc. They are surface structure notions and are uniquely definable in terms of a deep structure category plus the features it has acquired (cf. §0.1).

0.3.1.3 A derived part of speech should not be associated with any particular transformational rule since there are no transformations specialized for the sole purpose of deriving surface structure categories from deep structure categories. For instance, there is no need for an "active participle transformation" in Russian. Active participles are most often derived from a deep V as the result of the Relative Clause Reduction transformation (§2.12), but they are also derived as a result of Subject Raising (cf. §3.4.1);[4] both of these rules have independent motivation in the syntax of Russian, and neither can be called the "active participle rule". In other words, derived parts of speech cannot be associated with a particular transformational rule because: (a) a given surface structure category can

[2] It is therefore incorrect to claim that the base phrase-structure rules are the sole determiner of "part of speech".

[3] The morphophonemic rules thus give phonological shape to a lexical item and its features, both deep and acquired, in the final derived phrase marker. For example, these rules will "spell out" *čitala* f.sg. past 'read' from the deep structure [*čitaj*-]$_V$ plus the features of singular, feminine, and past.

[4] In the following example, the first active participle (*sidjaščaja* 'sitting') is the result of relative clause reduction, while the second one (*zaxvativšej* 'seized') is derived by Subject Raising (cf. § 3.4.1): *Ženščina, sidjaščaja naprotiv menja, kažetsja mne nezakonno zaxvativšej čužoe mesto* (lit.) 'The woman sitting opposite me seems to me illegally [having] seized another's place'.

be derived from a deep category by more than one rule (e.g. the active participle); (b) a given transformational rule may be involved in the derivation of more than one derived part of speech (e.g. Equi-NP Deletion results in either a gerund or an infinitive (§3.4.0). It might thus be said that derived parts of speech are a by-product of the transformational component. It must also be pointed out that a given surface structure category is always derived from a particular deep structure category; it can never have two deep structure sources.

0.3.2 THE REVISED THEORY

In the theory of parts of speech employed in *A Transformational Grammar of Russian Adjectives* (outlined above), it was assumed that a derived part of speech could be uniquely defined in terms of a deep structure category (V) plus the features it picked up in the transformational component. My recent work on Russian syntax (especially the syntax of gerunds) has made it appear quite certain that this theory is not able to account for all the derived verbal categories in modern Russian and, therefore, that it must be reformulated. In light of my recent work it now seems far more likely that a derived part of speech can be uniquely defined only in terms of a deep structure category (V) plus acquired features IN A PARTICULAR DERIVED SURFACE STRUCTURE PHRASE MARKER CONFIGURATION (notice then that this requires that the morphophonemic rules be able to take the constituent structure of the final derived phrase marker into account). Below it will be argued that the surface structure phrase marker CONFIGURATION is more important than FEATURES in determining a derived part of speech.

0.3.2.1 According to the revised definition of derived parts of speech just suggested, a FINITE VERB will result when a deep structure V (having acquired the features of gender, number, and person) appears in the following surface structure phrase marker configuration: $[\ldots[\ldots V\ldots]_{VP}\ldots]_{S}$.

The grammar of Russian will produce an ACTIVE PARTICIPLE whenever a deep structure V, having acquired the features of Subject-verb Agreement, is transformationally introduced into a NP, where it receives a case feature (cf. §0.3.1.3 and §2.12).[5] Accordingly, an active participle

[5] This last fact explains why active participles in modern Russian never have SF's: they are by definition always NP constituents and thus always have a case feature (recall that a LF is a SF with a case feature; recall also that PASSIVE participles have both a LF and SF (cf. §3.3.4)).

Notice also that this derivation automatically explains why active participles in modern literary Russian can never function as the predicate of the highest or "root" sentence: active participles are the main V's of reduced sentences, and, in order for the V to enter NP constituency when its S is reduced, THIS S MUST BE EMBEDDED. This same

will appear in Russian whenever the surface structure contains the derived configuration $[\ldots[\ldots[\ldots V\ldots]_{VP}\ldots]_{NP}\ldots]_S$.

The surface structure of Russian will contain a gerund (*deepričastie*) whenever a deep structure V is transformationally introduced into the constituency of an AP (adverbial phrase); a gerund phrase (*deepričastnyj oborot*) is therefore simply an entire VP embedded in an AP (in a similar manner, an active participle phrase is an entire VP embedded in an NP). A gerund in Russian must therefore be associated with the derived configuration $[\ldots[\ldots[\ldots V\ldots]_{VP}\ldots]_{AP}\ldots]_S$.[6]

---

type of argumentation can be employed to explain why GERUNDS can never be the predicate of the "main" sentence in literary Russian. The situation with infinitives, however, is far from clear, since it appears from sentences like the following that, at least superfically, infinitives can function as the main verb of root sentences:

Poslat' vaše pis'mo aviapočtoj?
(to send your letter by air)
'Shall I send your letter by air?'

[6] There are a great many unanswered questions about the syntactic derivation of gerunds. Probably the most crucial one is: does the gerund phrase ($[VP]_{AP}$) derive from a deeper sentence ($[S]_{AP}$) which is reduced by Equi-NP Deletion (and Complementizer deletion), or are gerund phrases derived from a deep structure $[VP]_{AP}$?

The complexity of accounting for gerunds in Russian can be further illustrated by the following sentences (the comma in these examples indicates a pause):

(a) *Utomlennaja, devuška poterjala interes k sudu.*
(exhausted girl lost interest in trial)
'Exhausted, the girl lost interest in the trial.'

(b) *Utomlennaja devuška poterjala interes k sudu.*
(exhausted girl lost interest in trial)
'The exhausted girl lost interest in the trial

Notice that the LF *utomlennaja* f.sg.nom. 'exhausted' has a different function in (a) and (b). In (a) it has the same function as the ADVERBIAL CLAUSE in (c); in (b) it has the same function as the RELATIVE CLAUSE in (d).

(c) *Devuška poterjala interes k sudu potomu, čto ona byla utomlena.*
(girl lost interest in trial because she was exhausted)
'The girl lost interest in the trial because she was exhausted.'

(d) *Devuška, kotoraja byla utomlena , poterjala interes k sudu.*
(girl who was exhausted lost interest in trial)
'The girl who was exhausted lost interest in the trial.'

Sentences (a) through (d) thus suggest that the LF in (b) has the same derivation as active participles (cf. (f)), and the LF in (a) has the same derivation as gerunds (cf. (e)) (recall that one source of the active participle is a deeper relative clause, and that the gerund derives from a deeper AP).

(e) *Utomivšis', devuška poterjala interes k sudu.*
(exhausted girl lost interest in trial)
'Exhausted, the girl lost interest in the trial.'

(f) *Utomivšajasja devuška poterjala interes k sudu.*
(exhausted girl lost interest in trial)
'The exhausted girl lost interest in the trial.'

(g) **Utomivšajasja, devuška poterjala interes k sudu.*

Utomivšis' is the gerund of *utomit'(sja)* 'to get exhausted'; *utomivšajasja* f sg nom. is its active participle. (e) and (f) derive from the deep structures underlying (h) and (i), respectively.

(h) *Devuška poterjala interes k sudu potomu, čto ona utomilas'.*
(girl lost interest in trial because she became exhausted)
'The girl lost interest in the trial because she became/got exhausted.'

(i) *Devuška, kotoraja utomilas', poterjala interes k sudu.*
(girl who got exhausted lost interest in trial)
'The girl who became / got exhausted lost interest in the trial'.

That sentence (a) does in fact involve a deeper gerund is made absolutely certain by the existence of sentences like that of (j), which is an intermediate structure in the derivation of (a) from an underlying structure like that of (c) (it is not crucial to this discussion whether (a) and (c) actually have identical deep structures).

(j) *Buduči utomlena, devuška poterjala interes k sudu.*
(being exhausted girl lost interest in trial)
'Being exhausted, the girl lost interest in the trial.'

Buduči 'being' is the gerund of the copula *byt'* 'to be'.

The sentences (a) through (j) demonstrate that any hypothesis concerning the syntactic derivation of gerunds in Russian must take "LF gerunds" like *utomlennaja* in (a) into account.

Notice that the derivation of the "LF gerund" involves a deeper SF (cf. *utomlena* SF f.sg. 'exhausted' in (c) and (j)), thus providing an important piece of supporting evidence for our main hypothesis, namely, a LF in modern Russian always derives from a deeper SF.

Our immediate task is to explain the origin of the nominative case, and why "LF gerunds" cannot appear in any other case:

(k) *Utomlennaja* [nom], *ona ne xotela bol'še čitat'.*
(exhausted she no want more read)
'She didn't want to read any more because she was exhausted.'

(l) *Ej ne xotelos' bol'še čitat'.*
(her no want more read)
'She didn't feel like reading any more.'

(m) **Utomlennoj* [dat], *ej* [dat] *ne xotelos' bol'še čitat'.*
(exhausted her no want more read)

In Chapter 2 it is demonstrated that the SF is the main (finite) verb of its sentence. In §2.12, on the basis of paradigms like (2.73) to (2.77) it is hypothesized that the LF is the active participle of the SF. This claim is ultimately based on two observations: (i) the LF and the active participle are both deeper V's that are introduced into NP

It becomes even clearer that the "feature" approach to determining part of speech is inadequate when we take the infinitive into consideration. This is because the two classes of "agreement" features that have been posited for Russian (Subject-verb Agreement features and case features) cannot account for the four-way surface structure distinction that we find in Russian verbal categories, namely, finite verb: active participle: gerund: infinitive. The "configurational" approach, on the other hand, can capture this four-way distinction, provided that we are able to discover the surface configuration that uniquely characterizes the infinitive phrase (recall that the configurations for the finite verb, gerund, and active participle were posited above). It seems at the present time that an infinitive complement can invariably be associated with the following surface structure configuration (cf. footnote 5): $[\ldots[\ldots[\ldots V\ldots]_{VP}\ldots]_{VP}\ldots]_{S}$ .For example, the derived structure of *Mal'čik ljubit pravit' mašinoj* 'The boy loves to drive the car' is $[[$*mal'čik*$]_{NP}$ $[$*ljubit* $[$*pravit' mašinoj*$]_{VP}]_{VP}]_{S}$. The four crucial configurations posited above are summarized in the table below; $[\ldots]_{S}$, which is common to all four, has been "factored out".

	$[\ldots]_S$
Finite verb	$[\ldots V\ldots]_{VP}$
Infinitive	$[\ldots[\ldots V\ldots]_{VP}\ldots]_{VP}$
Active Participle	$[\ldots[\ldots V\ldots]_{VP}\ldots]_{NP}$
Gerund	$[\ldots[\ldots V\ldots]_{VP}\ldots]_{AP}$

The table makes it clear why there are FOUR verbal parts of speech in Russian, and not three or seven: there is one verbal part of speech corresponding to V in each of the FOUR non-lexical nodes that can immediately dominate VP, namely, S, NP, VP, AP.[7] The reason that parts of speech are determined at the level of surface structure, and not deep structure, is that VP configurations appear in surface structure that are impossible in deep structure (which is determined by the phrase-structure rules). VP's greater

---

constituency where they acquire a case feature; (ii) both the LF and active participle have the same syntactic function and occur in exactly the same surface constructions. But a comparison of (a) and *(g) reveals that the latter observation (ii) is incorrect (cf. §3.9) and, consequently, requires that we abandon the claim that the LF is invariably the "active participle" of the SF. Sentences like (a) and (b) show that the LF may function in the surface structure of Russian as either the active participle or the gerund of the SF. The reason that the "LF active participle" and the "LF gerund" have the same FORM is that they have, in the final derived phrase marker, the same FEATURES (cf. §0.3.2.2).

[7] Notice that the surface structure configuration $[\mathrm{P}\ \mathrm{VP}]_{PP}$ is impossible in Russian, while the derived structure $[\mathrm{P}\ [\mathrm{VP}]_{NP}]_{PP}$, which is quite common, yields, as expected, an active participle: *On ne xočet govorit'* $[[$*o*$]_{P}$ $[[$*slučivšemsja*$]_{VP}]_{NP}]_{PP}$ 'He doesn't want to talk about what happened.'

"privileges of occurrence" in surface structure is, of course, due to the operation of the rules in the transformational component.

0.3.2.2 In addition to the evidence presented above, there exists yet another argument that a theory of parts of speech based exclusively on features is wrong.

Let us consider *interesno* 'interesting' in the following sentences.

(0.1) *On* interesno *govorit o vojne.*
(he *interestingly* speaks about war)
'He speaks about the war interestingly.'

(0.2) '*Govorit' s nim o vojne* interesno.
(to speak with him about war *interesting*)
'To speak with him about the war is interesting.'

(0.3) *Ego pis'mo o vojne očen'* interesno.
(his letter about war very *interesting*)
'His letter about the war is very interesting.'

In sentence (0.1) *interesno* is an ADVERB of manner; in (0.2) and (0.3) it is the "main verb", i.e. a "predicate adjective" in the SF[8] (the reason that the LF *interesnoe* cannot replace the SF in (0.2), but can if (0.3), is explained in Chapter 4).

The problem is this: how can a grammar of Russian capture the fact that *interesno* is not the same part of speech in (0.1) and (0.2)?

What is significant here is the fact that the manner adverb *interesno* in (0.1) and the SF in (0.2) have the SAME FORM FOR THE SAME REASON: both derive from a deep structure V (cf. §0.1) that has passed through the transformational component without acquiring either the features of Subject-verb Agreement or a case feature (cf. §3.3.3). They are both in the neuter, singular, third person, since this is the unmarked form of gender, number, and person, which is added by a late rule to items that have not previously received any "agreement" features (cf. §3.6.3). (Note that neither can be said to be in the nominative, the unmarked case, because neither is the constituent of a NP.)

The SF *interesno* in (0.2) is in the neuter, singular, third person because its surface subject is an infinitive phrase, which has no inherent features that can be copied by the Subject-verb Agreement transformation.

[8] Note that in *Govorit' s nim bylo trudno* 'To speak with him was difficult' *trudno* 'difficult' is unambiguously the predicate SF, since there is no ADVERB *trudno* in literary Russian; there is only *s trudom* 'with difficulty'.

The adverb *interesno* in (0.1) is in the neuter, singular, third person because there is no deep subject in its underlying structure from which Subject-verb Agreement can copy features. (It is patently incorrect to derive a sentence like *Ona poet krasivo* 'She sings beautifully' from a deep structure like [*ona poet* [[*ona krasiv-*$]_{S}]_{AP}]_{S}$ '[she sings [[she is beautiful$]_{S}]_{AP}]_{S}$'.)

It is only the predicate SF *interesno* in (0.3) that is the result of Subject-verb Agreement, since there is a neuter, singular subject (*pis'mo* 'letter') from which to copy these features.

In order to prove conclusively that the neuter, singular, third person ending is not necessarily the result of some form of Subject-verb Agreement, all we need to do is observe a sentence containing a V that is subcategorized as not having a subject NP (do not confuse this type of verb with a verb like *otkryvat'(-sja)* 'to open', which requires an EMPTY subject NP.[9] An example of such a verb is *znobit'* 'to feel feverish; to have the shivers' (or *tošnit'* 'to feel sick'). (*Znobilo* in (0.4b) is in the past neuter singular; *znobit* in (0.4a) is the present singular, third person.)[10]

(0.4a) *Ego znobit.*
(him fevers)
'He feels feverish.'

(0.4b) *Ego znobilo.*
(him fevered)
'He felt feverish.'

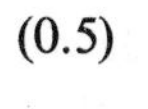
(0.5)

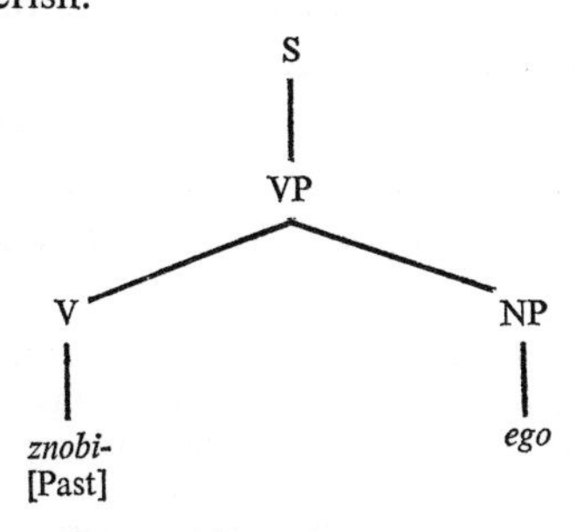

[9] The form in *-sja* (*otkryvat'sja*) is not found in the lexicon of Russian; it is transformationally derived. If there is no agent NP to fill the empty subject position, then the object NP will occupy it, leaving *-sja* behind as a "tracer" (cf. Channon, 1968 and Chvany, to appear). The transformational framework being employed in this section is basically that of John Bowers (cf. *Grammatical Relations*).

[10] Note that Russian verbs are formally marked for number and PERSON in the present tense, and for number and GENDER in the past singular (the plural in Russian excludes gender distinctions).

The verb *znobit'* requires that the person experiencing the fever and chills (*ego* 'him') be the direct object in the accusative case; there is no subject, overt or "understood". Accordingly, the subcategorization feature for *znobit'* is simply: . ______ NP (the line under the NP means that the object NP must be filled).[11] The underlying structure of (0.4b) is thus (0.5). There is no subject NP, filled or empty, from which the rule of Subject-verb Agreement can copy the features of gender, number, and person.

If there were an empty subject NP in the structure underlying (0.4b) (cf. (0.6a)), then Object Preposing, an OBLIGATORY rule that moves direct objects into an empty subject NP,[9] would derive the ungrammatical (0.6b) (the arrow in (0.6a) traces the path of Object Preposing).

(0.6a)

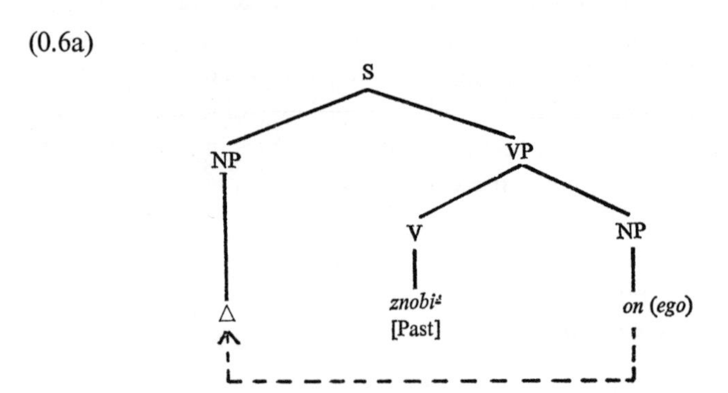

(0.6b) **On znobilsja.* (he fevered)

Thus in the surface structure both the SF "predicate adjective" *interesno* in (0.2) and the manner adverb *interesno* in (0.1), both of which derive from the same underlying category V, have the same features (and thus the same form [cf. end of footnote 6]); yet we do not want to claim that they are the same part of speech.[12] The "feature approach" to parts of

[11] If this analysis of verbs like *znobit'* is correct, then we are in effect claiming that the initial phrase-structure rule of Russian is S → (NP) VP, and, consequently, that Russian and English differ in a very essential way, since there is no evidence that the subject NP is optional in English.

This analysis provides an answer to the question posed in footnote 14, Chapter 3.

[12] Some Russian linguists have referred to words like *interesno* in sentences like (0.2) as "predicate adverbs" (*narečie predikativnoe*) or "category of state" and have claimed that they are "indeclinable" (*neizmenjaemyj*) words that are used exclusively as the predicate of impersonal sentences.

According to this, Russian linguists are actually claiming that *interesno* in (0.1), (0.2), and (0.3) are three different parts of speech, namely, adverb, category of state (cf. below), and adjective respectively. It is being demonstrated here that this analysis is incorrect and that *interesno* in all three sentences is the same underlying category, while

speech, however, DOES force us to make this claim, while the "configurational approach" does not, since the part of speech ADVERB is associated with the phrase marker configuration $[VP]_{AP}$ and the precidate SF is associated with the finite verb configuration $[\ldots[\ldots V\ldots]_{VP}\ldots]_S$. How the deep V got its features is irrelevant for determining part of speech.

The major points made in §0.3.2.2 are summarized in Table 1.

TABLE 1

Deep structure source	V ([+adj])		
Configuration	$[VP]_{AP}$	$[\ldots VP\ldots]_S$	
Part of speech	adverb	SF adjective	
Surface form	*interesno* in (1)	*interesno* in (2)	*interesno* in (3)
Mode of acquisition	features assigned by late rule		Subject-verb Agreement

0.3.2.3 It must be emphasized that the adverb in *–o* and the predicate SF in *–o* (especially when it has an finitive or sentential subject, or when it is the predicate of a "subjectless" sentence like *V sadu bylo pusto* 'The garden was empty') *are* in the third person neuter singular, and are not indeclinable or "frozen" forms (cf. footnote 12 and the preceding paragraph).

0.3.2.3.1 EVIDENCE THAT THE SF IN –O IS IN THE NEUTER SINGULAR. This becomes clear when a sentence like (0.7a) is embedded in a sentence whose main verb is *sčitat'* 'to consider', as in (0.7b).

(0.7a) Nužno *čitat' mnogo knig.*
(*necessary* to read many books)
'It is necessary to read many books.'

(0.7b) *Ona sčitala* nužnym *čitat' mnogo knig.*
(she considered *necessary* to read many books)
'She considered it necessary to read many books.'

---

in the surface structure *interesno* in (0.1) is an adverb ($[VP]_{AP}$) and a SF predicate adjective in (0.2) and (0.3). We are therefore claiming that there is no "category of state" (*kategorija sostojanija*; cf. Vinogradov 1947: chapter 4 for details). We are furthermore claiming that the manner adverb in *–o* and the SF in *–o* in sentences like (0.2) are not indeclinable, frozen forms, but are in the neuter singular (cf. §0.3.2.3).

(0.7c) *Ona sčitala { nužno / nužna / nužnoj } čitat' mnogo knig.

(0.7d) *Ona sčitala, čto* nužno *čitat' mnogo knig.*
(she considered that *necessary* to read many books)
'She considered that it is necessary to read many books.'

Nužno n.sg., the main verb of the underlying embedded sentence (cf. (0.7a) and (0.7d)), is put in the instrumental case (cf. (0.7b)) when (0.7d) is reduced, and we get *nužnym* n.sg.inst. just as we do when the main verb of the reduced embedded sentence acquires its features by Subject-verb Agreement (cf. chapter 2 for details):

(0.8a) *My sčitaem moloko neobxodimym dlja zdorov'ja.*
(we consider milk vital for health)
'We consider milk to be vital for (our) health.'

(0.8b) *My sčitaem ee nužnoj obščestvu.*
(we consider her necessary to society)
'We consider her to be necessary to society.'

The crucial point here is that if *nužno* in (0.7a) and (0.7d) were an indeclinable, frozen form, we could not explain the fact that it is in the instrumental case in (0.7b). If, however, it is the neuter singular, as we have claimed, then there is nothing strange about (0.7b): it is derived by the rules already required by the grammar for the derivation of the sentences in (0.8).

0.3.2.3.2 EVIDENCE THAT THE ADVERB IN –O IS IN THE NEUTER SINGULAR. It remains now to demonstrate that the adverb in *–o* is also in the neuter singular, and is not an indeclinable form. To do this, we must look briefly at the comparative construction in Russian.

(0.9a) *On govorit bol'še, čem ja govorju.*
(he speaks more than I speak)
'He speaks more than I speak.'

(0.9b) *On govorit bol'še, čem ja.*
(he speaks more than I)
'He speaks more than I (do).'

(0.9c) *On govorit bol'še menja.*
(he speaks more me)
'He speaks more than I (do) / me.'

(0.9d) **On govorit bol'še, čem menja.*
(He speaks more than me)

The sentences in (0.9) illustrate that the simple comparative in Russian is followed by an S embedded in an NP marked genitive. Sentence (0.9b) is derived from the structure underlying (0.9a) by a rule that deletes repeated constituents. Sentence (0.9c) is derived from (0.9b) by a rule which optionally deletes the complementizer *čem* 'than'. Once *čem* is gone, the embedded S node no longer branches and it deletes (cf. §3.1.1), making *ja* 'I' a constituent of the upper genitive NP; *menja* 'me' in (0.9c) is in the genitive.[13]

Now observe what happens when the sentence embedded in the NP marked genitive contains an adverb in *-o*.

(0.10a) *On segodnja govorit bol'še, čem on obyčno govorit.*
(he today speaks more than he usually speaks)
'He is speaking more today than he usually speaks.'

(0.10b) *On segodnja govorit bol'še, čem obyčno.*
(he today speaks more than usually)
'He is speaking more today than he usually does.'

(0.10c) *On segodnja govorit bol'še obyčnogo.*
(he today speaks more usual[ly])
'He is speaking more today than { (he) usually (does) / usual }.'

(0.10d) **On segodnja govorit bol'še* { *obyčno* / *čem obyčnogo* }.

In sentence (0.10c) we see that the adverb in *-o*, *obyčno* 'usually', acquires a case feature (genitive), and emerges as *obyčnogo* n.sg.gen. in precisely

[13] The subject of the embedded sentence *ja* 'I' is NOT in the nominative case when it is introduced into the upper genitive NP. The reason this must be so will become clear in §3.10.3.

the same way that *ja* in (0.9) became *menja.*[14] If the adverb in *–o* were an indeclinable, frozen form, there would be no way to explain the genitive singular "adjectival" form *obyčnogo* in (0.10c). If, however, *obyčno* in (0.10a) is the neuter singular, then (0.10c) is perfectly predictable, and our grammar explains in a natural way why Russian has this unusual construction.

Notice that (0.10) provides us with another case of a SF (*obyčno*), i.e. a deep V plus gender and number, becoming a LF (*obyčnogo*), i.e. a SF plus a case feature. Thus the derivation of the manner adverb in *–o* (*–ogo*), which is only hinted at in §3.3.3 furnishes us with further evidence that the main hypothesis of *A Transformational Grammar of Russian Adjectives* is correct.

SUMMARY OF §0.3

It has just been demonstrated that a part of speech in Russian must be defined in terms of a deep structure category, i.e. a category introduced by the base phrase-structure rules, and this category's position in the finial derived phrase marker (the surface structure). The FORM of a surface structure part of speech, including its grammatical ending, is a function of its syntactic features, both inherent and acquired. The data presented above in §0.3.2.2 provides particularly strong evidence in favor of this hypothesis.

Given this definition of "part of speech", it is not difficult to see why taxonomic classifications of parts of speech, which are based entirely on surface structure, are inadequate. Their one-level approach renders them incapable of explaining facts like the following: On the one hand, a form like *obyčno* can be either a SF adjective or an adverb; on the other hand, a form like *obyčnogo* can be either a LF adjective (*U menja net daže obyčnogo pera* 'I don't even have an ordinary pen') or an "adverb" (cf. (0.10c)).

[14] If the derivation just proposed for the sentences in (0.10) is correct, i.e. $[obyčno]_{AP}$ 'usually' receives a case feature when *čem* is deleted, then the claim that the AP (adverbial phrase) node acts like an S node in that it blocks a case feature from being copied onto any of its constituents from a higher NP is incorrect (cf §3.3.3).

Notice the English glosses in (0.10); it must be more than a mere coincidence that *usually* can alternate with *usual*, while in Russian the adverb *obyčno* 'usually' assumes the "adjectival" form *obyčnogo* when it receives a case feature.

1

ADJECTIVES AND RELATIVE CLAUSES

1.1 The purpose of this chapter is to determine where in the Base Rules (PS Rules) the symbol ADJ is introduced. It will be argued that prenominal adjective + noun (ADJ + N) is a transformationally derived surface structure constituent and not a Base Structure.[1]

This informal discussion of Russian follows similar arguments for English and other languages and is intended to provide additional evidence that these rules are universals or near universals.[2] One such bit of evidence that has not yet, to the best of my knowledge, been noticed is *obmykanie*, discussed in §1.6.

1.2 Russian grammar traditionally views both prenominal and predicate position of the adjective as basic; in so doing it fails to capture some very important generalizations. If we try to make this view more explicit by stating it in the form of a Phrase-structure Grammar, we have to introduce the symbol ADJ in two different expansions:

(1) NP ---→ DET + ADJ + N
(2) VP ---→ Copula + ADJ

In other words, the traditional treatment implicitly assumes that the adjective is both a NP and VP constituent at the level of deep structure. This fails to capture the fact that the selectional restrictions for ADJ + N and N + Copula + ADJ are the same. **Umnaja ložka* 'smart spoon' is unacceptable for the same reason that **ložka umna* 'the spoon is smart'

[1] It will be shown in Chapter 2 that at the level of deep structure the adjective (ADJ) is a verb (V) with the FEATURE [+ADJ]. In N + Copula + ADJ, ADJ corresponds only to the SF. The LF in the predicate is treated in Chapter 4. The Copula is discussed in Chapters 3 and 4.

[2] See Bach, 1965 for a discussion of these rules in several languages.

is unacceptable. If we insist on the symbol ADJ being introduced at two points in our PS Rules, these restrictions must be stated twice.

1.3 A transformational grammar can capture generalizations of this kind, while grammars without transformations have no way of expressing them. The repetition of selectional restrictions is a good indication that we are dealing with a transformational relationship.

1.4 Our evidence, then, seems to point to the fact that ADJ + N and N + Copula + ADJ are transformationally related. The selectional restrictions, consequently, need be stated only for the underlying structure and these restrictions will be maintained under all subsequent transformations. In the following paragraphs several arguments will be given to support the view that the symbol ADJ is introduced only as an expansion of the VP, i.e. N + Copula + ADJ is the underlying structure and ADJ + N is transformationally derived from it.

1.5 In Chapter 2 two important facts about modern Russian will be demonstrated: (a) adjective (SF) and verb are the same lexical category (Verbal); (b) active participles are derived by the same transformations that derive long forms (LF) of the adjective.

Assuming these two facts, let us examine the relations in (1.3):

(1.3a) *Devuška rabotaet.*
'The girl is working.'
(1.3b) *rabotajuščaja devuška.*
(working the girl)
(1.3c) **Kniga rabotaet.*
'The book is working.'
(1.3d) **rabotajuščaja kniga.*
(working the book)

(1.3) exhibits the same kind of selectional restrictions that we observe in (1.4).

(1.4a) *Devuška umna.*
'The girl is smart.'
(1.4b) *umnaja devuška*
'The smart girl'
(1.4c) **Ložka umna.*

'*The spoon is smart.'

(1.4d) **umnaja ložka*

'*The smart spoon'

If we accept the conclusions of Chapter 2 and wish to capture the syntactic parallels between (1.3) and (1.4), then we must recognize (1.4a) as underlying (1.4b), since the alternative solution ((1.4b) underlying (1.4a)) would require that (1.3b) underlie (1.3a), which is intuitively incorrect.

1.6 Another argument for N + Copula + ADJ as the deep structure of ADJ + N constructions can be found in *obmykanie*[3] constructions:

(1.5) *polnaja solnca komnata*

lit. 'the full-of-sun room'

(1.6) *gotovyj na vse student*

lit. 'the ready-for-anything student'

If we allow ADJ to be introduced in our Base Rules as an expansion of NP, then these rules will also have to generate the *obmykanie* constructions, which are potentially infinite in variety (cf. (1.9)).
The NP expansion needed to generate (1.5) and (1.6) can be represented by (1.7) and (1.8) respectively:

(1.7) DET + ADJ + N + N

(1.8) DET + ADJ + P + N + N
[+PRO]

(1.9) ... *iz monografij vtorogo roda nazovem napisannuju četvert' veka nazad, no svežuju i aktual'nuju po problematike rabotu Lavrova.*

lit. 'from monographs of the second type let us name Lavrov's written-a-quarter-of-a-century-ago-but-fresh-and-current-in-its--range-of-problems work.'

The absurdity of viewing the *obmykanie* construction in (1.9) as an NP expansion is obvious. If, however, we introduce ADJ in the VP, the *obmy-*

[3] The term *obmykanie* is used in Bauer, et al., 1966. An *obmykanie* construction is a NP in which the head noun is modified by an entire preposed VP ([(DET) — VP — N]$_{NP}$). This is illustrated by the following examples: [*vse*[*nužnye dlja stroitel'stva*]$_{VP}$ *materialy*]$_{NP}$ and *doznanie, kotoroe velos'* [*s* [[*zasluživajuščej byt' otmečennoj*]$_{VP}$ *bystrotoj*]$_{NP}$]$_{PP}$ 'the inquest, which was carried out with a promptness that deserves to be mentioned' (Aldanov). *Obmykanie* constructions are derived from deeper reduced relative clauses by the Modifier Shift transformation.

kanie constructions can easily be handled without special apparatus: they can be shown to be preposed adjectival complements and are introduced by the Base Rule in the same way that verb complements are introduced. This is another instance of parallelism between the adjective (SF) and verb (cf. 1.10)):

(1.10a) *Učitel' pridiraetsja k učenikam iz-za pustjakov.*
'The teacher finds fault with the students over trifles.'

(1.10b) *[pridirajuščijsja k učenikam iz-za pustjakov učitel']*$_{NP}$
([the finding-fault-with-the-students-over-trifles teacher]$_{NP}$)

Notice also that the order of elements in an *obmykanie* construction is identical to the order of elements in a verb complement (cf.(1.10)). If our grammar did not relate these two structures transformationally, there would be no meaningful explanation of this phenomenon.

1.7 If the adjective is introduced by an expansion of NP, there is no insightful way to explain the relations among (1.11)-(1.14).

(1.11) *[gotovaja na vse devuška]*$_{NP}$
lit. '(the) ready-for-anything girl'

(1.12) *Devuška gotova na vse.*
'The girl is ready for anything.'

(1.13) **Devuška gotovaja na vse.*

(1.14) **[gotova na vse devuška]*$_{NP}$

These relations will be dealt with in great detail in Chapter 2.

1.8 Consider the following examples:

(1.15) *umnaja devuška*
'a smart girl'

(1.16) *očen' umnaja devuška*
'a very smart girl'

(1.17) **očen' devuška*
'a very girl'

If ADJ is introduced in the NP by the Base Rules, i.e. is a deep structure NP constituent, then the rules must be constrained so as to allow the optional introduction of an adverb like *očen'* 'very' just in case ADJ is already modifying the head N (cf. (1.15)-(1.17)). In other words, if ADJ is a deep structure NP constituent, the Base Rules must be made context-sensitive in order to block NPs like (1.17) (cf. §4.2.1.2). If, however, ADJ is a deep structure VP constituent (and, consequently, prenominal adjectives that can be modified by a degree ADV like *očen'* are introduced into the NP by transformation), the non-occurrence of NPs like (1.17) can be accounted for by V-ADV constraints, which are required independently of any considerations in this paragraph. This provides us with another reason for accepting NP + Copula + ADJ as the underlying construction and ADJ + N as derived. The acceptance of ADJ + N as basic would entail an unmotivated complication of the grammar. In addition, it will be argued later (cf. §4.2.1.2) that the Base Rules must be context-free, thus providing us yet another reason for rejecting the NP-expansion origin of prenominal adjectives.

1.9 In §§1.2-1.7 we have presented some evidence that ADJ + N and N + Copula + ADJ are transformationally related and that N + Copula + ADJ is the underlying structure. We have not specified in what manner these two structures are related. More precisely, we have not claimed that ADJ + N is derived DIRECTLY from N + Copula + ADJ by some transformation. To do this would be equivalent to asserting that ADJ + N is a NOMINALIZATION of the underlying N + Copula + ADJ sentence.[4] The Nominalization of, for instance, *devuška krasiva* 'the girl is pretty' is $[$*krasota devuški*$]_{NP}$ 'the prettiness of the girl', and not $[$*krasivaja devuška*$]_{NP}$ 'the pretty girl'.

[4] A Nominalization is a transformation which changes a S into a NP and which preserves the grammatical relations of the S. Thus *Eë vyxod zamuž za Ivana menja očen' volnuet* 'Her marriage to Ivan worries me very much' is derived from a S whose subject clause (*ona vyšla zamuž za Ivana*) has undergone Nominalization. The deep structure may be schematically represented as

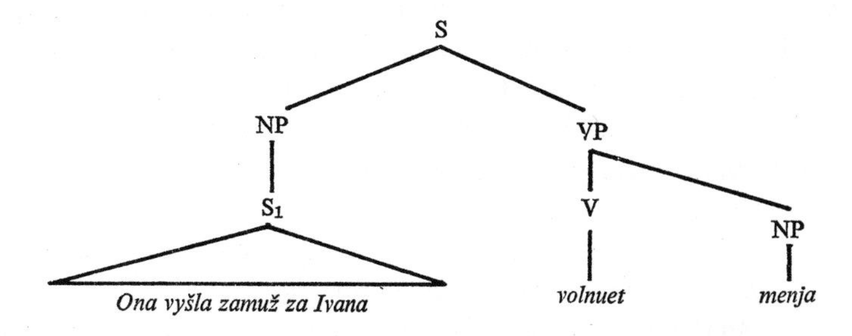

S_1 is transformed into $[$*eë vyxod zamuž za Ivana*$]_{NP}$.

The derivation of ADJ + N directly from N + Copula + ADJ also fails to reflect the fact that ADJ + N is, in most cases, semantically equivalent to a relative clause: *krasivaja devuška* is synonymous with *devuška, kotoraja krasiva* 'the girl who is pretty'. These considerations lead us to the conclusion that prenominal adjectives are derived from relative clauses, which, at the level of deep structure, are embedded sentences. The deep structure configuration of *krasivaja devuška* 'the pretty girl' is

(1.18)

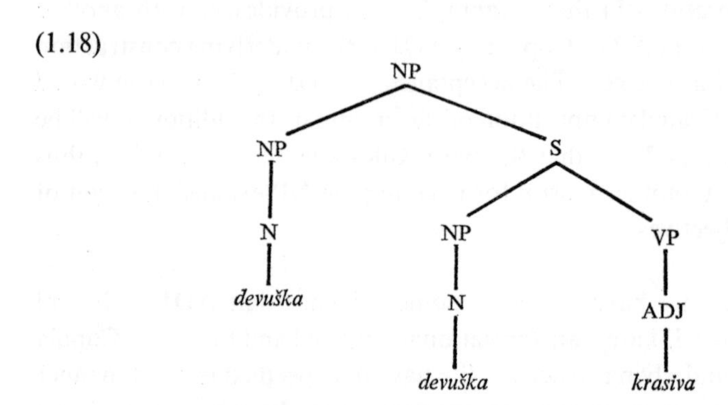

The set of transformations (Relative Clause Formation, Relative Clause Reduction, and Modifier Shift) that convert deep structures like (1.18) into ADJ + N (*krasivaja devuška*) will be discussed in detail in subsequent chapters.

These same rules relate the NPs (1.19) and (1.20).

(1.19) *čitajuščaja knigu devuška*
'the girl reading a book'

(1.20) *devuška, kotoraja čitaet knigu*
'the girl who is reading a book'

1.10 Our decision to derive prenominal adjectives from deep structure relative clause structures reflects the native speaker's intuitive feeling that ADJ + N and N + Relative Clause are related (cf. Boguslavskij, 1964: 19; Dudnikov, 1958: 32-33). Dudnikov cites (1.21) as an example of a pair of sentences where this relation is strongly felt.

(1.21a) *Vdali vidnelis' malen'kie domiki, kotorye byli edva zametny na fone beskonečnogo snežnogo prostora.*
'In the distance small houses could be seen, which were barely visible against the background of the endless stretch of snow.'

(1.21b) *Vdali vidnelis' edva zametnye na fone beskonečnogo snežnogo prostora malen'kie domiki.*
'In the distance could be seen barely-visible-against-the-background-of-the-endless-stretch-of-snow small houses.'

1.11 The relative clause source of prenominal adjectives outlined above enables us to explain several other facts of Russian syntax which could not be otherwise accounted for.

There are two kinds of relative clauses: RESTRICTIVE and NON-RESTRICTIVE (cf. Smirnickij, 1957: 94-95). If prenominal adjectives are derived from underlying relative clauses, we should expect them to possess precisely those distinctions that relative clauses do, i.e. a prenominal adjective should be ambiguous with respect to restrictive-appositive meaning. Jespersen (1958:112) has pointed out that prenominal adjectives are ambiguous in just this way:

(1.22) It may sometimes be doubtful whether an adjunct is of one kind or another kind ... *The industrious Japanese will conquer in the long run*; does this mean that the J. as a nation will conquer, because they are industrious [=non-restrictive adjunct], or that the industrious among the Japanese nation will conquer [=restrictive adjunct]?

Russian makes the same distinction. In (1.23) it is not clear whether only those workers who are industrious are fulfilling the plan (the lazy ones are not) or whether all the workers (and they are industrious) are fulfilling the plan.

(1.23) *Naši trudoljubivye rabočie vypolnjajut plan.*
'Our industrious workers are fulfilling the plan.'

If we did not view prenominal adjectives as deriving from relative clauses, there would be no way to account for this ambiguity.[5]

[5] In the version of transformational grammar being employed here, the rules of semantic interpretation operate only on deep structure P-markers; transformations do not alter meaning. An ambiguous sentence must correspond to as many deep structures as it has readings. A sentence containing a prenominal adjective is thus ambiguous in at least two ways and must have at least two deep structures, each containing a different relative clause configuration.

1.12 The relative-clause origin of prenominal adjectives also explains why personal pronouns (*on* 'he', *ja* 'I', etc.) cannot be modified by either an adjective or a relative clause. The unacceptability of a pronoun modified by a restrictive clause (**ja, kotoryj glup* 'I who am stupid') automatically predicts the unacceptability of a pronoun modified by an adjective (**glupyj ja* 'stupid I'), provided that we recognize a transformational relationship between the prenominal adjective and the clause.[6] If they were not transformationally related, we would not be able to explain why relative clauses and prenominal adjectives are both ungrammatical as pronoun adjuncts. It should be noted that if we chose to derive ADJ + N directly from N + Copula + ADJ we would no longer be able to account for the unacceptability of **glupyj ja*, since *ja glup* 'I am stupid' is a perfectly good sentence in Russian.

There are a number of other arguments supporting the view that prenominal adjectives are derived from relative clauses, but more groundwork must be laid before this material can be profitably discussed.

1.13 Implicit in previous transformational treatments of the relation between adjectives and clauses is the assumption that ALL prenominal adjectives are derived from relative clauses. Russian provides a great deal of evidence that seems to contradict this. We will limit ourselves to one concrete example.

It was pointed out in the beginning of this chapter that $[\text{ADJ} + \text{N}]_{\text{NP}}$ is ambiguous with respect to restrictive-appositive meaning. Prenominal adjectives can be ambiguous in still another way. The NP *otricatel'nye vyskazyvanija* 'negative utterances' has two readings: 'utterances negative in form' i.e. containing negative particles *ne, net*, etc. (*Otricatel'nye vyskazyvanija izučajutsja v sed'moj glave našego učebnika* 'Negated utterances are studied in the seventh chapter of our textbook'); and 'utterances negative or adverse in meaning, not form' (*Ego otricatel'nye vyskazyvanija*

[6] Sentences like *Izumlennyj, on ne srazu našel podxodjaščij otvet* 'Dumbfounded, he could not immediately find the appropriate answer' (B. T. Panov, 1967: 91-92) present a different set of problems. The "adjective" *izumlennyj* is not "prenominal" (note the pause *izumlennyj # on...* vs. **izumlennyj on...*) and does not derive from a relative clause. *Izumlennyj, on ne srazu našel podxodjaščij otvet* is probably a transformation of the structure underlying *On ne srazu našel podxodjaščij otvet, tak kak byl izumlen* 'He could not immediately find the appropriate answer, since he was dumbfounded'. *Izumlen(nyj)* is thus introduced into the subject NP not from a relative clause, but from what is traditionally called a subordinate clause (*pridatočnoe predloženie*), i.e. a sentence which is not embedded in the same NP as the head noun at the level of deep structure.

otnositel'no vojny spravedlivy 'His adverse comments on the war are just'). Furthermore, *otricatel'nyj*, when it means 'containing negative forms', cannot appear in the SF: *èti vyskazyvanija otricatel'ny* can only have the meaning 'adverse' (it will be crucial for our explanation of the LF in the predicate to note that the sentence *èti vyskazyvanija otricatel'nye* is ambiguous in just the same way that $[ADJ + N]_{NP}$ is). Our argument that prenominal adjectives have at least one source other than relative clauses is based on facts like these. These semantic and syntactic differences of *otricatel'nyj* cannot both be derived from the structure underlying *vyskazyvanija, kotorye otricatel'ny* 'utterances which are negative', especially since the 'negative in form' meaning cannot appear in the SF. English, on which the elaboration of transformational grammar is based, has not stimulated a discussion of these syntactic relations because it does not distinguish LF and SF.

The ambiguity under discussion here corresponds to the traditional Russian distinction between the qualitative (*kačestvennyj*) adjective, which has a SF, and the relational (*otnositel'nyj*) adjective, which does not. It has been widely recognized by Russian grammarians that relational adjectives may be used as qualitative adjectives. We have merely pointed out the fact that many qualitative adjectives can be used quite freely as relational adjectives.[7]

Prenominal adjectives, then, exhibit two kinds of ambiguity. What might be called the "path of disambiguation" is schematically given in (1.24).

(1.24)

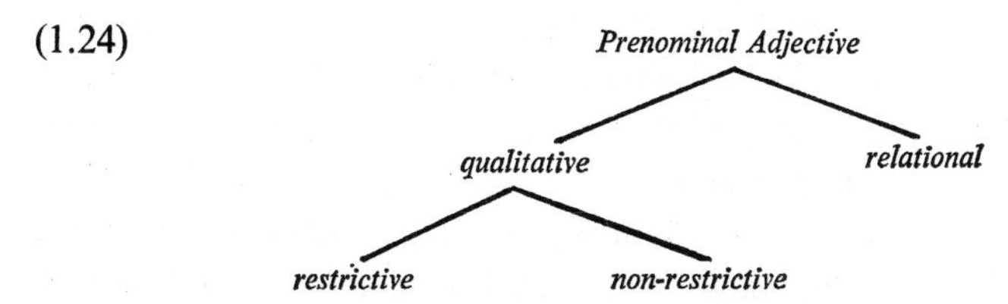

Since relational adjectives do not derive from relative clauses, they, predictably, do not display the clausal ambiguity discussed in §1.11.

[7] This study will deal only with the relationship between the SF and LF of "qualitative" adjectives. It seems at this stage in my research that "relational" adjectives like *vetrjanoj* in *vetrjanaja mel'nica* 'windmill', *stennoj* in *stennaja gazeta* (= *stengazeta*) 'wall newspaper', *dvernoj* in *dvernaja ručka* 'door-knob', *železnyj* in *železnaja doroga* 'railroad', etc., should be included in a transformational analysis of compounding, since despite their superficial resemblance to qualitative adjectives, they behave syntactically more like components of compound nouns. A similar view has been expressed by D. Bolinger (1967: 31-34) in the section "Attribution and Compounding" (cf. also A. Smirnickij, 1956: 114-137 and V. M. Pavlov, 1960).

2

ADJECTIVES AND VERBS

2.0 In Chapter 2 it will be argued that adjective and verb are members of the same category, Verbal (V), and differ only by a syntactic feature ([±ADJ]).

The association of the syntactic properties of adjectives and verbs is not new in Russian grammatical thought. For instance, Šaxmatov (1941: 190) suggested that the SF of the adjective is a *sprjagaemaja forma* (conjugated form). The syntactic similarities of verbs and adjectives were also discussed in Russian philosophical grammars of the nineteenth century (cf. Vinogradov, 1947:187, and 1947:266 for Vostokov's views). Jakubinskij (1953:216) was correct when he described the process by which the SF lost its declension and was restricted to predicate position as verbalization.

2.1 G. Lakoff in his doctoral dissertation (1965:Appendix A) presented a number of rules of English syntax in which adjectives and verbs are treated identically. This evidence makes it seem likely that adjective and verb are members of a single lexical category, Verbal (V). Lakoff worked on English, but his conclusions are not language-particular. Adjectives and verbs seem to behave this way in many languages, and this may prove to be a fact of natural language in general and not just of English or Russian.

I will briefly run through the arguments Lakoff has adduced for English and discuss them in terms of Russian material. I will then add some Russian phenomena that provide additional support for the view that adjective and verb constitute a single lexical category V and that Lakoff's findings are not language-particular.

2.2 GRAMMATICAL RELATIONS. There are pairs of sentences which are understood in the same way, one with an adjective, the other with a verb as the predicate.

(2.1a) *On (očen') padok na den'gi.*
'He is (very) fond of money.'
(2.1b) *On (očen') ljubit den'gi.*
'He likes money (very much).'

In Russian there are also many pairs of sentences where the adjective and verb seem to be the same lexical item at some level. It is particularly clear in these examples that the grammatical relations are exactly the same. In Russian, unlike English, the preposition may appear after the verb as well as the adjective (cf. Lakoff, 1965:A-3).

(2.2a) *Ivan poxodit na otca.*
'Ivan looks like his father.'
(2.2b) *Ivan poxož na otca.*
'Ivan looks like his father.'
NB: **Ivan byl poxodjaščij na otca.*
**Ivan byl poxodjaščim na otca.*
**Ivan byl poxožij na otca.*
**Ivan byl poxožim na otca.*
(2.3a) *Anna serditsja na menja.*
'Anna is angry at me.'
(2.3b) *Anna serdita na menja.*
'Anna is angry at me.'
(2.4a) *Ivan boleet grippom.*
'Ivan is sick with the flu.'
(2.4b) *Ivan bolen grippom.*
'Ivan is sick with the flu.'
(2.5a) *Anna prostudilas'.*
'Anna caught cold.'
(2.5b) *Anna prostužena.*
'Anna has a cold.'

In the above examples, the (a) and (b) sentences differ only in that the (a) sentence contains a verb, while the (b) sentence contains *byt'* 'be' (= Ø in the present tense) + ADJ. This difference, however, is superficial, since *byt'* in $[\left\{\begin{array}{c} \textit{byl} \\ (\emptyset) \\ \textit{budet} \end{array}\right\} + \mathrm{ADJ}]_{VP}$ serves only to carry the tense marker and is not a deep-structure constituent of the VP (cf. §3.3.0 and Lakoff, 1965:A-6, where tense is treated as a feature of the V and introduced as a surface segment by a rule called Tense-Spelling).

The (a) and (b) sentences are understood in the same way because they both have the same grammatical relations. This requires that they both be members of the same lexical category. Thus the deep-structure relations of (2.2a) and (2.2b) can be schematically represented by (2.6).

(2.6)

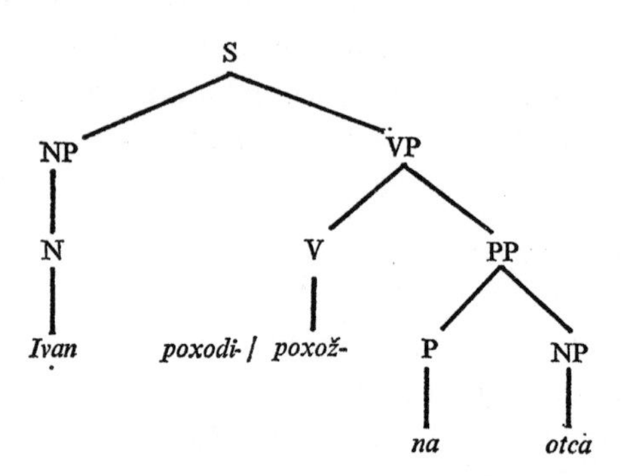

2.3 SELECTIONAL RESTRICTIONS One of the strongest arguments for assuming that adjective and verb are subcategories of the same lexical category is the fact that they have the same kinds of CONTEXTUAL RESTRICTIONS. An example of selectional restrictions and their significance may be found in §§1.2-1.3.

Under selectional restrictions Lakoff also mentions the fact that both adjectives and verbs may be either transitive or intransitive, i.e. either may have the feature $[+\_\_ \begin{Bmatrix} \text{NP} \\ \text{PP} \end{Bmatrix}]$ or $[+\_\_\#]$. The sentences of (2.7) contain intransitive adjectives and those of (2.8) contain transitive adjectives.

(2.7a) *Ivan živ.*
'Ivan is alive.'

(2.7b) *Moja sestra očen' krasiva.*
'My sister is very beautiful.'

(2.8a) *Ja dolžen emu bol'šuju summu.*
'I owe him a large sum.'

(2.8b) *Ix dom polon krasivyx kartin.*
'Their home is full of beautiful pictures.'

(2.8c) *On blagodaren emu.*
'He is grateful to him.'

(2.8d) *Ona ravnodušna k teatru.*
'She is indifferent to the theater.'

Russian grammar recognizes a further subdivision within transitive adjectives and verbs, thus strengthening our "transitivity" evidence for verb and adjective being the same category: *sil'naja perexodnost' / slabaja perexodnost'* (strong transitivity / weak transitivity) (cf. Peškovskij, 1938: 221). In transformational terms, verbs and adjectives with strong transitivity do not allow the rule of Object Deletion to operate (Lakoff discusses this rule on page A-17). In other words, the V must have an object. The sentences of (2.9) seem "incomplete" to a native speaker because the adjectives are strongly transitive.

(2.9a) (*)*On byl sposoben.*[1]
'He was capable (of).'
(2.9b) (*)*On byl sklonen.*
'He was prone (to).'
(2.10a) *On byl sposoben na obman.*
'He was capable of deceit.'
(2.10b) *On byl sklonen k p'janstvu.*
'He was prone to drunkeness.'
(2.11a) **On byl sposobnyj na obman.*
(2.11b) **On byl sklonnyj k p'janstvu.*

Thus (2.12) is to be judged deviant for the same reason as (2.9a) and (2.9b): the V is strongly transitive.

(2.12a) (*)*On ulovil.*
'He caught.'
(2.12b) (*)*On ubil.*
'He killed.'

In (2.13)-(2.15) there are a number of adjectives that are weakly transitive, i.e. Object Deletion is possible with them; (2.16)-(2.17) contain verbs with the same property.

[1] Sentences like (2.9a) and (2.9b) can occur in dialogues:

— *Dumaete, čto on sposoben na obman?*
Do you think he is capable of deceit?
— *Da, da* [*on*] *sposoben* [*na obman*].
Yes, he is.

The object of the adjective *sposoben* is deleted not by the rule of Object Deletion, but, most likely, by a later "gapping" rule which deletes repeated surface structure constituents.

(2.13a) *Ego slova byli ponjatny studentu.*
'His words were understandable to the student.'
(2.13b) *Ego slova byli ponjatny.*
'His words were understandable.'
(2.14a) *Usvoenie jazykov trudno dlja studenta.*
'Mastering languages is difficult for the student.'
(2.14b) *Usvoenie jazykov trudno.*
'Mastering languages is difficult.'
(2.15a) *Ix idei byli sxodny s našimi.*
'Their ideas were similar to ours.'
(2.15b) *Ix idei byli sxodny.*
'Their ideas were similar.'
(2.16a) *Ivan mnogo dumaet o ljubvi.*
'Ivan thinks a great deal about love.'
(2.16b) *Ivan mnogo dumaet.*
'Ivan thinks a great deal.'
(2.17a) *Ona ljubit čitat' prikljućenčeskie romany.*
'She loves to read adventure novels.'
(2.17b) *Ona ljubit čitat'.*
'She loves to read.'

The LF, in its function as a predicate, is never transitive. In this respect there is a certain parallelism between (2.18) and (2.19) (cf. §2.12).

(2.18a) *On čitaet knigu.*
'He is reading a book.'
(2.18b) **On čitajuščij knigu.*
(2.19a) *On dolžen mne bol'šuju summu.*
'He owes me a large sum.'
(2.19b) **On dolžnyj mne bol'šuju summu.*

Summarizing, adjectives and verbs are completely parallel with respect to transitivity: they both have the same restrictions and are both subject to Object Deletion.

Adjectives and verbs take the same kind of adverbs.

TIME ADVERBIALS

(2.20a) *Ivan byl v tot moment bolen.*
'Ivan was ill at that moment.'
(2.20b) *Ivan rabotal v tot moment.*

'Ivan was working at that moment.'

NB: **Ivan byl v tot moment bol'noj.* (cf. Peškovskij, 1938:221)

LOCATIVE ADVERBIALS

(2.21) *Deti byli šalovlivy v sadu, no potom, v gostinoj, oni veli sebja xorošo.*
'The children were (being) mischievous in the garden, but later, in the livingroom, they were well-behaved.'

(2.22) *Deti sideli v sadu.*
'The children were sitting in the garden.'

MANNER ADVERBIALS

(2.23a) *Ona oslepitel'no krasiva.*
'She is dazzlingly pretty.'

(2.23b) [*ee oslepitel'naja krasota*]$_{NP}$
'her dazzling beauty'

(2.24a) *Oslepitel'no blestit more.*
'The sea shines dazzlingly.'

(2.24b) [*oslepitel'nyj blesk morja*]$_{NP}$
'the dazzling brilliance of the sea'

Details aside, what is of real significance here is the fact that both adjectives and verbs co-occur with a wide range of adverbs, while deep structure nouns do not. Even more striking for our claim that adjective and verb comprise a single category V is the fact that adverbs that modify both adjectives and verbs themselves become adjectives upon Nominalization (cf. (2.23b) and (2.24b)).

2.4 STATIVE AND NON-STATIVE VERBS AND ADJECTIVES. Lakoff states that "adjectives and verbs can be subcategorized with respect to the feature Stative (or Non-activity) and as a result both can undergo, or fail to undergo, rules conditioned by these features". He offers several tests for determining whether an adjective or verb is stative or non-stative.[2] One of the tests involves formation of the command imperative: only non-stative verbs and adjectives can form the command (or true) imperative:[3]

[2] A more detailed treatment of the distinction stative / non-stative can be found in Lakoff, 1966.

[3] Many of the tests that Lakoff proposes, unlike the command imperative test, do not

(2.25a) **Bud'te živy.*
'Be alive.'

(2.25b) **Bud'te mertvy.*
'Be dead.'

---

apply in Russian. For instance, Russian does not have a Progressive tense which enables us to make distinctions like *I'm being noisy* and **I'm being tall.*

Moreover, there is a test that permits us to distinguish stative and non-stative verbs in Russian, but this test does not work for adjectives: the conjunction *čtoby* 'in order to' of a purpose clause containing an infinitive of a non-stative verb may be optionally deleted.

(i a) *Ja podošel k oknu, čtoby posmotret', čto delaetsja na ulice.*
'I went to the window in order to see what was happening in the street.'

(i b) *Ja podošel k oknu posmotret', čto delaetsja na ulice.*
'I went to the window to see what was happening in the street.'

(ii a) *Ja podošel k oknu, čtoby videt', čto delaetsja na ulice.*
'I went to the window in order to see what was happening in the street.'

(ii b) **Ja podošel k oknu videt', čto delaetsja na ulice.*

(iii a) *Ja rabotal ves' den', čtoby byt' gotovym vovremja.*
'I worked all day in order to be ready on time.'

(iii b) **Ja rabotal ves' den' byt' gotovym vovremja.*
'I worked all day to be ready on time.'

It will be shown in §3.5.0 that if *gotov* 'ready' is a V, then *byt' gotovym* 'to be ready' is its infinitive. The deep structure of (iii) is (iv) (irrelevant details omitted).

(iv)

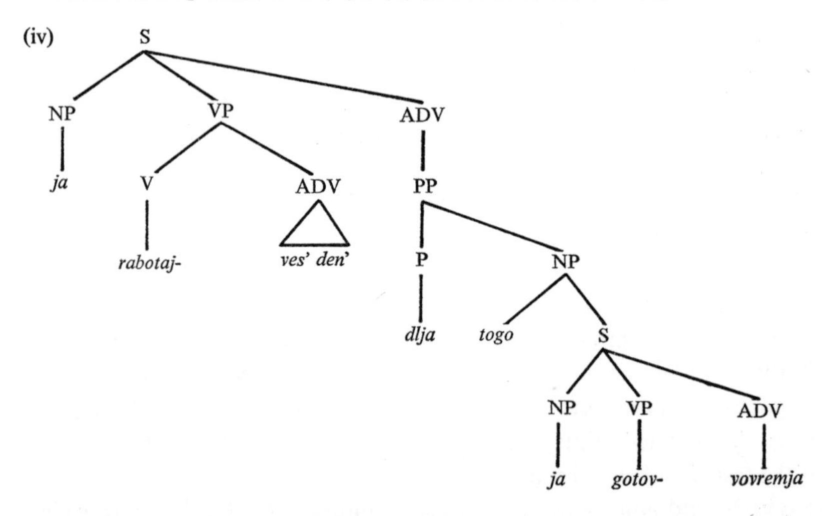

Since many of Lakoff's tests depend on phenomena peculiar to English, and Russian fails to provide additional evidence that adjectives may be non-stative, a more detailed investigation for non-stative adjectives (especially in Russian) would seem to be in order.

(2.26) *Bud'te gotovy.*
'Be ready.'
(2.27) *Slušajte, kak ona xorošo poet.*
'Listen to how nicely she is singing.'
(2.28) **Slyš'te, kak ona xorošo poet.*
(2.29a) **Vid'te kartinu.*
'See the picture.'
(2.29b) *Smotrite (na) kartinu.*
'Look at the picture.'

2.5 MODIFIER SHIFT. The rule of Adjective or Modifier Shift, which permutes a reduced relative clause and its head noun, provides another syntactic parallel between the adjective and verb, and thereby strengthens our claim that they are members of the same lexical category V.

(2.30a) *V zale stojat škafy, kotorye polny knig.*
'In the hall stand shelves which are full of books.'
(2.30b) *V zale stojat škafy, polnye knig.*
'In the hall stand shelves, full of books.'
(2.30c) *V zale stojat polnye knig škafy.*
lit. 'In the hall stand full-of-books shelves.'
(2.31a) *V zale sidit student, kotoryj čitaet knigu.*
'In the hall is sitting a student who is reading a book.'
(2.31b) *V zale sidit student, čitajuščij knigu.*
'In the hall is sitting a student reading a book.'
(2.31c) *V zale sidit čitajuščij knigu student.*
'In the hall is sitting a reading-a-book student.'

Modifier Shift in Russian, however, is not an instance of a rule's SD mentioning both adjective and verb, since, as the *obmykanie* constructions clearly demonstrate (cf. §1.6), it is not an adjective or verb that is shifted to prenominal position, but the entire VP remaining after Relative Clause Reduction. The English rule of Modifier Shift does mention adjective and verb, since the rule must stipulate that either adjective or verb must be the last constituent of the VP, thus blocking NPs like **the reading-a-book student* from [*the student who is reading a book*]$_{NP}$.

The Modifier Shift Rule in Russian makes the claim that the surface structure of (2.32) is (2.33).

(2.32) *sposobnyj student* 'the capable student'

(2.33)

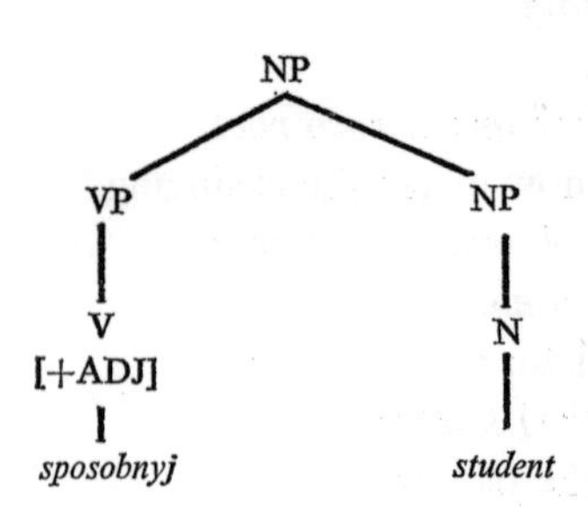

There is some question, however, as to whether VP | V [+ADJ] is the correct derived structure for (2.32). It seems quite probable that a VP-Deletion convention must be added to our grammar. This convention would delete the node VP if it no longer branched, thus changing (2.33) to (2.34).

(2.34)

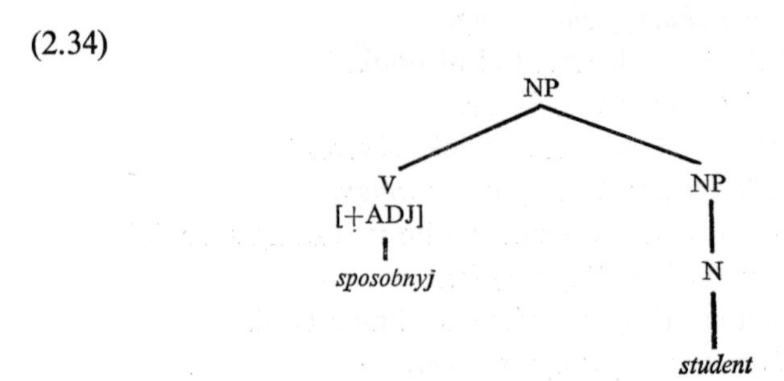

The proposed VP-Deletion is motivated not only by the need for intuitively correct surface structures, but also by the fact that the VP's function is quite different from that of the NP: the sole function of the VP seems to consist of providing INTERMEDIATE CATEGORIZATION (cf. Chomsky, 1965: 197 for this term). We must capture the fact that in a NP like [*každyj sposobnyj k muzyke mal'čik*]$_{NP}$ 'each boy gifted in music' (from [*každyj mal'čik, kotoryj sposoben k muzyke*]$_{NP}$), *sposobnyj k muzyke* is an immediate constituent: (2.35a) is the correct structure, not (2.35b).

The absence of a complement or an ADV removes the need for intermediate categorization and, in these cases, the VP is deleted (cf. *každyj sposobnyj mal'čik*).

The NP, on the other hand, is vital to Case Marking, (cf. §3.1.3) and as

(2.35a)

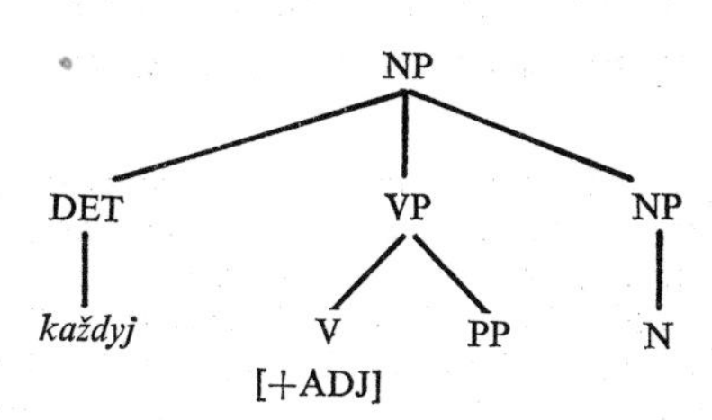

(2.35b)

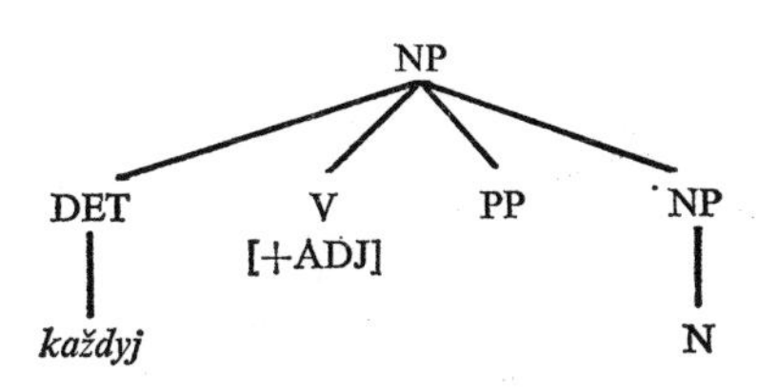

will be seen in the following chapters it is necessary whether or not it branches and whether or not it dominates a N. It therefore seems very unlikely that any form of NP Deletion will prove to be necessary (cf. §4.2.3).

2.6 NOMINALIZATION. Nominalizations were discussed in §1.9 (cf. especially Chapter 1, footnote 4) where it was pointed out that both adjectives and verbs undergo a transformation (or possibly a set of transformations) that converts a S to a NP. This is very strong evidence for the claim that adjectives and verbs are the same category at the level of deep structure: the SD of the Nominalization Transformation need only specify V. The fact that both adjectives and verbs are modified by adverbs and that these adverbs "become" adjectives as a result of a Nominalization is another piece of evidence supporting the claim.

2.7 SUBJECT-OBJECT INTERCHANGE OR FLIP. This transformation interchanges or "flips" the subject and object NPs of sentences containing predicate adjectives and verbs. The rule's SD must therefore mention verb and adjective, and thus serves as another piece of evidence that they are the same category.

Flip is needed in the grammar of Russian to account for the relationships between pairs of sentences like:

(2.36a) *Ja vspominaju mamu očen' krasivoj.*

'I remember mother as being very pretty.'

(2.36b) *Mama vspominaetsja mne očen' krasivoj.*[4]

[4] Example (2.36) is particularly interesting, since it gives us some clue as to which sentence has the underlying structure on which the Flip transformation must operate. At the level of deep structure, there must be an embedded sentence *Mama očen' krasiva* 'Mother is very beautiful'. Thus (2.36b) is derived from the structure underlying (2.36a) after the subject NP of the embedded sentence has been transformationally introduced into object position in the matrix sentence by the rule of Subject Raising. The deep structure of (2.36a) is (i) (details omitted).

(i)

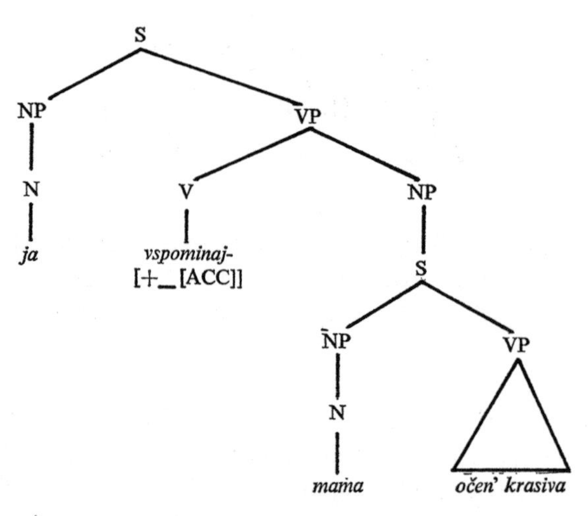

Flip applies to P-marker (ii), which is derived from (i) by Subject Raising (the NPs in squares are the ones interchanged to give (2.36b)). A configuration like (ii) is needed to account for surface *krasivoj* from deep structure *krasiva* (cf. §3.5.1).

(ii)

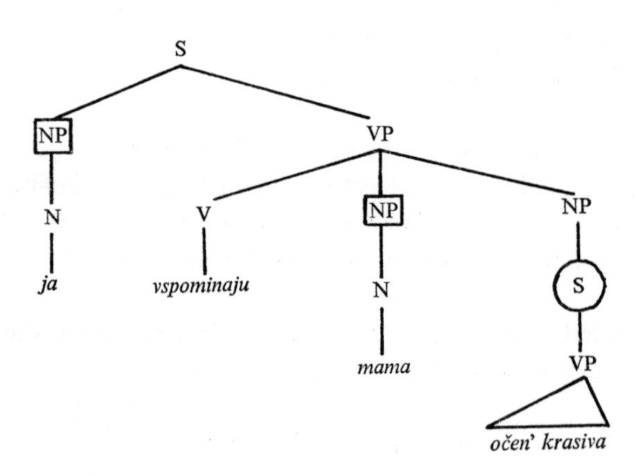

	lit. 'Mother is recalled to me as being very pretty.'
(2.37a)	*Èto razdražalo otca.*
	'That annoyed father.'
(2.37b)	*Otec ot ètogo razdražalsja.*
	'Father was annoyed at that.'
(2.38a)	*To, čto on delaet, udivljaet menja.*
	'What he is doing amazes me.'
(2.38b)	*Ja udivljajus' tomu, čto on delaet.*
	'I am amazed at what he is doing.'

Lakoff's example of Flip applied to a sentence containing an adjective is:

(2.39a)	*I enjoy movies.*
(2.39b)	*Movies are enjoyable to me.*

Relations like those in (2.39) are common in Russian:

(2.40a)	*Ja nenavižu ego slova.*
	'I despise his words.'
(2.40b)	*Ego slova nenavistny mne.*
	'His words are hateful to me.'
NB:	**Ego slova nenavidjatsja {mnoju / mne}.*
(2.41a)	*Ja vižu otsjuda požar.*
	'I see a fire from here.'
(2.41b)	*Mne viden otsjuda požar.*
	'A fire is visible to me from here.'
(2.42a)	*Ja znaju ego.*
	'I know him.'
(2.42b)	*On znakom mne.*
	'He is known to me.'

To accept a transformational relation (Flip) between the (a) and (b) sentences of examples like (2.40) to (2.42), as I am inclined to do, is in effect to make a number of rather interesting attendant claims.

For instance, many cases of Flip involve the transformation of a S containing a verb into a sentence containing an adjective. This involves an entirely new source of surface-structure adjectives (cf. Chapter 1). This is a problem only if ADJ is viewed as a category. If ADJ is considered to be a feature, however, we need only to have our Flip rule change $\underset{[-\text{ADJ}]}{\text{V}}$ to $\underset{[+\text{ADJ}]}{\text{V}}$. This solution is not at all radical, since the Passive transformation, which resembles Flip in many ways, must also change [—ADJ] into [+ADJ] if the verb in the Base Structure is perfective.

(2.43a) *Vse učeniki pročitali ètot učebnik.*
'All the students read this textbook.'
(2.43b) *Ètot učebnik (byl) pročitan vsemi učenikami.*
'This textbook was read by all the students.'

Pročitan 'read' in (2.43) is an "adjective" (= $\underset{[+\text{ADJ}]}{\text{V}}$): once the Passive transformation has produced *pročitan*, there seem to be no rules of Russian syntax that make a distinction between deep-structure and derived adjectives.

In these transformations, the "flipped" deep-structure subject is marked [+DATIVE]. A similar marking takes place in English (cf. *to me* in (2.39); cf. Rosenbaum, 1967:98-99).

The Flip transformation in Russian is far more complex than it has been stated here. It does not, for instance, easily account for relations like those in (2.44) (cf. Rothstein, 1966):

(2.44a) *Èti knigi interesujut menja.*
'These books interest me.'
(2.44b) *Èti knigi interesny mne.*
'These books are interesting to me.'
(2.44c) *Ja interesujus' ètimi knigami.*
'I am interested in these books.'

If (2.44c)'s underlying structure is viewed as the source for (2.44a) and (2.44b), then perhaps (2.44a) and (2.44b) can be accounted for by making the feature change [—ADJ] → [+ADJ] optional with *interesovat'sja.* Clearly, Flip in Russian must be more thoroughly studied.

2.8 AGENT NOMINALS. Russian and English both form agent nominals from verbs and adjectives.

(2.45a) *presledovat'* 'to persecute' – *presledovatel'* 'persecutor'

(2.45b) *uprostit'* 'to simplify' – *uprostitel'* 'simplifier'
(2.45c) *uxaživat'* 'to court' – *(uxaživatel') uxažër* 'suitor'
(2.66a) *umen / umna* 'smart' – *umnica* 'smart person'
(2.46b) *vesel* 'happy' *vesel'čak* 'happy person'
(2.46c) *zdorov* 'sound' *zdorovjak* 'strong person'

Notice once again (cf. §2.6) that an adverb becomes an adjective when its VP is converted into a NP.[5]

[5] We are assuming here that agent nominals are formed by a transformational rule that converts a VP to a NP (Nominalization transforms a S to a NP, cf. §2.6). It is not at all clear that this is the correct approach. While the transformation of (i) to (ii) presents no immediate difficulties, agent nominals like *moreplavatel'* 'seafarer' and *zemlepol'zovatel'* 'land-user' do.

(i)

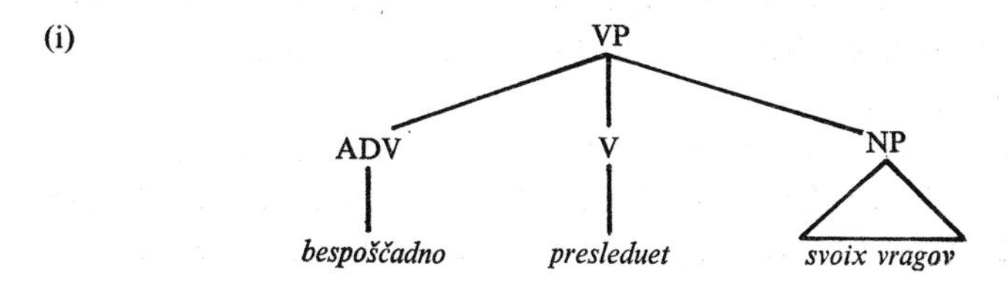

(ii)

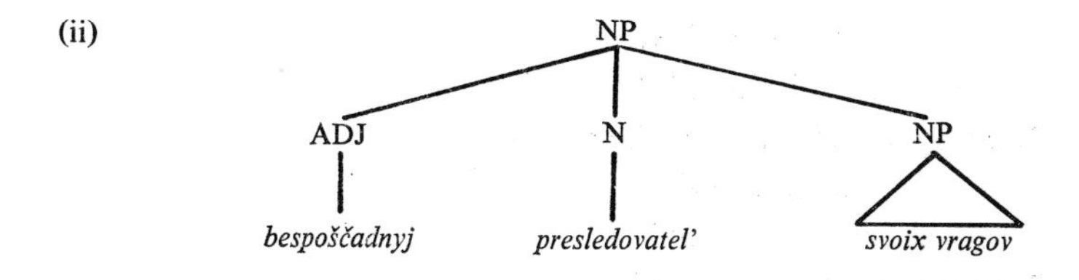

Are we to assume that (iii) is syntactically derived from (iv)?

(iii) *On zemlepol'zovatel'.*
'He is a land-user.'
(iv) *On pol'zuetsja zemlëj.*
'He is using the land.'

This would require that the syntactic component contain a rule to change (iv) to

(v) **On zemlëj pol'zovatel'.*

and then another rule to change the VP in (v) to *zemlepol'zovatel'*. This last rule must evidently also change NP to N, since we do not wish to claim that *zemlepol'zovetal'* is a NP. Also, (vi) is not derived from (vii).

(vi) *On staryj zemlepol'zovatel'.*
'He is an old land-user.'

(2.47a) *On bespoščadno presleduet svoix vragov.*
'He mercilessly persecutes his enemies.'

(2.47b) *On bespoščadnyj presledovatel' svoix vragov.*
'He is a merciless persecutor of his enemies.'

(2.48a) *Ivan užasno grub.*
'Ivan is awfully rude.'

(2.48b) *Ivan užasnyj grubijan.*
'Ivan is an awful churl.'

(2.49a) *Ona potrjasajušče krasiva.*
'She is strikingly beautiful.'

(2.49b) *Ona potrjasajuščaja krasavica.*
'She is a striking beauty.'

2.9 COMPLEMENTS. Both verbs and adjectives take the same kind of subject and object complements. This is an extremely compelling argument for recognizing verb and adjective as the same lexical category.

Here again it must be emphasized that it is the SF that possesses the verbal properties being discussed in Chapter 2. The LF is syntactically quite different (cf. §2.12 and Chapter 4). Of immediate interest is the fact that only SF can take predicate complements:

(2.50a) *Ona byla slaba zdorov'em.*
'She was weak in health.'

(2.50b) **Ona byla slabaja zdorov'em.*

(2.51a) *Ona byla gotova uexat'.*
'She was ready to leave.'

(2.51b) **Ona byla gotovaja uexat'.*

Not only do both adjectives and verbs take the same kind of complements, but also the transformational rules that map deep structures containing ADJECTIVE complements into surface structures, are precisely those rules that map deep structures containing VERB complements into surface structures.[6]

(vii) **On staro pol'zuetsja zemlëj.*
lit. 'He uses the land oldly.'

Whatever the process by which agent nominals are formed, it is the same for adjectives and verbs, and is therefore a valid argument for grouping them together into a single category.

[6] In the following examples, only object complements will be discussed; subject complements with adjectives will be touched upon in Chapter 3.

For example, in purely surface-structure descriptive terms, it is usually stated (cf. Ušakov, 1935) that the adjective *nameren* 'intend' and the verb *namerevat'sja* 'intend' both require an infinitive phrase complement. Furthermore, it is understood that the subject of *nameren* or *namerevat'sja* and the complement infinitive are identical.

(2.52) *Ja nameren čitat' ètu knigu.*
'I intend to read this book.'

(2.53) *Ja namerevajus' čitat' ètu knigu.*
'I intend to read this book.'

Within a generative-transformational framework, these relations may be stated more explicitly. (2.54) is the deep structure of (2.52); the deep structures of (2.52) and (2.53) are identical except for the feature [+ADJ] in (2.52) and [—ADJ] in (2.53).

(2.54)

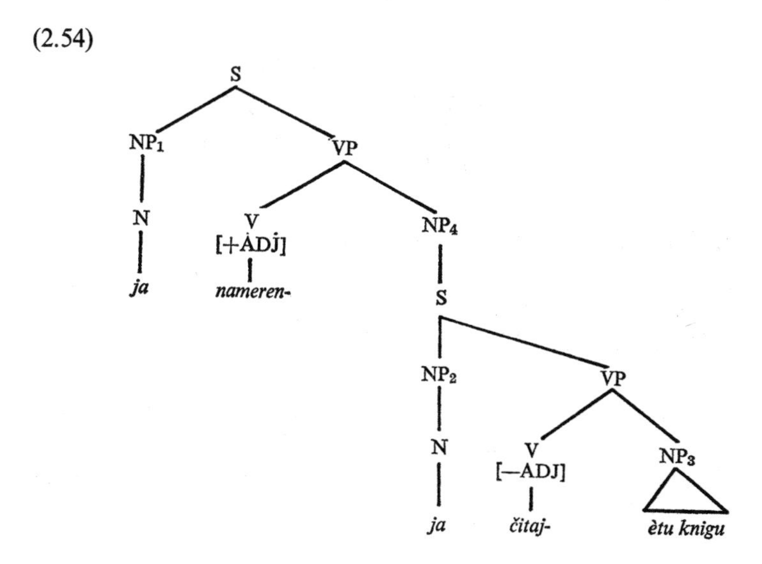

The lexical item *nameren* (and *namerevat'sja*) must specify that the subject NP of the complement sentence is identical to the matrix subject NP. Both (2.52) and (2.53) are derived by the same transformations. Details aside, these transformations are:

EQUI-NP DELETION, which deletes NP_2 under identity with NP_1.

S-NODE DELETION (cf. §3.1.1), which deletes a node S when the NP it immediately dominates is transformationally removed from its domination (by Equi-NP Del, Subject Raising, Relative Clause Reduction, etc.).

In (2.54), the S-node embedded in NP_4 is subject to S-Node Deletion.

INFINITIVE FORMATION (cf. §3.4.0), which converts the underlying verb into an infinitive (*čitat'* 'to read') after S-Node Deletion.

CASE-MARKING (cf. (3.24) and Appendix to Chapter 3) and SUBJECT-VERB AGREEMENT (cf. §4.5.4.2).

The transformational rules sketched above convert the deep-structure P-marker (2.54) into the surface structure (2.55).

(2.55)

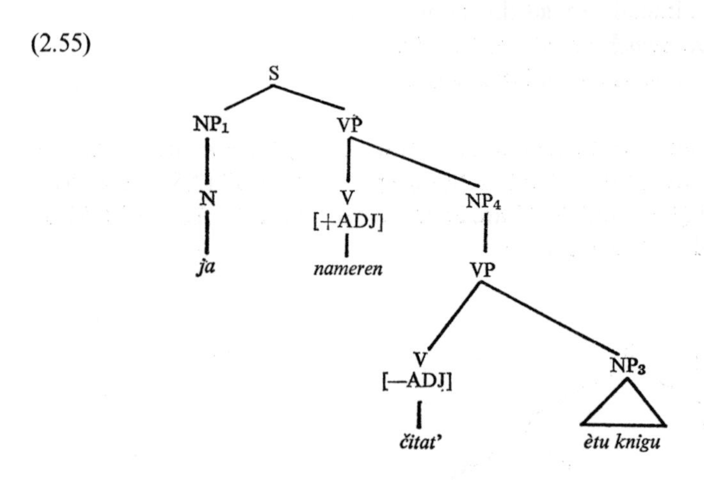

Sentence (2.56) is a more complicated example.

(2.56) *On sposoben obmanut' nas.*
'He is capable of deceiving us.'

Descriptive statements usually include the fact that *sposoben* 'capable of' requires either a PP (*V otčajanii on sposoben na vsë* 'When desperate he is capable of anything') or an infinitive phrase as its complement. These facts can be correlated by (2.57), the deep structure of (2.56).

Besides the transformations already mentioned in connection with (2.52) and (2.53), the derivation of (2.56) from (2.57) requires additional transformations, all of which are needed independently to derive sentences containing $\underset{[-\text{ADJ}]}{\text{V}}$.

The rule of Expletive Deletion deletes *to* in the configuration $[to - S]_{NP}$. In the case of *sposoben* (2.56), Expletive Deletion is optional (cf. *On sposoben na to, čtoby obmanut' nas*), while in (2.58) *soglasen* and *sog-*

(2.57)

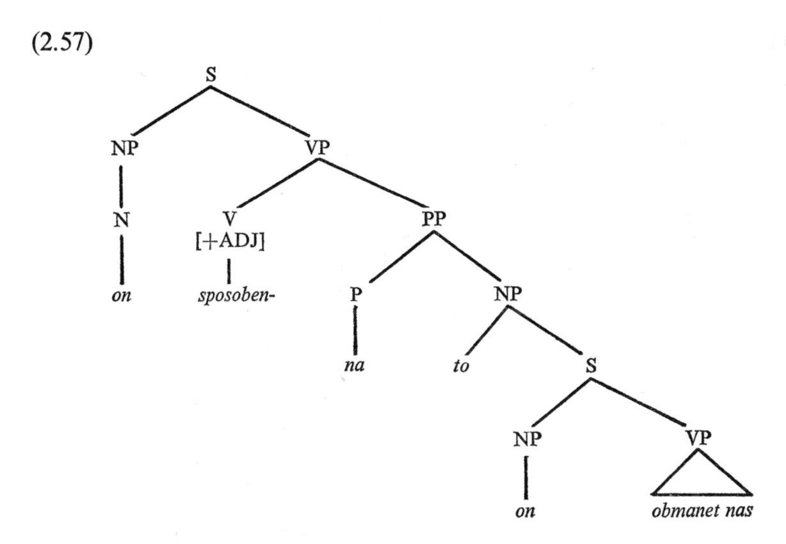

lašat'sja must be marked so as not to undergo Expletive Deletion. In (2.60) Expletive Deletion seems to be optional.

(2.58a) *Ja ne soglasen s tem, čto ona skazala.*
'I don't agree with what she said.'

(2.58b) *Ja ne soglašajus' s tem, čto ona skazala.*
'I don't agree with what she said.'

(2.59) **Ja ne* {*soglasen* / *soglašajus'*}, *čto ona skazala.*
lit. 'I don't agree what she said.'

(2.60a) *Mne ne nravitsja to, čto on delaet.*
'I don't like what he is doing.'

(2.60b) *Mne ne nravitsja, čto on delaet.*
'I don't like what he is doing.'

After Expletive Deletion, the rule of Preposition Deletion applies, obligatorily deleting a P in the configuration $[P - S]_{PP}$ (or perhaps $[P - S]_{NP}$). The surface structure restriction that a preposition cannot govern a sentence is a reflex of this transformation.

This set of transformations will generate the derived structure:

(2.61)

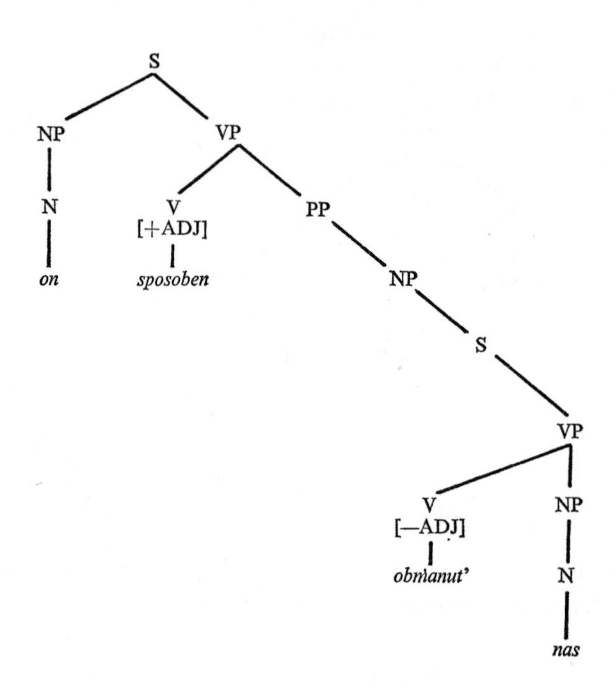

Pruning conventions will give:[7]

(2.62)

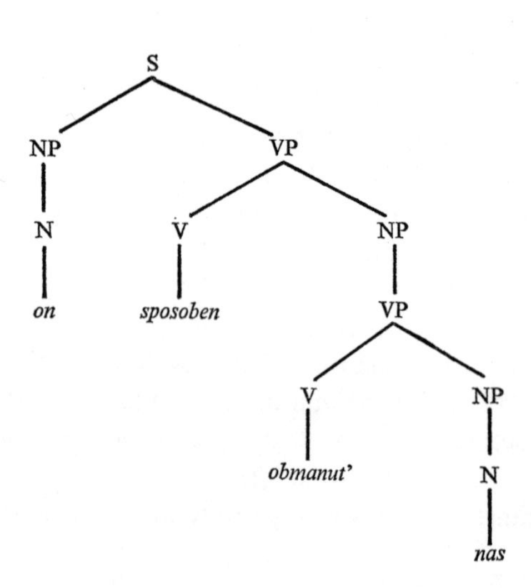

[7] No attempt has been made to justify every detail of the deep structures proposed in §2.9. For instance, no evidence has been offered that *nameren* (cf. (2.54)) requires a

NP complement and not a VP complement ([V — S $]_{VP}$). More precisely, what evidence is there that NP_4 is justifiable in (2.54) and (2.55)? Similarly, is there any evidence that the lowest VP in (2.62) is dominated by a NP?

There is, in fact, some evidence that the NP is there (cf. Rosembaum's (1967) introduction on the status of VP complementation in English). This evidence will be presented in Chapter 3 in connection with our discussion of the instrumental case in sentences like:

(i) *Ona ne namerena byt' gotovoj v tri časa.*
'She has no intention of being ready at three.'

(ii) *On ne xotel byt' poxožim na mat'.*
'He didn't want to resemble his mother.'

There is another, tenuous piece of evidence for the presence of NP in (2.62). (iii) is not possible in the Russian literary language, but it is in certain dialects (cf. Ušakov, 1935).

(iii) *Ètak mne rabotat' ne sposobno.*
'I am not capable of working this way.'

If we assume that (iii) is derived by Flip from the structure underlying *Ja ne sposoben rabotat' ètak* 'I am not capable of working like this', then *rabotat'* must be dominated by a NP, since the SD of the rule of Flip specifically mentions the two NPs to be interchanged. If these assumptions are correct, the intermediate structure of (iii) to which Flip applies must be (iv).

(iv)

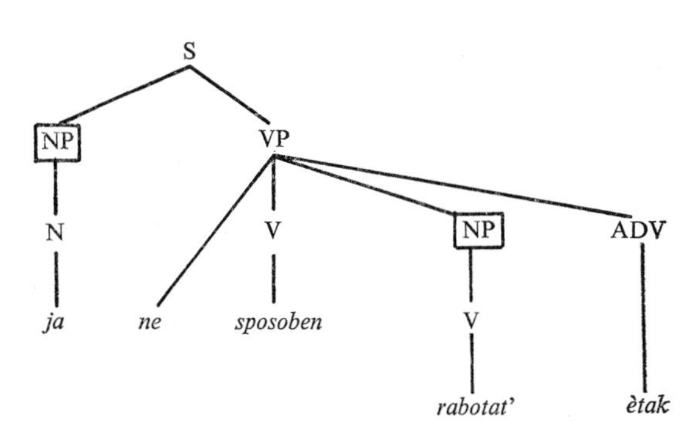

Observe that the final surface structure word order in Russian is not a function of the transformations being discussed here. The final word order depends on several factors which are too complex to be gone into at this time (cf. §3.8.1 for some discussion of the relation between constituent complexity and word order; the primary function of word order in Russian seems to involved anaphoric relations with constituents of preceding sentences.)

There is also some evidence justifying NP_4 in (2.54). If (2.54) is negated, then *Ja (voobšče) ne nameren čitat' ètoj knigi* 'I do not intend to read this book' can be derived from it. We are faced with the problem of accounting for the genitive ([+GEN]) *ètoj knigi* 'this book,' when in the deep structure the direct object of *čitaj-* 'read' must be in the accusative. The genitive *ètoj knigi* can be explained in a non-ad hoc manner if we assume that NP_4 dominates *čitat' ètu knigu* in (2.55). The general rule that marks the direct object of a negated transitive verb with the feature [+GEN] will mark NP_4

In §§2.2-2.9 it has been demonstrated with some degree of certainty that the evidence that Lakoff has presented for English holds, *mutatis mutandis*, for Russian as well. In the following paragraphs I will present several more instances where adjective and verb display a more than coincidental syntactic parallelism, offering additional support to the claim that adjectives and verbs are members of the same lexical category V. These phenomena, which are particularly vivid in Russian, were not mentioned by Lakoff.

2.10 IMPERSONAL SENTENCES. Both verbs and adjectives (NB: SF only) may serve as the predicate of impersonal sentences (cf. Vinogradov, 1947:267).

(2.63a) *Na ulice temno.*
'It is dark out.'
(2.63b) **Na ulice temnoe.*
'It is dark out.'
(2.63c) *Na ulice temneet.*
'It is getting dark out.'
(2.64a) *Kogda ja prosnulsja, bylo uže svetlo.*
'When I awoke, it was already light.'

---

as being [+GEN]. The NP *ètu knigu* is a constituent of NP_4 and it is changed to *ètoj knigi* by the Rule of Case Marking (cf. (3.24)). The *ètogo* in *On ne mog ètogo sdelat'* 'He could not do it' is most likely to be accounted for in the same way that *ètoj knigi* is. Note that *ètogo* for *èto* in *Počemu ja byl tak uveren, čto ètogo ne možet slučit'sja* 'Why was I so sure that this could not happen' has a different source.

If we accept the suggestions just made, certain problems arise concerning the nature of case marking (cf. §3.10.3).

There is a distinct possibility that the genitive *ètoj knigi* in *Ja (voobšče) ne nameren čitat' ètoj knigi* 'I do not intend to read this book (at all)' is to be explained by Neg Raising, a transformation that moves the *ne* from an embedded sentence to the matrix sentence. If this is true, the deep structure of this sentence contains the embedded sentence *Ja ne čitaju ètoj knigi* 'I am not reading this book', thus explaining *ètoj knigi* in familar terms. The *ne* is then transformationally introduced into the position before *nameren*. This explanation is possible only if we accept the semantic equivalence of *Ja nameren ne čitat' ètoj knigi* 'I intend not to read this book.' and *Ja ne nameren čitat' ètoj knigi* 'I do not intend to read this book.' The need for a Neg Raising transformation in the Grammar of Russian is made obvious by the synonymy of *On velel mne ne xodit' tuda* and *On ne velel mne xodit' tuda* 'He told me not to go there' (cf. Izrailevič, 1955: 426).

If it turns out that the Neg Raising solution is the correct one, this does not mean that we have found evidence disproving the presence of NP_4. It simply means that we cannot use the genitive *ètoj knigi* to prove that it is there.

(2.64b) **Kogda ja prosnulsja, bylo uže svetloe.*
(2.64c) *Kogda ja prosnulsja, uže svetlelo.*
'When I awoke, it was already getting light.'

There is a rule of Russian syntax which has to mention adjective and verb in its SD and which is related to the impersonal sentences just discussed. A small class of verbs and adjectives, when negated, may optionally undergo a transformational rule which marks the SUBJECT NP genitive ([+GEN]) (cf. §3.6.3., in which the "neuter" ending *-o* in sentences like (2.65b), (2.66b) and (2.68) and the Subject-Verb Agreement transformation are discussed).

(2.65a) *Požar otsjuda ne viden.*
'The fire is not visible from here.'
(2.65b) *Požara otsjuda ne vidno.* (more common than (2.65a))
(2.65c) **Požar otsjuda ne vidnyj.*
(2.65d) **Požara otsjuda ne vidnoe.*[8]
(2.66a) *S tex por ne prošel i god.*
'Since then not even a year has passed.'
(2.66b) *S tex por ne prošlo i goda.*
'Since then not even a year has passed.'

[8] Example (2.65) is complicated by the fact that adjectives like *vidno* 'visible' and *slyšno* 'audible' also appear in constructions where they take direct objects in the accusative.

(i) *Iz okna vidno rečku.*
'A little river can be seen from the window.'
NB: **Iz okna vidnoe rečku.*
(ii) *Slyšno pesnju.*
'A song can be heard.'

It is therefore a possibility that the genitive (*požara*) in (2.65b) is to be accounted for by the general rule that optionally marks the DIRECT OBJECT of a negated transitive verb with [+GEN], i.e. (2.65b) may be the negation of *Požar* [Acc] *otsjuda vidno* 'the fire is visible from here'. In other words, it is not yet clear to me whether *sčast'ja* in (iii) is the deep-structure subject or object of *zametno*.

(iii) *Sčast'ja osobennogo ne zametno.* (Aldanov)
'No particular happiness is noticeable.'

Whatever the correct solution may be, it must support our claim that adjectives and verbs are the same category, for either explanation involves a transformation that applies to both verbs and adjectives.

(2.67a) *Neuželi ne najdutsja želajuščie?*
'Is it possible that people who desire (it) cannot be found?

(2.67b) *Neuželi ne najdetsja želajuščix?*
'Is it possible that people who desire (it) cannot be found?'

(2.68) *Toski ne dolžno byt' v moem serdce! A ona est'....*
'There should not be (any) melancholy in my heart! But there is....'

(Zoščenko)

It is clear from sentence pairs like (2.69) that transformations which mark the SUBJECT NP with an oblique case are indeed necessary in Russian.

(2.69a) *Volna razbila lodku.*
'The wave smashed the boat.'

(2.69b) *Volnoj razbilo lodku.*
lit. 'By-the-wave smashed the boat.'

2.11 PREDICATE POSITION AND THE NOMINATIVE CASE. Another important syntactic parallel between verb and adjective (SF) has been obscured in Russian grammar by the force of tradition and the pragmatism of pedagogical formulations. Pedagogical grammars of Russian usually state that the SF appears only in the nominative case, while the LF may appear in any case. The LF, even in predicate position, is felt by speakers of Russian to agree in case with the subject NP (cf. Kubik, 1968: 67; in the sentence *Mama dobraja* 'Mama is (a) kind (person)', the predicate LF *dobraja* is felt to agree with the subject *mama* in gender, number, and case). In modern Russian, however, there is as little justification for calling the forms of the SF (*krasiv*, *–a*, *–o*; *–y*) nominative case forms (i.e. claiming that the SF agrees in case with the subject NP) as there is for calling the past tense forms of the verb (*znal*, *–a*, *–o*; *–i*) nominative (cf. Vinogradov, 1947:265; Peškovskij, 1938:220). By the same token, there is no real justification for calling the SF of past passive participles nominative case forms. The persistence with which Russian grammar holds the view that the forms of the SF are nominative case forms has, most likely, several reasons:

(a) The SF in Old Russian was declined, so that there was justification for viewing forms like *krasiv*, *krasiva*, etc., as being in the nominative case. This view has persisted even in modern Russian.

(b) The SF makes gender distinctions, and in Russian gender distinctions are associated with the declension rather than the conjugation.[9]

(c) There are complex syntactic structures containing the instrumental of adjectives (=LF) which, in a simple sentence, can appear in the SF only:

(2.70a) *Ja xotel by byt' poleznym vam.*
'I would like to be useful to you.'
(2.70b) *Ja polezen vam.*
'I am useful to you.'
(2.70c) **Ja poleznyj vam.*
(2.70d) **Ja byl* {*poleznyj* / *poleznym*} *vam.*
(2.70e) *Ja byl polezen.*
'I was useful.'
(2.71a) *Ja zastal ego ešče živym.*
'I found him still alive.'
(2.71b) *On ešče živ.*
'He is still alive.'
(2.71c) **On ešče živoj.*
(2.71d) *On byl ešče živ.*
'He was still alive.'
(2.71e) **On byl ešče* {*živoj* / *živym*}.
(2.72a) *Oni sčitajut, čto oni pravy.*
'They think that they are right.'
(2.72b) **Oni sčitajut, čto oni pravye.*[10]
(2.72c) *Oni sčitajut sebja pravymi.*
'They consider themselves to be right.'

The relations shown in (2.70)-(2.72) motivate an association between the SF and the instrumental, thus providing some basis for considering the SF to be nominative (cf. §3.10.3). Observe that the past tense in *–l* (*znal, znala*, etc. 'knew') does not enter into syntactic relations like those de-

[9] This also holds true for the past tense forms (*znal, znala*, etc.), but adjectives in *-l* (*ustarelyj* 'obsolete', *gorelyj* 'burnt', *byvalyj* 'experienced', etc.) are no longer syntactically related to the verbal forms in *-l* (*ustarel* 'became obsolete'), so that the considerations contained in (b) are insufficient to make the native speaker feel that the past tense forms are nominative. The SF, on the other hand, is syntactically related to LF adjectives (cf. point (c); §2.12).

[10] Sentence (2.72a) is more common than (2.72c). (2.72b) is possible if *pravye* is interpreted as 'right-winger'. (2.72c) is therefore ambiguous.

scribed in (2.70)-(2.72). The relations in (c) will be discussed in Chapter 3.

Significantly enough, some Russian linguists, explicating their native intuitions, have claimed that the SF (but not the LF) is marked for person (cf. Vinogradov, 1947:267 for a summary of this view), thus completing the parallelism between verb and adjective (SF) with respect to the Subject-Verb Agreement transformation.

Therefore by discarding the unjustified notion of case in the SF it becomes possible to capture a significant generalization in modern Russian and simplify the grammar by reducing the number of transformations needed to account for the sentences of Russian. Both adjective (SF only) and verb undergo Subject-Verb Agreement (i.e. agreement in number, person, and, in the past tense, gender). The rule of Subject-verb Agreement is treated in more detail in §4.5.4.2. Hence we see another instance when the SD of a rule must mention adjective and verb, thus providing another reason for recognizing the category V.

2.12 ACTIVE PARTICIPLES. So far I have limited myself to enumerating the syntactic parallels between the SF and the verb, and have merely pointed out in passing that the LF has none of the verbal properties that characterize the SF. An examination of active participle formation will not only provide us with another parallel between verb and SF; it will shed some light on the SYNTACTIC relationship between the SF and the LF (and between the LF and active participle).

The following pairs of sentences all seem to involve the same grammatical relations and syntactic processes. The (b) sentences are derived from the (a) sentences by the same transformation: Relative Clause Reduction.

(2.73a) *Mal'čik, kotoryj bolen anginoj, dolžen ležat' celuju nedelju.*
'The boy who is sick with tonsillitis has to stay in bed for a whole week.'

(2.73b) *Mal'čik, bol'noj anginoj, dolžen ležat' celuju nedelju.*
'The boy sick with tonsillitis has to stay in bed all week.'

(2.73c) **Mal'čik, bolen anginoj, dolžen ležat'*[11] *celuju nedelju.*

[11] Constructions like (2.73c) are no longer possible in modern spoken Russian; they are occasionally found in poetry, where their archaic status serves a stylistic function (cf. *Grammatika russkogo jazyka AN SSSR*, 1960: vol. II, §731). The impossibility in modern Russian of a SF in a reduced relative clause like (2.73c) is not an isolated fact. The (a) sentences in the following examples were possible as recently as the nineteenth century. Only the (b) sentences are possible in modern Russian.

(i a) **On prišel domoj goloden.*

(2.74a) *Vnutrennost' rošči, kotoraja byla vlažna ot doždja, besprestanno izmenjalas'.*
'The interior of the grove, which was wet from the rain, was incessantly changing.'

(2.74b) *Vnutrennost' rošči, vlažnoj ot doždja, besprestanno izmenjalas'.*
'The interior of the grove, wet from the rain, was incessantly changing.'

(2.75a) *V vozduxe, kotoryj čist i svež, paxnet grečixoj.*
'The air, which is pure and fresh, smells of buckwheat.'

(2.75b) *V vozduxe, čistom i svežem, paxnet grečixoj.*
'The air, clean and fresh, smells of buckwheat.'

(2.76a) *On ljubit dorogu, kotoraja vedet k reke.*
'He loves the road that leads to the river.'

(2.76b) *On ljubit dorogu, veduščuju k reke.*
'He loves the road leading to the river.'

(2.77a) *Devuška, kotoraja sidit okolo pal'my, očen' krasiva.*
'The girl who is sitting near the palm is very pretty.'

(2.77b) *Devuška, sidjaščaja okolo pal'my, očen' krasiva.*
'The girl sitting near the palm is very pretty.'

From sentences (2.73)-(2.77) it is clear that the same transformation that derives active participles from verbs (Relative Clause Reduction) also derives LFs from SFs. This fact suggests what may be a very important generalization about modern Russian: if the SF is viewed as a verb (more precisely, a V), then the LF may be considered its active participle (i.e. SF:LF::verb:active participle).

With this in mind, let us look more closely at the syntactic processes involved (details are omitted).

The deep structure of (2.78) is (2.79). (*Kotoryj* 'who' is transformationally derived from *mal'čik* by Relative Clause Formation.)

'He came home hungry.'

(i b) *On prišel domoj* {*golodnyj* / *golodnym*}.

(ii a) **Derevnja pokazalas' emu dovol'no grjazna.*
'The village seemed quite dirty to him.'

(ii b) *Derevnja pokazalas' emu dovol'no grjaznoj.* (cf. Sprinčak, 1960: 69; §3.6.0)

These examples illustrate the same process: the final stage of the "verbalization" of the SF during the nineteenth century. A finite V cannot appear in a reduced predicate in the surface structure of modern spoken Russian.

(2.78) $[$*mal'čik kotoryj poxož na otca*$]_{NP_1}$

(2.79)

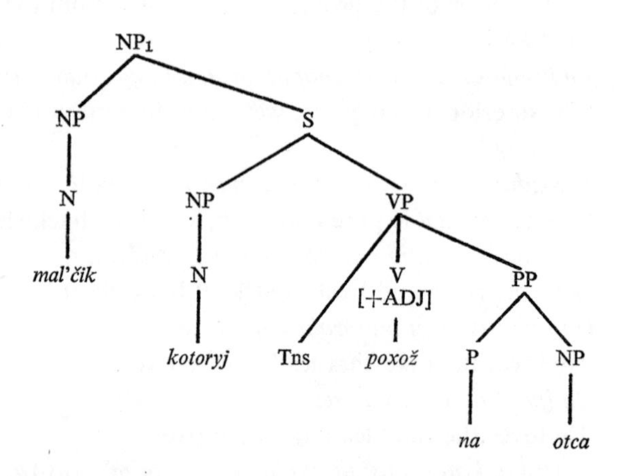

The Tense Marker (Tns) will be discussed in Chapter 3.

Relative Clause Reduction, which deletes *kotoryj* + Tns, transforms (2.79) into (2.80).

(2.80)

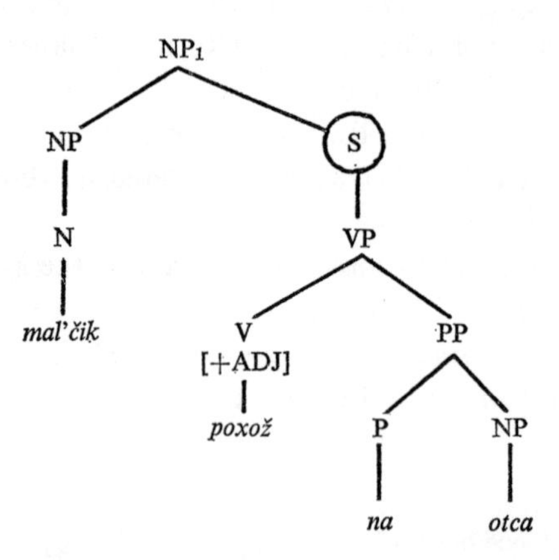

Tree Pruning (or S-Node Deletion; cf. §3.1.1) converts the P-marker (2.80) into (2.81).

Tree Pruning has the effect of introducing the SF into NP constituency. In other words, the head noun (here: *mal'čik*) and the reduced relative clause (*poxož(–ij) na otca*), after the node S is deleted, are constituents of

(2.81)

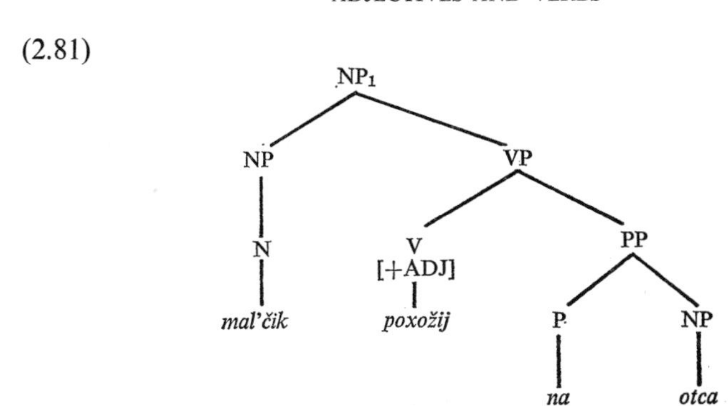

the same higher NP (NP_1). The SF, upon introduction into a NP, automatically undergoes Case Marking, since all "markable" elements of a NP must receive the same case feature as the highest NP (NP_1; cf. (3.24) and §3.10.3 for Case Marking and a discussion of why *otca* ([+GEN]) is not in the same case as NP_1 ([+NOM])). Note that the VP node that intervenes between NP_1 and the SF is "transparent" with respect to NP constituency and, consequently, with respect to Case Marking (cf. §2.5 for the primary function of the VP).

We are thus claiming that the LF is derived from the SF when the latter is, as a result of the operation of transformations, introduced into a NP. Recall that the Base PS-Rules introduce the SF or, more precisely, V [+ADJ] as an expansion of the VP only (cf. Chapter 1). A corollary of this is that the SF in contemporary Russian exists only outside of the NP, and the LF exists only within the NP. It might be said that the LF and SF are in complementary distribution with respect to NP constituency. This predicts the impossibility of surface structures like *[*bolen mal'čik*]$_{NP}$ (cf. *[*čitaet knigu mal'čik*]$_{NP}$) in modern Russian.

The configuration in (2.81) also explains the traditional dictum that the reduced relative clause agrees with its antecedent in case: they are both constituents of the same higher NP. The prenominal adjective / participle agrees with its head noun for the same reason. Modifier Shift, which transforms P-marker (2.81) into (2.82), moves the LF / participle around the head noun (*mal'čik*), and the affect of this transformation is merely to change the order of the elements in the upper NP (NP_1), not to change the constituency.

SUMMARY OF §2.12. This section has demonstrated that, in derivations involving Relative Clause Reduction, the surface structure LF is a deep

(2.82)

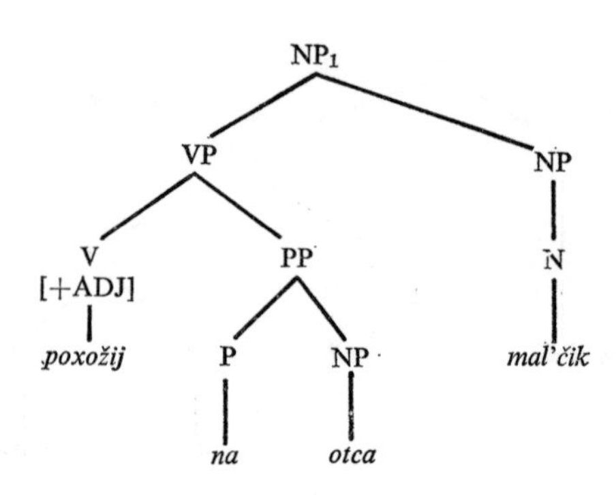

structure SF which has been transformationally introduced into a NP.

In a very real sense the rest of this study is devoted to determining whether this derivational relationship can account for other surface structures containing a LF. The possibility will be investigated that the syntactic relations between SF and LF shown in §2.12 (that the LF is a SF that has undergone Case Marking) may be elevated to the status of a general rule of Russian grammar which would be valid for all surface structures containing LF / participles, and not just for surface structures derived by Relative Clause Reduction.

SUMMARY OF CHAPTER 2. The evidence presented in Chapter 2 makes it quite probable that verbs and adjectives (SF) are the same deep structure category V, and differ by the feature [ADJ]. What is traditionally called the LF is, at least in the structures examined in Chapter 2, derived from V [+ADJ] and may be considered its active participle.

3

ADJECTIVES AND NP CONSTITUENCY

3.0 In §2.12 it was shown that a surface structure LF resulted from the introduction of a deep-structure SF into a NP as the result of Relative Clause Reduction and S-Node Deletion. The NP into which the SF was introduced also had as its constituent the head noun (antecedent) of the relative clause. The result was "agreement in case" between the LF and the head noun (cf. §3.10.2 for a discussion of Agreement).

In Chapter 3 we will deal with structures in which the SF is moved into a NP that has no constituent other than the resulting LF in its final derived P-marker.

The main purpose of Chapter 3 will be to demonstrate that the derivational relationship between the SF and LF revealed in §2.12 is not limited to the results of the Relative Clause Reduction sequence of transformations. Any transformation or sequence of transformations (Subject Raising, Equi-NP Deletion) which results in S-Node Deletion will produce a surface-structure LF by introducing an underlying SF into a higher NP where it undergoes Case Marking. This constitutes further evidence that any occurrence of a LF in a Russian sentence can be traced back to an underlying SF.

Traditional, taxonomic Russian grammar has been unable to uncover this relation between the SF and LF since it does not operate with synchronic derivation. The syntactic relation between the SF and LF has been further obscured by the fact that traditional Russian grammar has studied the LF with reference to the SF only in the predicates of simple sentences containing a finite form of the copula *byt'* (cf. §3.3.0) and only in the nominative case. This is due partly to the fact that the predicate is the only position where the LF and SF are opposed or co-occur, and partly to the mistaken notion that the SF is in the nominative case (cf. §2.11 and §3.10). Only when this arbitrary limitation is removed and the SF is considered in its relation to the LF in all cases and positions, can an insightful analysis be made. Chapter 3 is devoted to this task. Chapter 4 will go on to show that LF and SF in predicate position is only a special case of the more general relation of LF and SF: LF=SF (or, more precisely, $\underset{[+\text{ADJ}]}{\text{V}}$ + the features acquired by Subject-V Agreement) + any Case feature.

3.1 Sentences (3.1) and (3.2) are semantically equivalent and have the same deep structure; (3.1) is stylistically more neutral than (3.2).

(3.1) *Oni sčitali, čto oni pravy.*
'They considered that they were right.'

(3.2) *Oni sčitali sebja pravymi.*
'They considered themselves (to be) right.'

(3.3) **Oni pravye.*
'They are right.'

(3.4) **Oni sčitali, čto oni (byli) pravye.*

(3.5) **Oni sčitali, čto oni (byli) pravymi.*

(3.6) **Oni sčitali sebja pravy.*

(3.7) **Oni sčitali sebja pravyx.*

(3.8) **Oni sčitali sebja byt' pravymi.*[1]
'They considered themselves to be right.'

The approximate deep structure of (3.1) and (3.2) is (3.9).[2]

(3.9)

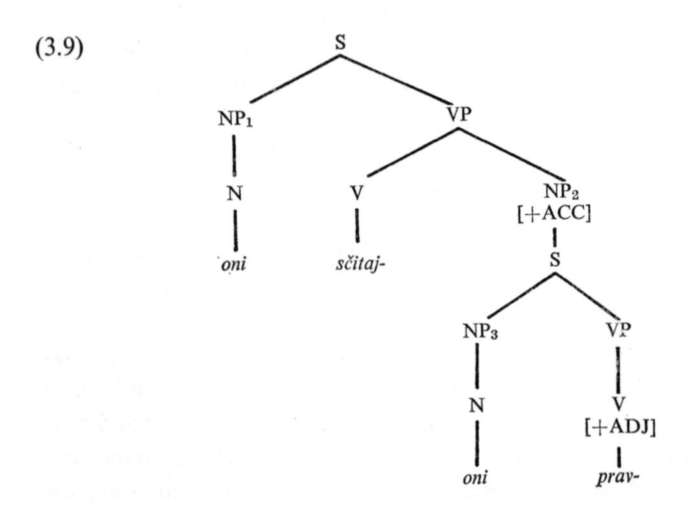

[1] Sentences like (3.8) were possible in the late eighteenth and early nineteenth centuries. See §3.6.2 where sentences like... *o takom čeloveke, kotoryj sčital sebja byt' sčastlivym* 'about the kind of man who considered himself to be happy' are discussed.

[2] The representation of tense in (3.1) and (3.2) is treated in §3.7.

Sentence (3.1) is derived from (3.9) by Complementizer Placement, which introduces *čto* 'that', and the Subject-Verb Agreement transformation, which copies certain inherent features from the subject onto the V (cf. §3.10).

The final derived P-marker of (3.1) is (3.10).

(3.10)

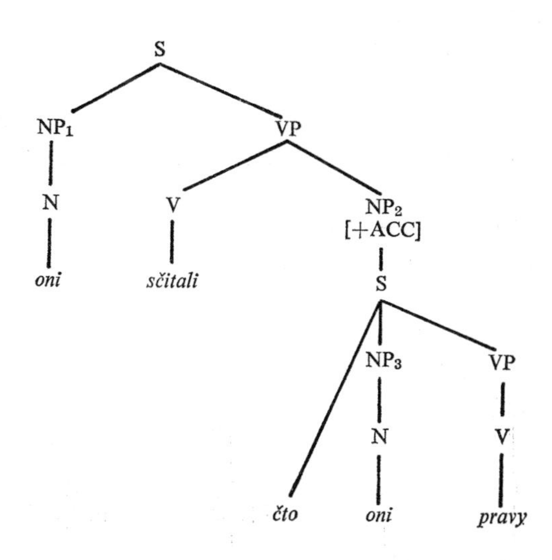

The derivation of (3.2) from (3.9) involves the following: on Cycle I, Subject-V Agreement applies giving *pravy*; on Cycle II, the rule of Subject Raising operates.

The Subject Raising transformation moves the subject of an embedded sentence up into the matrix sentence (cf. §3.6.1 for a detailed discussion of Subject Raising in Russian). In the case of (3.9), the constituent sentence subject NP_3 (*oni*) is raised into direct object position in the matrix sentence where it is marked [+ACC], since the lexical item *sčitaj-* 'consider' has the contextual feature [+___[ACC]] (NP_2 was marked [+ACC] in the deep-structure P-marker in the same way. cf. §3.10.1).

It may thus be said that the verb *sčitaj-* "governs" the rule of Subject Raising. The fact that this rule is optional is responsible for the fact that both (3.1) and (3.2) derive from the same deep structure. Note also that *sčitaj-* cannot govern the rule of Equi-NP Deletion. This fact accounts for the ungrammaticality of sentences like

(3.11) **Oni sčitali pravymi.*

After the constituent subject NP *oni* is raised into the matrix sentence, the rule of Reflexivization converts it to *sebja* 'themselves'. Reflexivization is obligatory in this type of structure, and accounts for the ungrammaticality of sentences like (3.12) when *oni* 'they' and *ix* 'them' have the same referent.

(3.12) **Oni sčitali ix pravymi.*
'They considered them right.'

Since Reflexivization can operate only within a simple sentence, the presence of *sebja* is evidence that the subject of the embedded sentence has been introduced into the matrix sentence.

(3.13) is the intermediate P-marker derived from the deep structure (3.9) by the transformations just mentioned.

(3.13)

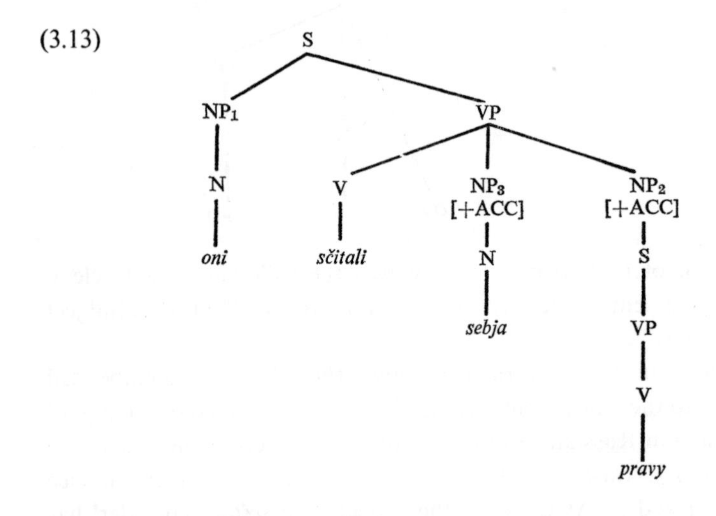

(3.13) is not a possible final derived P-marker of modern Russian (cf. **Oni sčitali sebja pravy* and **Oni sčitali sebja pravyx*), and, furthermore, it makes the counterintuitive claim that *pravy* is a S.

This is precisely the problem we encountered in Chapter 2 (cf. esp. §2.12) in conjunction with Relative Clause Reduction and the derivation of prenominal adjectives from underlying relative clauses. For instance, the derivation of [*poxožij na otca mal'čik*]$_{NP}$ from an underlying [*mal'čik, kotoryj poxož na otca*]$_{NP}$ 'the boy who resembles (his) father' involved an intermediate P-marker (2.80) (repeated here for convenience as (3.14) that makes the claim that *poxož na otca* is a S.

(3.14)

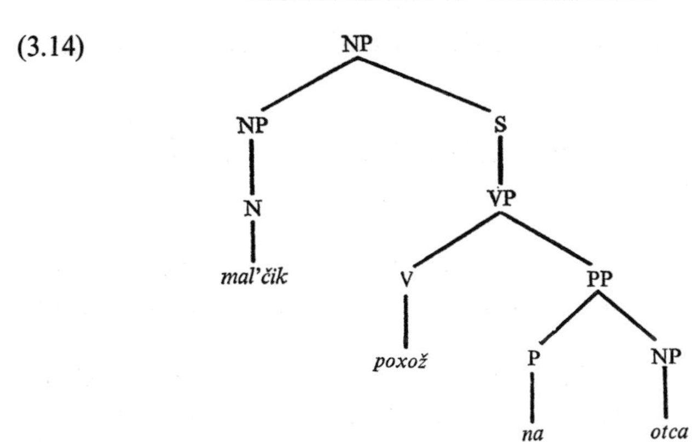

The convention of S-NODE DELETION was applied to Russian in (2.80) without discussion, in order to give a more intuitively correct surface structure and to account for the surface structure LF (*poxožij*) from the deep structure SF (*poxož*) (cf. (2.81)). Yet S-Node Deletion is crucial both to our explanation of the syntactic relationship between the LF and SF, and to Case Marking, Infinitive Formation, and Reflexivization, so we need to examine it in detail.

3.1.1 S-NODE DELETION OR TREE PRUNING. John R. Ross (1969:288-299) proposed the convention or meta-rule of S-Node Deletion in order to eliminate an inadequacy in the derived structure of P-markers containing adjectives. In English, as in Russian, prenominal adjectives are derived from deep-structure relative clauses by a set of transformations which include Relative Clause Reduction and Modifier Shift. As a result of the operation of these transformations, adjectives are dominated by S-nodes in the final derived P-marker. For example, Ross notes that *yellow* in the NP *his yellow cat* would look like:

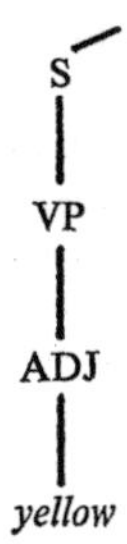

The same problem arises in the derivation of prenominal adjectives in Russian (cf. (3.14) and (2.79)-(2.81)).

It is clearly counterintuitive to claim that *yellow* in *his yellow cat* or *poxožij na otca* in *poxožij na otca mal'čik* are sentences. To avoid this,

Ross proposed the convention of S-Node Deletion, which he formulates as follows:

(3.15) Delete any embedded node S which does not branch (i.e. which directly dominates only NP or VP).

S-Node Deletion operates whenever a sequence of transformations produces a node S that no longer branches. It has no fixed place in the order of transformational rules.

In Russian, besides helping to make derived P-markers containing adjectives intuitively correct, S-Node Deletion provides an explanation of how an underlying SF emerges in the surface structure as a LF: S-Node Deletion results in the introduction of a SF into the next highest NP and the ensuing rule of Case Marking produces the LF. Thus S-Node Deletion is crucial to Russian syntax in a way Ross could not have foreseen. These Russian facts provide additional evidence that Ross's formulation of S-Node Deletion is correct and is needed in the theory of grammar, not merely in the grammar of English. The following section offers further proof that S-Node Deletion is necessary in Russian grammar.

3.1.2 REFLEXIVIZATION AND S-NODE DELETION IN RUSSIAN. The reflexive pronoun *sebja* 'themselves' in (3.2) may serve as proof that Subject Raising has taken place, but it tells us nothing about the node S of the embedded sentence from which it has been raised. There is, however, a class of sentences in which Reflexivization provides unquestionable evidence that S-Node Deletion is necessary in a transformational grammar of Russian.[3] Consider the following sentences:

[3] Absence of Reflexivization does not prove that a given pronoun is not in the same simple sentence as a coreferential noun. In sentences like:

(i) *Ja soveršenno uveren v dostovernosti provodimyx* mnoju *faktov.*
'I am absolutely certain of my facts.'

(ii) *V každom iazyke est' zvuki, prisuščie tol'ko* emu.
'Every language has sounds which are unique to it alone.' (Vinokur)

(iii) *V* svoem *dnevnike, napisannom v poslednie gody* ego *žizni, Sevčenko vspominaet ob odnoj devuške.*
'In *his* diary, written in the last years of *his* life, Sevčenko recalls a certain girl.' (Zoščenko)

there are no embedded S nodes to block Reflexivization, yet it does not take place (for reasons which are not clear to me). Thus the absence of Reflexivization is noncommittal with respect to the presence or absence of embedded S nodes. The PRESENCE of Reflexivization is proof positive that there are no embedded S nodes intervening between the reflexive pronoun and its coreferential N.

(3.16) *On ne pozvoljaet* sebja *duračit'*.
'He does not allow (anyone) to make a fool of *him*.'

NB. *He does not allow anyone to make a fool of *himself*.'
'He does not allow *himself* to be made a fool of.'
*'He does not allow *him* to be made a fool of.' (*him* = *he*)

(3.17) *On prikazal ubit'* svoju *lošad'*.
'He had *his* horse killed.'

(3.18) *Ona pozvolila misteru Franklinu otvesti* sebja *obratno v komnatu.*
(3.18) is a Russian translation of the English 'She suffered Mr. Franklin to lead *her* back into the room.'

(3.19) *...on exal xoronit' tovarišča, a ona pozvoljala celovat'* sebja *Igumnovu.* (Panova)
'He went to bury a friend, and she let Igumnov kiss *her*.'

The deep structure of (3.18) is (3.20); irrelevant details are omitted.

(3.20)

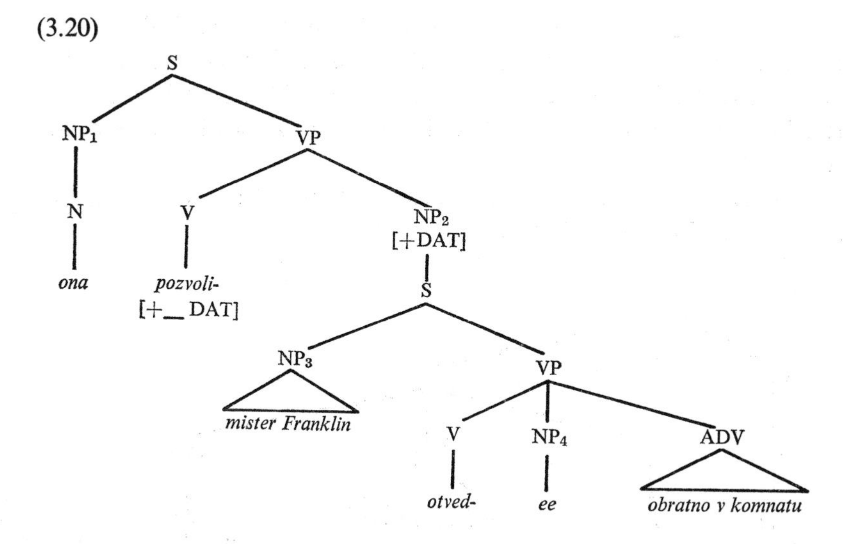

Subject Raising derives (3.21) from (3.20); the origin of the infinitive (*otvesti* 'to lead') is dealt with in §3.4.1.

[*Misteru Franklinu*]$_{NP_3}$, the deep-structure subject of the embedded S, has been introduced by Subject Raising into object position in the matrix S and, accordingly, is marked [+DAT], since *pozvoli-* "governs" the dative (cf. deep structure (3.20) and (3.13)).

The embedded S-node in (3.21) no longer branches, and according to

(3.21)

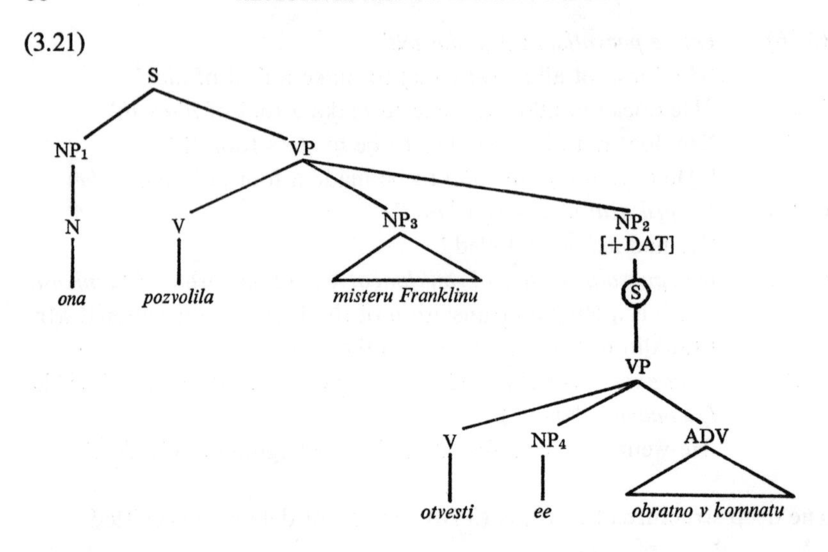

(3.15) it is deleted. That the convention of S-Node Deletion is in fact necessary in Russian can be seen in the Reflexivization of $[ee]_{NP_4}$ 'her' to *sebja* 'herself'. If the S-node were not deleted, *ee* would not be in the same simple sentence as $[ona]_{NP_1}$ 'she', and it would be impossible to account for the Reflexivization.

S-Node Deletion and Reflexivization convert (3.21) into (3.22), the final derived P-marker of (3.18).

(3.22)

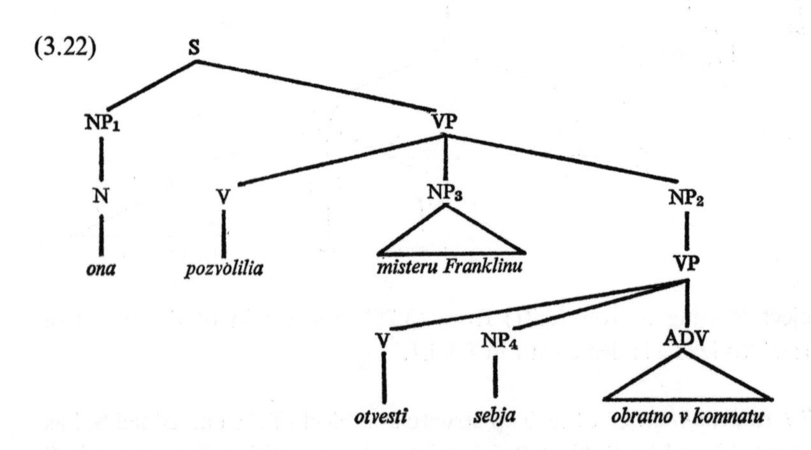

3.1.3 S-Node Deletion and Case Marking in Sentence (3.2): §3.1 Continued. According to (3.15), S-Node Deletion applies to (3.13), producing P-marker (3.23).

(3.23)

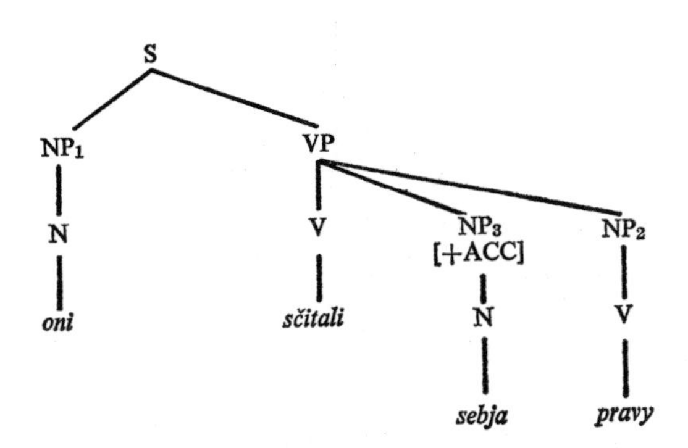

The node VP in NP_2 is also deleted (cf. §2.5).

Note that in §2.12 we encountered S-Node Deletion that was occasioned by Relative Clause Reduction. Here it is Subject Raising that leads to a situation where an S-node directly dominates only a VP and is therefore deleted. Later on sentences where this situation is created by Equi-NP Deletion will be discussed. From facts like these it must be concluded that the derivation of the LF from the SF cannot be associated with any one transformation. It is S-Node Deletion that is the common denominator in all derivations involving the LF.

S-Node Deletion in (3.23) has had the effect of introducing the SF into the domination of NP_2, which at a deeper level was the direct object of *sčitaj-* and, consequently, received the feature [+ACC]. Once it is a NP constituent, the SF *pravy* must undergo Case Marking, the transformation that copies the case feature of the upper NP on to all its markable constituents. A rule of Case Marking that accounts for the distribution of case in Russian was formulated by Ross (1967:80-87) as follows:

(3.24)	$[_{NP_i}$ X	—	Y	—	Z	—	$[+CASE_j]]_{NP_i}$	Obligatory
SD:	1		2		3		4 ⇒	
SC:	1		2		3		4	
			$[+CASE_j]$					

CONDITION: it is not the case that $NP_i > S_k$ and $S_k > Y$.

Ross's "condition" on (3.24) merely stipulates that the case feature of NP_i cannot go down into an embedded S. In other words, node S_k blocks the rule of Case Marking from copying the case feature of NP_i on to any of its constituents:

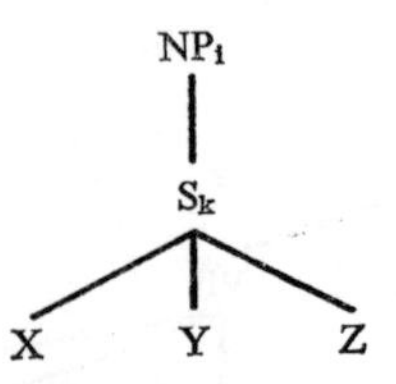

It is this condition, for instance, that accounts for the SF in (3.1) (*Oni sčitali, čto oni pravy.*) and blocks (3.4) and (3.5) (cf. P-marker (3.10)).

These considerations are extremely important, since the LF differs from the SF only in that it has acquired a case feature, and, consequently, the proper formulation of Case Marking in Russian automatically produces the correct surface-structure distribution of the LF and SF, given the other facts presented in Chapter 3.

It would seem appropriate at this point to provide an explicit statement of the status of Case Marking and Case in a generative-transformational grammar of Russian. However, since transformations are required that cannot be justified until the end of Chapter 3, the material is presented in §3.10 as an appendix.

Thus in (3.23) *pravy* or, more precisely, the lexical item *prav-* plus the features acquired by it through Subject-V Agreement has become a constituent of NP_2 as a result of S-Node Deletion and must undergo Case Marking. This produces P-marker (3.25), which does not, however, underlie (3.2). If (3.25) is interpreted as a final derived P-marker, it is seen to be the surface structure of the ungrammatical (3.7).

(3.25)

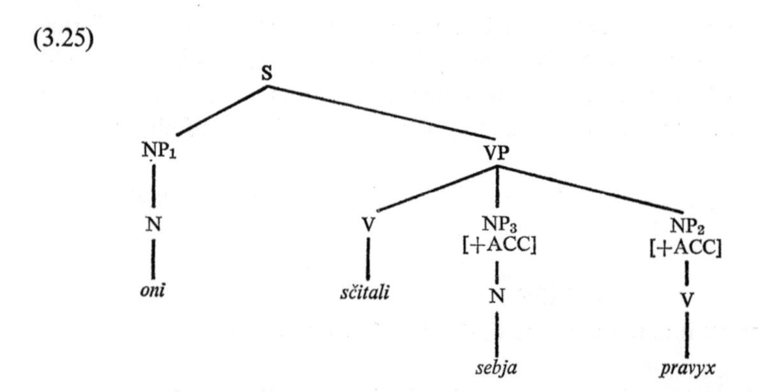

We are thus faced with the problem of accounting both for the ungrammaticality of (3.7) and of accounting for the instrumental *pravymi* in (3.2).

One possible solution immediately suggests itself. As recently as the first third of the nineteenth century sentences like (3.26) were common.

(3.26) *Oni našli ego mertvogo.*
'They found him dead.'
NB: **Oni našli mertvogo ego.*
'They found (a) dead him.'

(3.27) is the deep structure of (3.26) and (3.28) is its surface structure (details omitted).

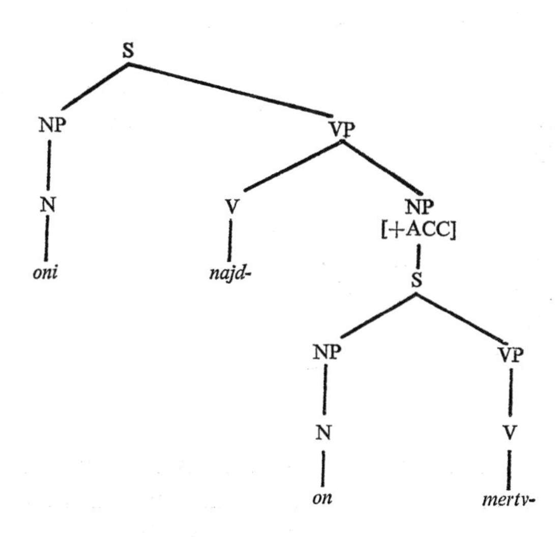

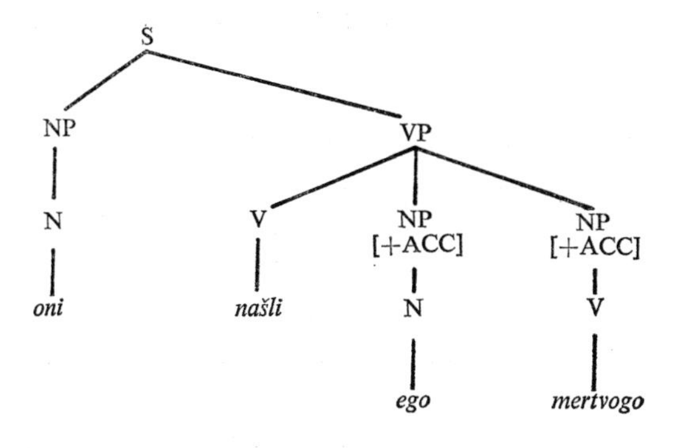

In modern colloquial Russian, sentences like (3.26) are no longer possible (they are, however, still found in poetry). (3.26) has been replaced by (3.29), which also has (3.27) and (3.28) as underlying P-markers.

(3.29) *Oni našli ego mertvym.*
'They found him dead.'

(3.30) and (3.31) further illustrate this use of the instrumental; (3.31) is another instance of the parallelism between the LF and the active participle.

(3.30a) *Ja zastal ego uže mertvym.*
'I found him already dead.'
(3.30b) **Ja zastal ego uže mertv.*
(3.30c) **Ja zastal ego uže mertvogo.*
(3.31) *Elena na dnjax zastal menja celujuščim ruki u Zoi.*
'Elena recently found me kissing Zoja's hand.' (Turgenev)

Note also that when the final position in these three-place predicates is occupied by a noun, it too must be in the instrumental, which replaces an older accusative.

(3.32a) *Oni izbrali ego prezidentom.*
'They elected him president.'
(3.32b) *On byl izbran prezidentom.*
'He was elected president.'
(3.33a) **Oni izbrali ego prezidenta.*
(3.33b) **On byl izbran prezidenta.*

These facts suggest that the grammar of Russian requires a transformational rule which reflects the process that eliminated the second accusative of the old construction (cf. V. L. Georgieva, 1968: §33, where the elimination of the *vtoroj vinitel'nyj* is discussed). Rule (3.34) seems to account for these facts.

(3.34) OBLIGATORY INSTRUMENTAL RULE

	X	[V	—	NP	—	$NP]_{VP}$	Y	
SD	1	2		3		4	5 ⇒	Obligatory
SC	1	2		3		4	5	
						[INST]		

CONDITION: the two NPs are immediately dominated by the same VP.[4]

The fact that (3.24) is obligatory in modern Russian accounts for the ungrammaticality of (3.7).

Sentences (3.35) and (3.36) demonstrate that *odin*, *odna*... 'alone' is an exception to (3.34).

[4] Rule (3.34) will be subsequently rejected (cf. §3.5.1). The two versions of the Obligatory Instrumental rule are compared and discussed in §3.6.4.

(3.35a) *Ja našel ego odnogo.*
'I found him alone.'
(3.35b) **Ja našel ego odnim.*
(3.36a) *Ja zastal ee odnu.*
'I found her alone.'
(3.36b) **Ja zastal ee odnoj.*

The Obligatory Instrumental rule as stated in (3.34) merely CHANGES the second NP in the configuration $[\text{V NP NP}]_{VP}$ to [+INST], without regard to which case feature the NP has already received. This allows Case Marking to operate without any constraints since (3.34), which must follow Case Marking, will change any case to [+INST]. Case Marking alone will produce (3.35a) and (3.36a); rule (3.34) does not apply because *odin* is marked as an exception to rule (3.34).

Having introduced the Obligatory Instrumental rule we can return to the problem encountered in the derivation of (3.2). (3.25) meets the SD of (3.34) and, accordingly, the case feature on *prav-* is changed from [+ACC] to [+INST]. This gives the correct surface-structure form *pravymi* and is the final transformation in the derivation of (3.2) from the deep structure (3.9).

The derivation of (3.2) is extremely important because it provides us with another instance of the LF (*pravymi*) being derived from an underlying SF (*prav-* + syntactic features acquired by Subject-V Agreement). The sequence is essentially the same as that noted in §2.12: acquisition of a case feature by a SF as a result of S-Node Deletion and Case Marking. The derivation in §2.12 differs from the derivation of (3.2) in the following ways. (i) In §2.12 the transformation that occasioned S-Node Deletion was Relative Clause Reduction; in (3.2) it was Subject Raising. (ii) In §2.12 rule (3.34) did not apply. (iii) In the derivation of (3.2) the SF is introduced into a NP that has no other constituent; in §2.12 the SF is introduced into a NP that also has the deep-structure relative clause head noun as its constituent. None of these three differences bears on the main point being made here.

3.2 In this section, we will examine another type of Russian sentence which reveals a derivational relationship between the SF and LF (instrumental).

Consider the sentences in (3.37)-(3.39).

(3.37a) *Ivan xotel byt' poxožim na otca.*

'Ivan wanted to resemble his father.'

(3.37b) **Ivan xotel byt' poxož na otca.*

(3.37c) **Ivan xotel byt' poxožij na otca.*

(3.37d) **Ivan xotel byt' poxožego na otca.*

(3.38a) *Ivan xotel, čtoby Igor' byl poxož na otca.*
'Ivan wanted Igor to resemble his father.'

(3.38b) **Ivan xotel, čtoby Igor' byl poxožim na otca.*

(3.38c) **Ivan xotel, čtoby Igor' byl poxožij na otca.*

(3.39a) *Ivan byl poxož na otca.*

(3.39b) **Ivan byl poxožim na otca.*

(3.39c) **Ivan byl poxožij na otca.*

Note that in a simple sentence, embedded or not, only the SF (*poxož*) is possible: in (3.37) only the LF instrumental is possible.

The lexical item *xote-* 'want' can take an object clause (sentential object) and governs the rule of Equi-NP Deletion, which deletes a subject NP in an embedded sentence if it is identical to the nearest NP in the matrix sentence. Furthermore, the ungrammaticality of (3.40) demonstrates that, unlike its English equivalent *want*, *xote-* does not allow Subject Raising in the event that Equi-NP Deletion does not apply.

(3.40) **Ivan xotel Igorja byt' poxožim na otca.*
'Ivan wanted Igor to resemble (his) father.'

NB: **Ivan xotel ego byt' poxožim na otca.*
'Ivan wanted *him* to resenble (his) father.'
Ivan xotel, čtoby on byl poxož na otca.

This fact accounts for a statistically important surface-structure difference between English and Russian.

The deep structure of (3.37) is (3.41).

(3.41) meets the SD for Equi-NP Deletion ($NP_1 = NP_3$), which maps it into (3.42).[5]

[5] Since Subject-V Agreement is obligatory in every S there is no need to mention it specifically in every derivation.

(3.41)

(3.42)

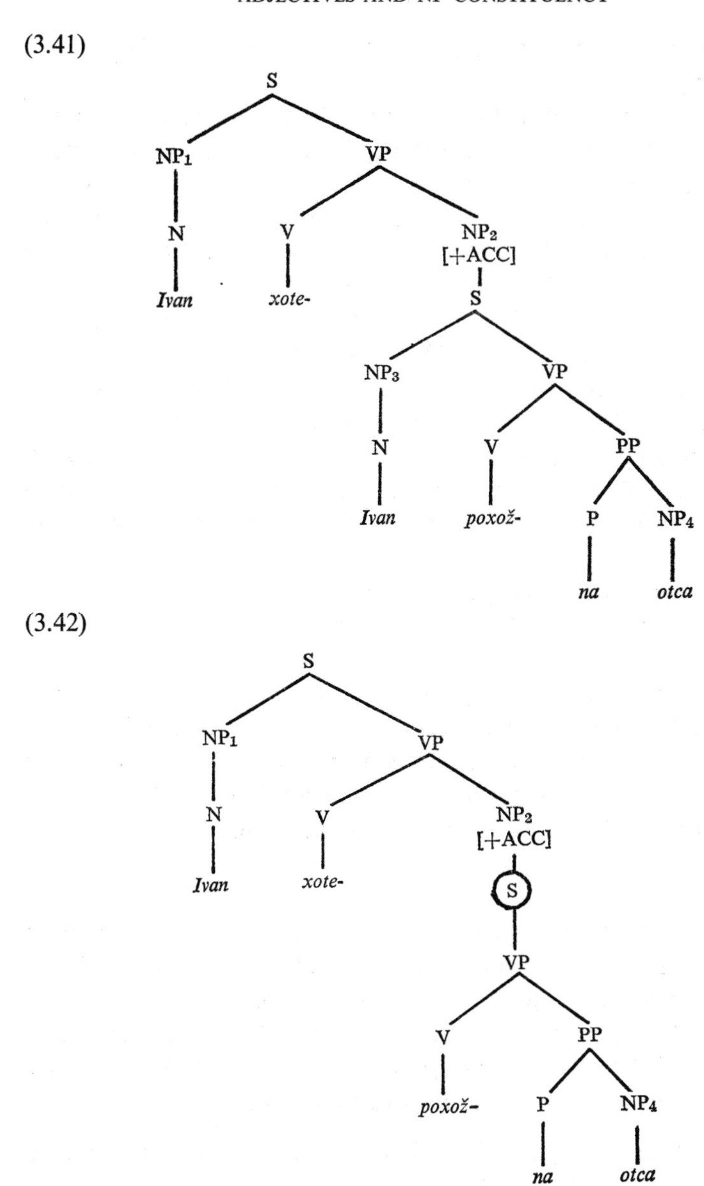

In (3.42) the embedded S-node (circled) no longer branches and is deleted by S-Node Deletion (cf. (3.15)). After the S-node is deleted, *poxož* becomes a constituent of NP_2, undergoes Case Marking, and, therefore, becomes a LF in precisely the same way that it did in the two types of derivations already examined (cf. §2.12 and (3.2)).

Note, however, that the intermediate P-marker (3.42) is defective in at least two ways.

First, it does not allow us to account for the instrumental *poxožim*; it tells us only that *poxož* will receive the case feature [+ACC]. In the derivation of (3.2), the instrumental (*pravymi*) was accounted for by (3.34), the Obligatory Instrumental rule. P-marker (3.42) does not, however, contain the configuration $[V — NP — NP]_{VP}$ and, consequently, rule (3.34) cannot be applied to (3.42) to derive (3.37a).

Second, P-marker (3.42) does not permit us to account for the presence of the infinitive *byt'* 'to be' in (3.37) (or *byl* in (3.38)).

These two defects require us to discuss the status of the copula *byt'* (*byl, budet,...*) in a transformational grammar of Russian. Further, they force us to re-examine deep structures of sentences (3.1) and (3.2), since in accounting for *byt'* in (3.37) and *byl* in (3.38) we must make certain that our rules do not produce sentences like (3.8), which we repeat here for convenience:

(3.8) **Oni sčitali sebja byt' pravymi.*
'They considered themselves to be right.'

The fact that rule (3.34) is not general enough to account for the instrumental in (3.37a) makes it seem likely that it is incorrect and must be replaced by a more general rule. Thus, in the following sections I will examine the synchronic origin of *byt'* in sentences like (3.37) and the instrumental of *poxožim*, and I will try to show that these two problems are closely related.

3.3.0 THE STATUS OF *byt'* IN A GENERATIVE GRAMMAR OF RUSSIAN. In recent work on transformational syntax, two views as to the nature of what is traditionally called the copula have been expressed.

According to one view (e.g. G. Lakoff, 1965: Appendix A, and J. Lyons, 1968: §7.6.3), the copula (*byl, budet*, etc., in Russian) is merely a semantically empty morpheme that serves to carry tense in surface structures containing adjectives ($\underset{[+ADJ]}{V}$), and is not a verb at the level of deep structure. Adherents of this view of the copula differ in details. For instance, Lakoff considers the copula a deep-structure tense-feature which, WITH ADJECTIVES, becomes a segment by a transformation which he calls Tense Spelling (cf. A-6). This same deep-structure tense-feature WITH VERBS ($\underset{[-ADJ]}{V}$) never becomes a segment (cf. *like* vs. *fond* on p. A-6).

It will make no difference in the problems of Russian syntax being investigated here whether the surface-structure copula *byl* (*budet*, #, *byt'*, *bud'*, etc.) is a deep-structure tense-feature on a $\begin{matrix}\text{V}\\ [+\text{ADJ}]\end{matrix}$ or a deep-structure constituent of the auxiliary. The important fact is that *byl* in the deep structure is a tense-marker, not a verb.

Accordingly, the deep structure of (3.43) is (3.44).

(3.43) *Ivan byl poxož na otca.*
'Ivan resembled his father.'

(3.44)

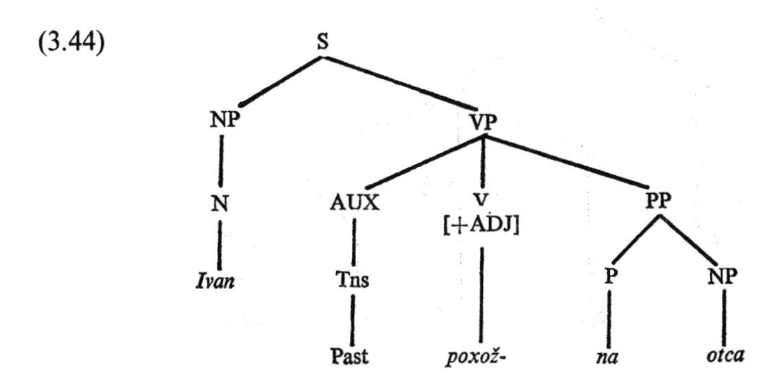

The deep structure of (3.45) is (3.46).

(3.45) *Ivan poxodil na otca.*
'Ivan resembled his father.'

(3.46)

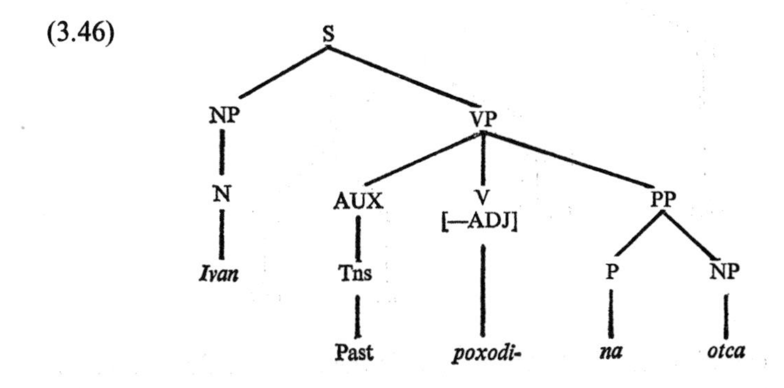

The only transformational rule that applies to (3.44) and (3.46) is Subject-V Agreement, which copies inherent features from the subject N on to the V. After the rules of the transformational component have applied, the rules of the phonological component apply to the final derived P-marker. These rules will convert Past + $\genfrac{}{}{0pt}{}{\text{V}}{[+\text{ADJ}]}$ in (3.44) to *byl* + $\genfrac{}{}{0pt}{}{\text{V}}{[+\text{ADJ}]}$, while Past + $\genfrac{}{}{0pt}{}{\text{V}}{[-\text{ADJ}]}$ in (3.46) will emerge from the phonological component as *poxodil.* The only difference between (3.44) and (3.46) is the feature [ADJ], while their surface structures are quite different as a result of the phonological rules. The surface structure of (3.43) is (3.47).

(3.47)

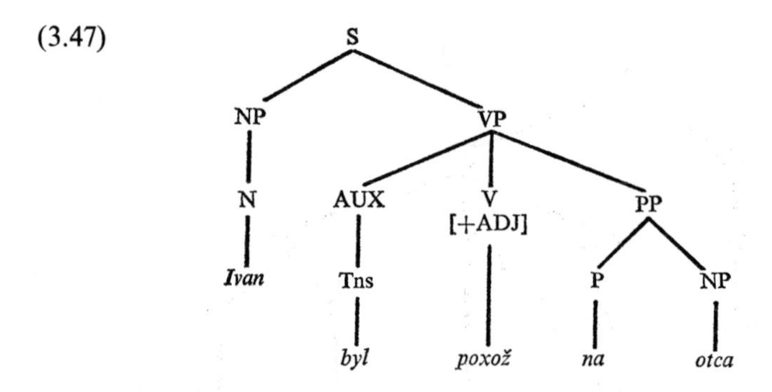

We are thus making the claim that the tense-marker in (3.44) underlies *byl* in (3.43).

The surface structure of (3.45) is (3.48).

(3.48)

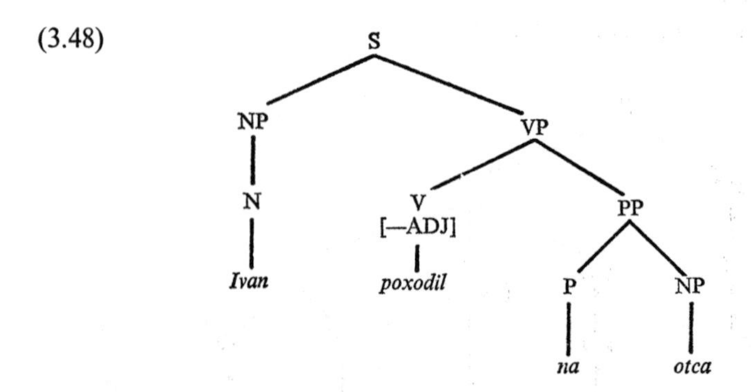

We are thus claiming that in (3.45) *poxodil* is the result of the operation of the morphophonemic rules of the phonological component on the input LEXICAL ITEM *poxodi–* + FEATURES ACQUIRED BY *poxodi–* AS A RESULT OF SUBJECT-V AGREEMENT + TENSE-MARKER. If the SF of the adjective is viewed as a verb ($\underset{[\pm ADJ]}{V}$), as it is here (cf. Chapter 2), then it is quite natural and intuitively satisfying to interpret *byl* in sentences like (3.43) not as a verb, but as a tense-carrier (cf. *do* in English). Further, there is a considerable amount of empirical evidence in Russian supporting the tense-marker origin of the copula. This evidence is presented later on in this section, after the second origin of the copula *byl,...* is discussed (cf. esp. the copula in sentence pairs like *My pročitali knigu – Kniga byla pročitana nami*; *On xotel, čtoby ego priglasili na večer – On xotel byt' priglašennym na večer* (§3.5)).

According to the second view, the copula is a verb in the deep structure (cf. Ross, 1969:352-360; this is also the position taken by traditional Russian grammar). There are sentences in Russian where the copula in fact seems to be a deep-structure verb with semantic content. In:

(3.49) *Ivan byl v sadu.*
'Ivan was in the garden.'

byt' has the meaning *naxodit'sja* 'to be located', and (3.49) has the same meaning and structure as:

(3.50) *Ivan naxodilsja v sadu.*
'Ivan was in the garden.'

This "existential" meaning of *byt'* is particularly clear in the following lines by Cvetaeva:

(3.51) *Ja ne xotela byt' milym rebenkom, romantičeskim monarxistom, monarxičeskim romantikom, –ja xotela* byt'.
'I did not want to be a nice child, a romantic monarchist, a monarchical romantic', – I wanted to be / exist.'

According to these considerations, the deep structure of (3.49) is (3.52) (cf. A. Isačenko, 1965:267-269, for a similar analysis of *Otec byl doma* 'Father was at home').

After the operation of the rules of the transformational component (Subject-V Agreement), the morphophonemic rules are applied. These rules will "spell out" *bud–* ($\underset{[-ADJ]}{V}$) + FEATURES ACQUIRED BY SUBJECT-V

(3.52)

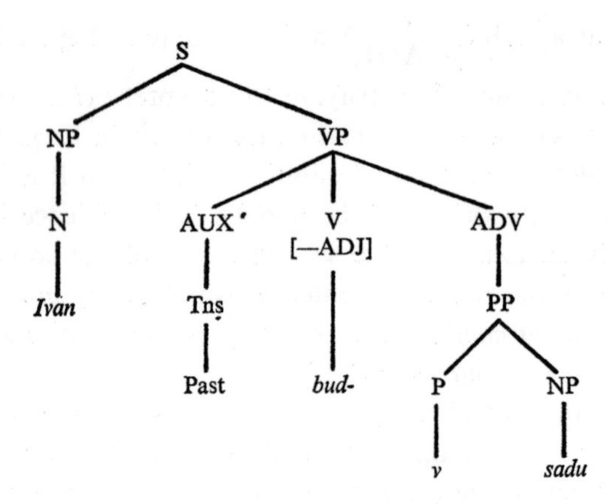

AGREEMENT + PAST as *byl* in precisely the same way that they produced *poxodil* in the derivation of (3.45). The surface structure of (3.49) is (3.53).

(3.53)

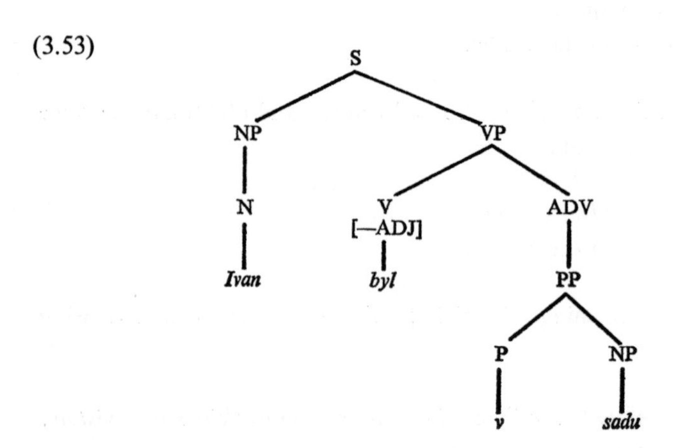

Compare (3.53), where *byl* is a verb, to (3.47), where it is a tense-marker.

SUMMARY OF §3.3.0. Russian material therefore makes it seem likely that the surface-structure copula *byl, byt',*... has two deep-structure sources.[6] It is either a deep-structure verb with existential meaning (i.e. it signals location, class membership, equivalence, or existence), or it is the surface-structure realization of a deep-structure tense-marker.

3.3.1 Russian grammarians have long recognized the dual nature of the copula *byl* (cf. Vinogradov, 1938:311 and Gvozdev, 1961:62-63), but

[6] The analysis of the copula offered §3.3.0 is highly tentative. It may, for instance, prove necessary to posit several deep-structure verbs that are realized as *byl*, *budet*, etc. I hope these remarks will serve as the basis for a more detailed study of the Russian copula.

they have limited themselves to purely semantic accounts, since their one-level, classificatory approach to syntax does not allow the kind of analysis we have just proposed. For instance, B. A. Dmitriev (1964:14) notes that in *Ona byla zdes'* 'She was here' *byla* is a "lexically full" verb [*polnoznačnyj glagol*] with the meaning *naxodi-sja* 'to be located'. The same is true of *byt'* in *Ona mogla byt' zdes'* 'She was able to be here'. However, Dmitriev further notes, in *Ona byla nedurna* 'She wasn't bad-looking', *byla* is not a "lexically full" verb, but is an "abstract copula" [*otvlečennaja svjazka*]. The same is true of *byt'* in *Ona mogla byt' nedurna* 'She was able to be not bad-looking' (cf. §3.4.0 for mention of the relation between underlying tense-marker and the infinitive *byt'*).

The transformational analysis of the copula proposed in §3.3.0 is not only more explicit than the Russian taxonomic analysis; it enables us to account for a wide range of syntactic phenomena that other kinds of analysis cannot explain or relate. Some of these phenomena will be discussed in the immediately following sections (§3.3.2-§3.3.4).

The semantic differences between the two copulas which were noted by Russian grammarians can be given a natural explanation when it is recalled that in a generative-transformational grammar the rules of the semantic component apply to the deep structure, not the surface structure. At the level of deep structure, the "existential" *byl* is a lexical item (a verb) and is consequently interpreted by the semantic rules differently from the "tense-carrier" *byl*, which is not a lexical item at the level of deep structure.

3.3.2 It was pointed out in §2.10 that sentences containing existential verbs may, when negated, optionally undergo a transformation that marks the subject NP with the case feature [+GEN]; Subject-V Agreement subsequently places the verb in the third person neuter singular (or "non-agreement", cf. §3.6.3). As an illustration, we repeat (2.67) here as (3.54) (cf. (2.65)-(2.68)). ((3.54a)=(3.54b))

(3.54a) *Neuželi ne najdutsja želajuščie?*
'Is it possible that people who desire (it) cannot be found?'

(3.54b) *Neuželi ne najdetsja želajuščix?*

Sentences containing the *byl*, which according to our analysis is a deep-structure existential verb (*bud*–), may also undergo this transformation:

(3.55a) *On byl doma.*
'He was at home.'

(3.55b) *On ne byl doma.*
'He was not at home.'

(3.55c) *Ego ne bylo doma.*[7]
'He was not at home.'

Sentences in which surface-structure *byl* is a deep-structure tense-marker will, predictably, not undergo this transformation:

(3.56a) *On byl poxož na otca.*
'He resembled (his)father.'

(3.56b) *On ne byl poxož na otca.*
'He did not resemble (his) father.'

(3.56c) **Ego ne bylo poxože na otca.*

The facts of §3.3.2 provide syntactic evidence that *byl* in sentences like (3.55) is a deep-structure existential verb and that the *byl* in sentences like (3.56) is not. Paragraph 3.3.2 therefore provides us with concrete SYNTACTIC evidence for assigning the surface-structure *byl* two distinct deep-structure sources.

3.3.3 Consider the following sentences.

(3.57a) *Ja byl* daleko *ot Moskvy.*
'I was far away from Moscow.'

(3.57b) **Ja byl* dalek *ot Moskvy.*
'I was far away from Moscow.'

(3.58a) *Ja žil* daleko *ot Moskvy.*
'I was living far away from Moscow.'

(3.58b) *Ja rabotal* daleko *ot Moskvy.*
'I was working far away from Moscow.'

(3.58c) *Aèroport naxoditsja* daleko *ot goroda.*
'The airport is far from the city.'

(3.59a) *Ja* dalek *ot togo, čtoby predpolagat' (zdes') obman.*
'I am far from assuming (a) fraud (here).'

(3.59b) **Ja* daleko *ot togo, čtoby predpolagat' (zdes') obman.*

(3.60a) *Ja živu* blizko *ot vas.*

[7] The validity of this argument depends on the assumption that (3.55b) and (3.55c) are synonymous. It is not, however, certain that they are. As H. G. Lunt and R. Rothstein (personal communication) have pointed out, sentences like (3.55b) are usually followed by the subject's location, while sentences like (3.55c) are not. More work must be done on the definition of synonymy before this problem can be solved.

'I live near you.'

(3.60b) *Kažetsja, čto gory sovsem* blizko.
'The mountains seem quite near.'

(3.60c) *Doč'* blizka *s mater'ju i* daleka *s otcom.*
'The daughter is close to (her) mother, but not to (her) father.'

Any Russian grammar must be able to account for the facts of agreement in the above sentences (i.e. *Ja byl dalek* vs. *Ja byl daleko*).

Ušakov (1935, cf. entry *dalekij*) attempted to capture facts like these by claiming that the adjective *dalekij*, in the meaning *naxodjaščijsja na bol'-šom rasstojanii otkuda-n.* 'located at a considerable distance from somewhere' is REPLACED by the adverb *daleko* 'far' when used in the predicate. Ušakov's suggestion is patently incorrect (adverbs by definition are not predicates) and would lead to unavoidable complications if adopted in an explicit grammar of Russian.

If the dual origin of the surface-structure copula *byl* proposed in §3.3.0 is accepted, these agreement facts can be accounted for without having to incorporate any new transformations into our grammar and, therefore, without having to deal with the complications that Ušakov's "transformation" would entail.

Byl in (3.57), according to the analysis of the copula in §3.3.0, is a deep-structure verb (*bud-*) and *daleko* is an adverb[8] just as it is in (3.58).

The deep structure of (3.57) is (3.61), which is also the deep structure of (3.58) except for the lexical verb.

(3.61)

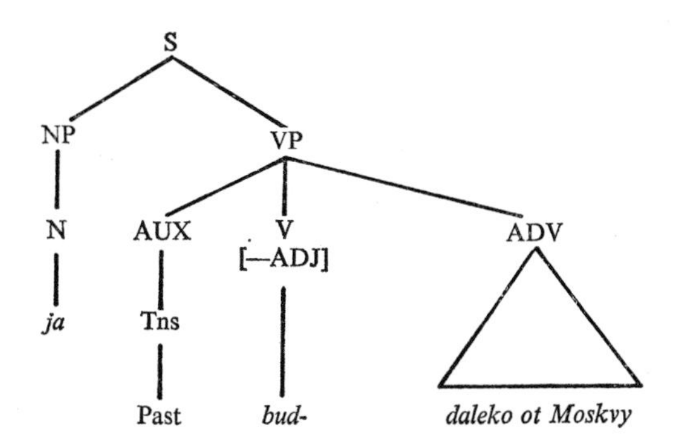

[8] H. G. Lunt (personal communication) has suggested that perhaps a separate class of locatives is called for. If this suggestion is justified by future research, it will force us to abandon the argument presented in §3.3.3.

Daleko in (3.57) is indeed an adverb, but it is not simultaneously the main verb as Ušakov has suggested and it has not "replaced" *dalekij*. Subject-V Agreement copies the features of the subject (gender, number, person, animate, etc.) on to *bud-*; the morphophonemic rules will subsequently "spell out" *bud-* + Subject-V Agreement features + past as *byl* in the same way that they "spell out" *žil* from an underlying *živ-* + Subject-V Agreement features + past.

The deep structure of sentences like (3.59) is:

(3.62)

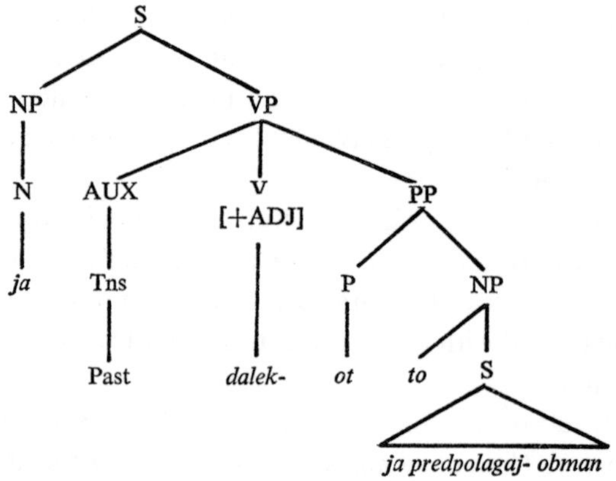

S
NP VP
N AUX V [+ADJ] PP
ja Tns P NP
Past *dalek-* *ot* *to* S
ja predpolagaj- obman

In (3.59) *dalek-* is the main verb and *it* receives the features from Subject-V Agreement; *byl* is the surface-structure realization of the deep-structure tense-marker.

The analysis of the copula proposed in §3.3.0 (deep-structure V *bud-* vs. tense-marker) thus enables us to account for the agreement phenomena (*ja byl daleko* vs. *ja byl dalek*) in (3.57)-(3.60) in terms of an independently motivated transformation: Subject-V Agreement. *Dalek* m.sg. SF 'far' in (3.59) has undergone this transformation, while *daleko* in (3.57) has not. At this point a few words should be said about the form of the adverb *daleko*.

The deep structure of the adverb is a complex problem that awaits solution (cf. §0.3.2.2). It is for this reason that the details of the internal structure of the adverb in (3.57) were omitted. Yet some ideas about the adverb in *-o* have suggested themselves in this study of Russian syntax, and I present them here merely as a programmatic suggestion for future study.

Note that the adverb *daleko* itself takes a complement (*daleko ot*

Moskvy 'far from Moscow') and, furthermore, it is the same complement that the V *dalek-* takes. This phenomenon is not an isolated fact in Russian as the sentences in (3.63) demonstrate (*poxože* and *nesorazmerno* are adverbs of manner).

(3.63a) *Možet byt' russkie, čexi i poljaki smejutsja* poxože *drug na druga.*
'Perhaps Russians, Czechs and Poles laugh alike.'
(L. Uspenskij)

NB: *Oni poxoži drug* na *druga.*
'They resemble each other.'

(3.63b) *...a drugie sobytija vyrosli* nesorazmerno *svoemu značeniju....*
'...while other events grew out of all proportion to their significance'

It seems that these facts can be best explained by assuming that the lexicon of Russian contains only the item *dalek-* + *ot* without specifying whether it is a surface-structure verb or an adverb. Its place in the deep-structure P-marker determines what "part of speech" *dalek-* will be in the surface structure.

Once this suggestion is accepted, it becomes possible to account for the surface-structure *daleko* from a deep-structure *dalek-* (+ *ot*) without complicating the grammar with additional transformational apparatus.

In §2.12 and Chapter 3 I have, in effect, accounted for the SF (verb) and LF (adjective or participle) in terms of agreement. Lexical item + features acquired by Subject-V Agreement + any case feature acquired by the Case Marking rule emerge as a LF. The ADV-node behaves very much like an S-node in that it blocks Case Marking: adverbs in Russian do not distinguish case. Adverbs in Russian do not agree with any noun in gender, person, or number. In other words, adverbs do not undergo Subject-V Agreement. Therefore, a deep-structure $\underset{[+\text{ADJ}]}{\text{V}}$ that has not undergone either Subject-V Agreement or Case Marking will emerge in the surface structure in the third-person neuter singular (*–o*), which in Russian signals non-agreement (cf. §3.6.3).

In other words, a deep-structure lexical item will emerge from the phonological component as a verb (SF), adjective / participle (LF), or adverb (*–o*) depending on what features it has acquired by the two "agreement" transformations. These relations are graphically represented by (3.64).

(3.64)

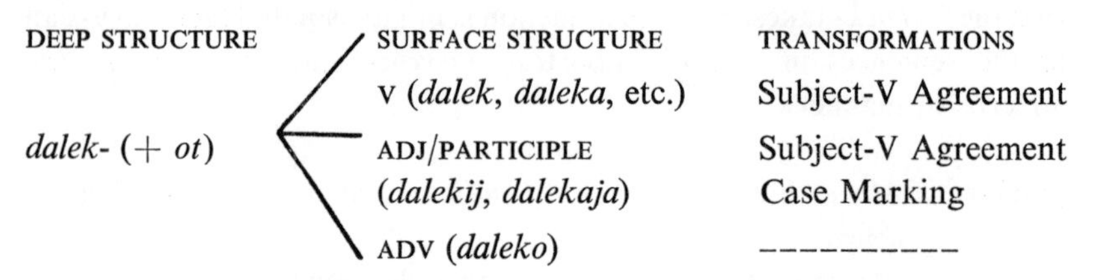

Gerunds in Russian can probably be accounted for in a similar way.

This analysis of the three-way surface-structure distinction VERB – ADJECTIVE/PARTICIPLE – ADVERB is strongly reminiscent of Jespersen's (1958: Chapter 7) notion of "the three ranks".

SUMMARY OF §3.3.3 Our assumption of a dual deep-structure source of the copula has allowed us to account for agreement (*daleko* vs. *dalek*) in sentences (3.57)-(3.60) quite naturally and this may serve as evidence that our analysis of the copula is correct.

3.3.4 THE PASSIVE TRANSFORMATION AND THE TENSE-MARKER. Paragraph 3.3.2 provided concrete evidence that *byl* in sentences like (3.55) is a deep-structure verb (*bud-*). Paragraph 3.3.4 will offer evidence that *byl* in sentences like (3.66) is a deep-structure tense-marker. The facts presented in this section constitute the strongest argument of the three offered (§§3.3.2-3.3.4) that the "copula" *byl*, *budet*, *byt'*... must, in certain sentences, be a deep-structure tense-marker.

Examples (3.65) and (3.66) are semantically equivalent and have the same deep structure (3.67).

(3.65) *Oni priglasili menja na večer.*
'They invited me to the party.'

(3.66) *Ja* byl *priglašen (imi) na večer.*
'I was invited (by them) to the party.'

(3.67)

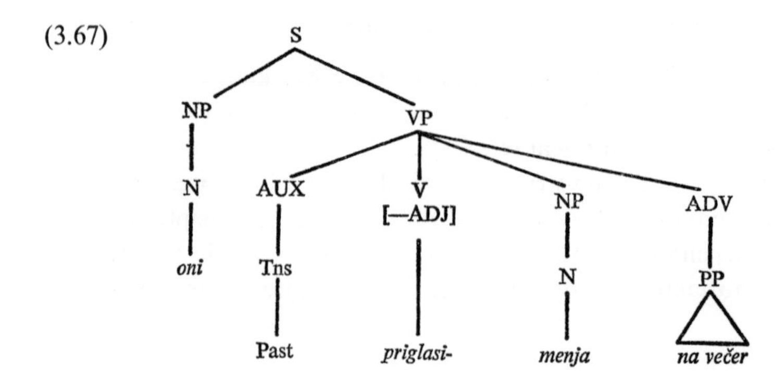

(3.65) is derived from (3.67) by Subject-V Agreement. The morphophonemic rules subsequently "spell out" *priglasi-* + features acquired by Subject-V Agreement + past as *priglisili.*

A passive participle in Russian is syntactically identical to a "SF adjective" (i.e. $\overset{\text{V}}{[+\text{ADJ}]}$): there is no rule of Russian syntax that makes a distinction between a SF and a passive participle. This fact can be best captured in our grammar of Russian by formulating the Passive transformation so that it changes the [—ADJ] feature on the perfective V governing the transformation to [+ADJ]. Once the Passive transformation changes $\overset{\text{V}}{[-\text{ADJ}]}$ to $\overset{\text{V}}{[+\text{ADJ}]}$, there is no subsequent transformation that is capable of distinguishing a DEEP-STRUCTURE $\overset{\text{V}}{[+\text{ADJ}]}$ (SF) from a DERIVED $\overset{\text{V}}{[+\text{ADJ}]}$ (passive participle).

The formulation of the Passive transformation just suggested accounts for the Russian speaker's intuitive association of "SF adjectives" and "SF (past) passive participles" (cf. *objazan* 'obliged', *uveren* 'sure, assured'). It can also account for the broader syntactic opposition of SF (deep and derived $\overset{\text{V}}{[+\text{ADJ}]}$; *poxož* 'resembles', *priglašen* 'invited') and LF (*poxožij, priglašennyj*). If the Passive transformation operates before the transformations that occasion S-Node Deletion (Relative Clause Reduction, Subject Raising, Equi-NP Deletion) the "LF of passive participles" will be derived in exactly the same way that "LF adjectives" are, since these transformations will have the effect of introducing $\overset{\text{V}}{[+\text{ADJ}]}$, regardless of its origin, into a NP where it receives a case feature. Compare the derivation illustrated by the sentences in (3.68) with the derivation of (2.78).

(3.68a) *Volk, kotorogo vysledil oxotnik, zabralsja v čašču.*
'The wolf which the hunter tracked down ran into the thicket.'

(3.68b) *Volk, kotoryj* byl *vysležen oxotnikom, zabralsja v čašču.*
'The wolf which was tracked down by the hunter ran into the thicket.'

(3.68c) *Volk, vysležennyj oxotnikom, zabralsja v čašču.*
'The wolf tracked down by the hunter ran into the thicket.'

Note that the Relative Clause Reduction transformation deletes *kotoryj* + TENSE-MARKER, which accounts for the fate of *byl* when (3.68b) is reduced to (3.68c).

Note also that the facts concerning the change of [—ADJ] to [+ADJ] by the Passive transformation is strong evidence supporting our decision to treat adjective as a feature and not a category: in the present theory of grammar, transformations may alter features, not categories (cf. Chapter 2).

Now that we have discussed some aspects of the Passive transformation we can return to the derivation of (3.66) from (3.67). The Passive transformation, which is optional, may apply to the deep-structure P-marker (3.67), producing P-marker (3.69).

(3.69)

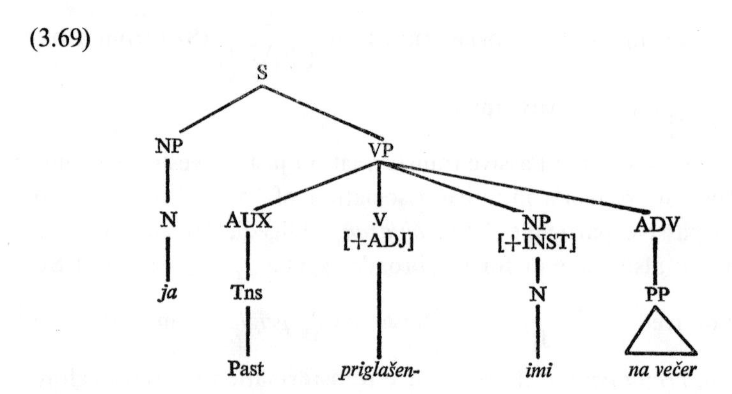

After Subject-V Agreement has applied to (3.69), the morphophonemic rules will "spell out" past + $\begin{array}{c}\text{V}\\ [+\text{ADJ}]\end{array}$ as *byl* + $\begin{array}{c}\text{V}\\ [+\text{ADJ}]\end{array}$ just as they did in the derivation of (3.43) from (3.44). The surface structure of (3.66) is thus (3.70).

(3.70)

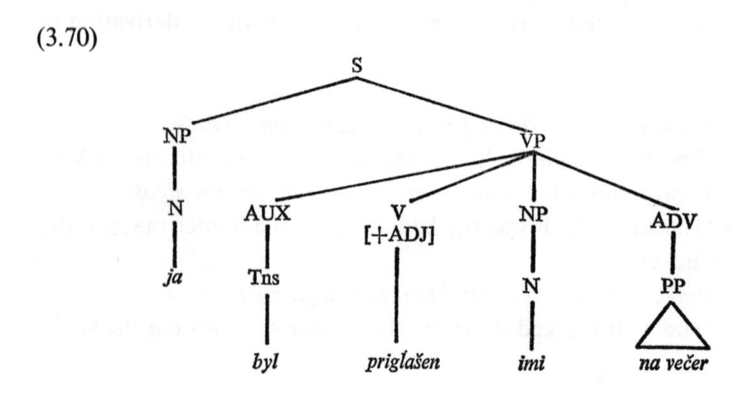

If *byl* in (3.66) were analyzed as a surface-structure constituent derived from an underlying V *bud-*, it would be impossible to relate (3.65) and (3.66) by deriving them from a common deep structure (3.67), since the deep structure of (3.66) would have to contain two verbs, while the deep structure of (3.65) would contain only one.

The analysis of *byl* in sentences like (3.66) is further supported by the existence of sentences like

(3.71a) *Ja budu priglašen na večer.*
'I will be invited to the party.'
(3.71b) *Ja priglašen na večer.*[9]
'I have been invited to the party.'

These sentences can be quite easily derived, given the analysis of (3.66). The Passive transformation will derive *priglasen* ([+ADJ]) from an underlying *priglasi-* ([—ADJ]) and the morphophonemic rules will spell out present + $\genfrac{}{}{0pt}{}{\text{V}}{[+\text{ADJ}]}$ as *priglašen*; future + $\genfrac{}{}{0pt}{}{\text{V}}{[+\text{ADJ}]}$ as *budu priglašen*, etc.. The deep structure of the sentences in (3.71) will be identical to (3.67), except for the tense-marker. These considerations make it clear that the traditional term "past passive participle" applied to *priglašen* is not appropriate, since it is not inherently past, present, or future. "Perfective passive participle" might better reflect its status in modern Russian grammar.

SUMMARY. §3.3 has attempted to demonstrate that *byl*, *budet*, etc with $\genfrac{}{}{0pt}{}{\text{V}}{[+\text{ADJ}]}$ (what is traditionally called the SF of the adjective and the past passive participle) is not a deep-structure verb, but a tense-marker. Further evidence is presented in §3.5, where sentence-pairs like *On xočet, čtoby ego priglasili na večer* / *On xočet byt' priglašennym na večer* will be discussed.

3.4.0 INFINITIVE FORMATION. When the derivation of (2.52) (*Ja nameren čitat' ètu knigu* 'I intend to read this book') was given (cf. §2.9), the details

[9] The "perfect" in Russian is discussed in Gvozdev (1955: §404), F. Papp et al. (1968: 482) and Rozental' (1965: 322: "Inogda pričastie bez svjazki oboznačaet sostojanie bezotnositel'no k momentu soveršenija dejstvija, naprimer: Biblioteka otkryta ežednevno". [Sometimes the participle without copula denotes a state without reference to completion of the action; for example: The Library (is) open daily.]). The treatment of tense and aspect in this study is oversimplified and requires a far more detailed analysis.

of the formation of the infinitive *čitat'* 'to read' from the underlying *čitaj-* were omitted. The analysis of the tense-marker proposed in §3.3 now makes it possible for us to account for surface-structure infinitives in an insightful manner.

According to the considerations discussed in §3.3, the deep structure of (2.52), repeated here as (3.72), is (3.73).[10]

(3.72) *Ja nameren čitat' ètu knigu.*

(3.73)

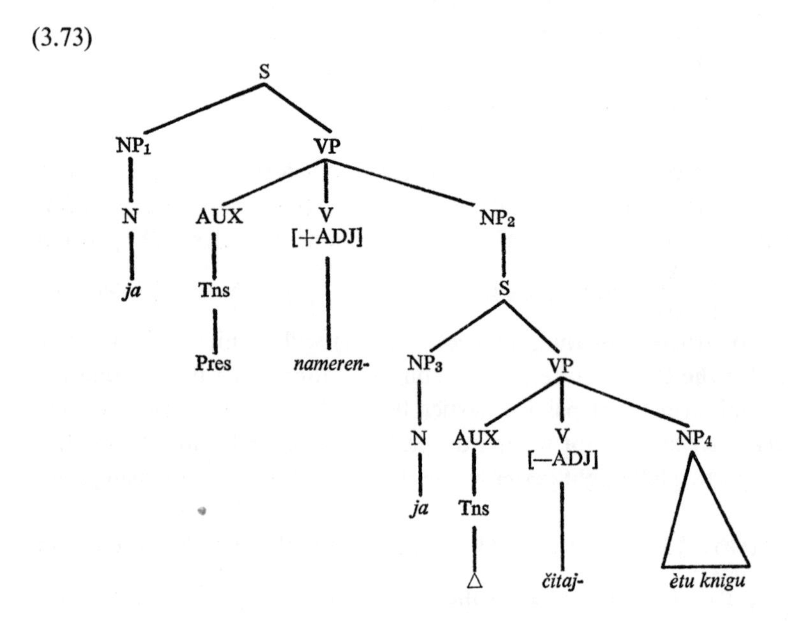

The derivation of (3.72) from (3.73) involves the following transformations (all obvious or irrelevant details omitted):

Equi-NP Deletion, which causes NP_3 to be deleted, maps P-marker (3.73) into P-marker (3.74).

The embedded node S, circled in (3.74), no longer dominates both NP and VP and is automatically deleted by the convention of S-Node Deletion (cf. §3.1.1). It is in terms of intermediate P-markers like (3.74) that we can account for the formation of infinitives.

P. Kiparsky (1968:12) made the following observation about the derivation of infinitives:

[10] See Chomsky, 1965: 222 for a discussion of the symbol Δ.

(3.74)

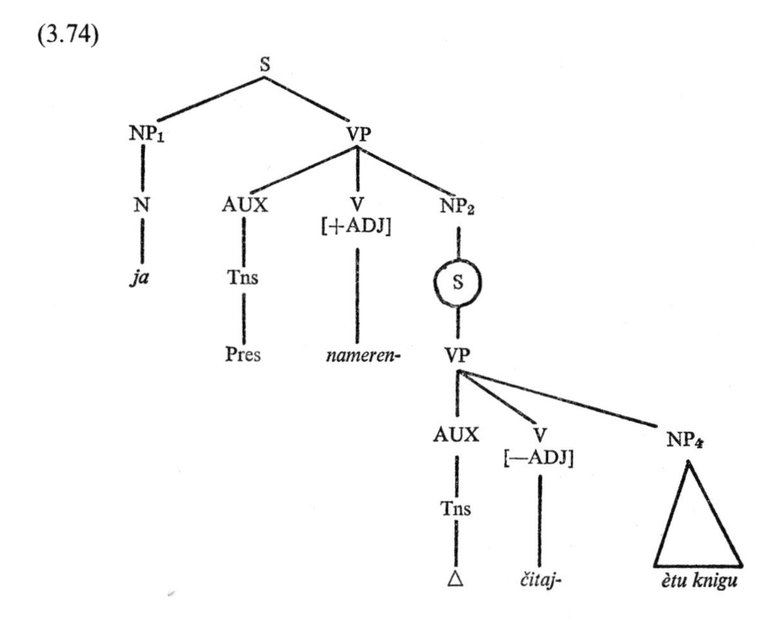

Infinitives arise regularly when the subject of an embedded sentence is removed by a transformation, or else placed into an oblique case, so that in either case agreement between subject and verb cannot take place.

Equi-NP Deletion has removed the subject NP of the embedded S in (3.73), and, accordingly, we get an infinitive in (3.72). It is not the case, however, that all the transformations that remove or delete the subject NP of an embedded S give rise to infinitives. Equi-NP Deletion and Subject Raising do invariably result in the formation of infinitives. Relative Clause Reduction, however, never results in an infinitive in Russian (it may in English: *She has an abundance of men from whom to select / to select from.*), even though it removes the subject of a embedded S. It is therefore obvious that it is not the removal of a subject NP alone that is responsible for infinitives. The crucial difference between Relative Clause Reduction and the other transformations that remove a subject NP is that Relative Clause Reduction deletes not only the subject NP, but the TENSE MARKER (cf. §3.3.4). Equi-NP Deletion and Subject Raising remove only the subject NP of an embedded S, but the tense-marker remains. There is little doubt that this fact is the key to infinitive formation.

In the derivation of (3.72) S-node Deletion, occasioned by Equi-NP Deletion, produces a P-marker in which there are TWO tense-markers in the same simple sentence (cf. (3.74)). It is this configuration that invariably gives an infinitive. Just those transformations that remove the subject

NP of an embedded S and, in addition, leave the tense-marker of the embedded S behind, produce infinitives. Relative Clause Reduction never results in a P-marker in which there are two tense-markers in the same simple sentence, and, consequently, a reduced relative clause never contains an infinitive. Note that these facts help to account for the presence of an active participle versus an infinitive in the surface-structure of Russian.

The rule of Infinitive Formation (3.75) is only a first approximation. Future research on the "infinitive sentence" and the morphophonemic rules in Russian will undoubtedly require its modification. But I believe the principles involved in its formulation to be correct.

(3.75) INFINITIVE FORMATION.

	X —	[Tns —	V —	$Y]_{VP}$ —	Z	Obligatory
SD:	1	2	3	4	5	⇒
SC:	1	0	3	4	5	
			[infin]			

CONDITION: 2 is in the same simple sentence as a higher tense-marker.

The morphophonemic rules will "spell out" a V with [infin] as an infinitive (*čitat'* from an underlying *čitaj-* in the derivation of (3.72)).[11]

Thus the intermediate P-marker (3.74) meets the SD of Infinitive Formation, which accounts for the infinitive in (3.72). The surface structure of (3.72) is (3.76). The surface-structure *nameren* is derived by the morphophonemic rules from pres. + *nameren-* after Subject-V Agreement.

(3.76)

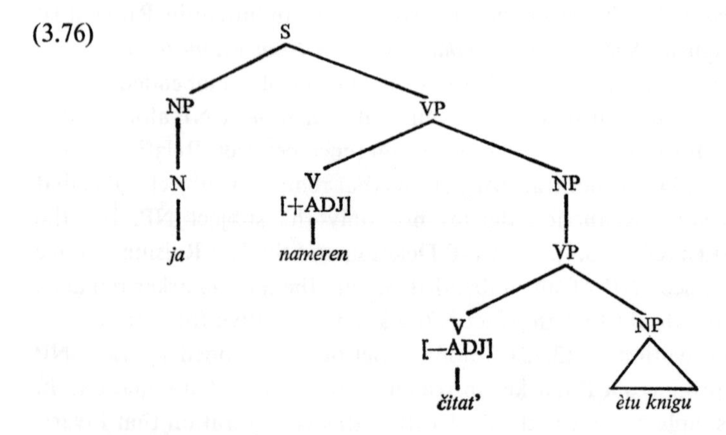

[11] The rules of Russian syntax that have been presented here give us some notion of

3.4.1 Subject Raising and Infinitive Formation. Another transformation that removes the subject NP from an embedded S and produces an infinitive is Subject Raising. In §3.1.2 we discussed sentence (3.18) but did not account for the infinitive *otvesti*. In light of §3.3, the deep structure of (3.18) is (3.77).

(3.18) *Ona pozvolila misteru Franklinu otvesti sebja obratno v komnatu.*

(3.77)

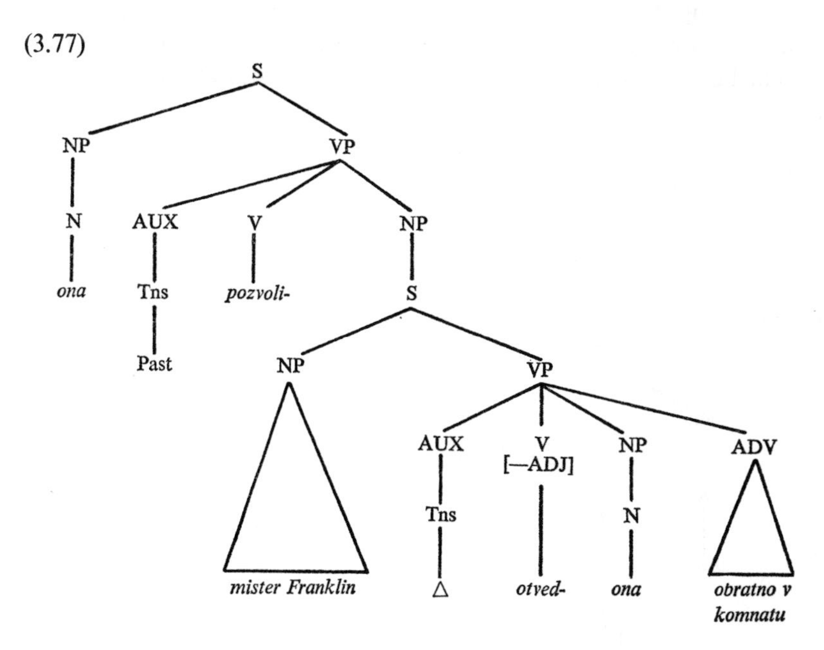

Mister Franklin, the subject NP of the embedded S, is raised into object position in the matrix S by the rule of Subject Raising. S-node Deletion then operates with the result that the tense-marker of the embedded S

---

what a V ([+ADJ] and [—ADJ]) will look like in a deep-structure P-marker. It must be NON-FINITE, since it will not yet have undergone Subject-V Agreement, which is responsible for agreement in number, person and, in the past tense, gender. The infinitive cannot be the "basic form" of the verb, since it is itself transformationally derived (cf. rule (3.75)). What we are left with as a basic or "lexicon" form of the verb looks very much like Roman Jakobson's "one-stem verb" (cf. R. Jakobson, 1948). The rules of the transformational and phonological components will produce surface-structure finite and infinite verb forms from the deep-structure / lexicon basic stems. We have merely extended the notion of a basic stem to include $\underset{[+\text{ADJ}]}{\text{V}}$ (*nameren-*, *sposob #n-*, *poxož-*) along with $\underset{[-\text{ADJ}]}{\text{V}}$ (*čitaj-*, *pozvoli-*).

comes under the domination of the matrix S. Rule (3.75) then operates and the morphophonemic rules produce *otvesti* from the underlying Tns + *otved-*.

If the interpretation of the infinitive presented in the derivation of (3.18) and (3.72) is correct, it can serve as another piece of evidence that the analysis of the tense-marker presented in §3.3 is correct.

3.5.0 Having discussed the tense-marker in deep and surface structure (§3.3) and introduced the rule of Infinitive Formation (§3.4), we have enriched our grammar sufficiently to enable us to return to the derivation of sentence (3.37).

(3.37) *Ivan xotel byt' poxožim na otca.*

(3.78) is the deep structure that our grammar assigns to (3.37).

(3.78)

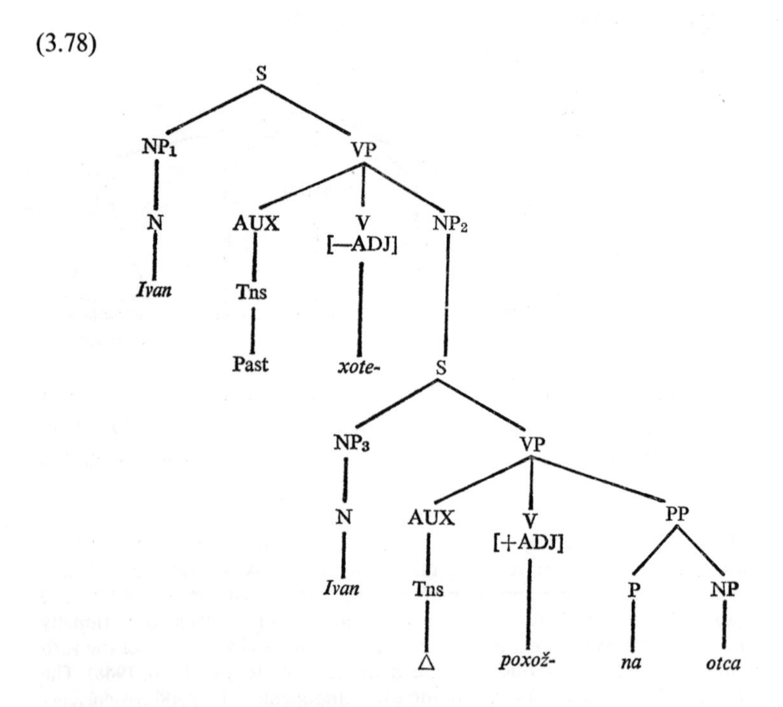

The following transformations map P-marker (3.78) into (3.79):

Cycle I: SUBJECT-V AGREEMENT between *Ivan* (NP_3) and *poxož-*.

Cycle II: EQUI-NP DELETION deletes NP_3 under identity to NP_1. This occasions the deletion of the embedded S-node by (3.15).

(3.79)

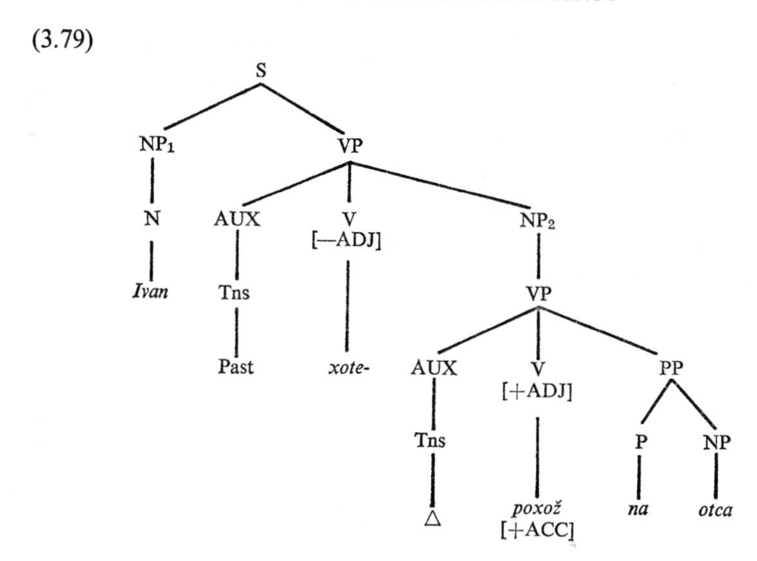

After S-node Deletion, *poxož* is a constituent of NP_2 and, accordingly, picks up its case feature. As in the other derivations studied in Chapter 3, this will give a LF in the surface structure.

(3.79) meets the SD for Infinitive Formation (cf. rule (3.75)), since there are two tense-markers in the same simple sentence. However, $\underset{[+\text{ADJ}]}{\text{V}}$ does not form infinitives in the same way that $\underset{[-\text{ADJ}]}{\text{V}}$ does. Notice that in the SD of rule (3.75), term 3 does not specify whether the feature on the V is [+ADJ] or [—ADJ]. If (3.75) has applied, the morphophonemic rules will convert Tns + $\underset{[-\text{ADJ}]}{\text{V}}$ to an infinitive in *-ti* (*pojti, čitat'*, *pomoč'*) as in the derivation of (3.72) from (3.73). Tns + $\underset{[+\text{ADJ}]}{\text{V}}$ will emerge from the morphophonemic rules as *byt'* + $\underset{[+\text{ADJ}]}{\text{V}}$. In other words, the infinitive *byt'* in sentences like (3.37) is a deep-structure tense-marker, not a deep-structure verb, just as *byl* in *byl* + $\underset{[+\text{ADJ}]}{\text{V}}$ is a deep-structure tense-marker in the derivation of (3.66) from (3.67) and (3.43) from (3.44).

This solution seems intuitively correct, since *byt'* + $\underset{[+\text{ADJ}]}{\text{V}}$ is felt by speakers of Russian to be an infinitive:

(3.80a) *Izbrat' i byt' izbrannym--pravo každogo sovetskogo graždanina.*
'To elect and to be elected is the right of every Soviet citizen.'

(3.80b) *On zaxotel byt' uslyšannym i zakričat'* "*vo ves' golos.*"
'He wanted to be heard and to shout at the top of his voice.'

The behavior of the tense-marker with respect to Infinitive Formation (two tense-markers in the same simple sentence) provides an exact parallel to the behavior of the tense-marker in §3.3 (one tense-marker per simple sentence). This parallel is graphically represented by the following table:

TABLE 2

	V [—ADJ]	V [+ADJ]
One tense-marker per simple S	Tns + *poxodi-* > *poxodil*	Tns + *poxož-* > *byl* + *poxož*
Two tense-markers per simple S	Tns + *poxodi-* > *poxodit'*	Tns + *poxož-* > *byt' poxožim*

Speaking in more general terms, the tense-marker itself emerges from the morphophonemic rules as *byl, budet, ø, byt', bud'*, etc., when its V has the feature [+ADJ], while the very same deep-structure tense-marker is incorporated into a V with the feature [—ADJ]: *poxodi-l* (*byl poxož*), *poxodi-t'* (*byt' poxožim*), etc.

A very strong argument for accepting *byt'* as an underlying tense-marker will be presented in the derivation of sentence (3.87). However, first we must account for the instrumental *poxožim* in sentences like (3.37).

3.5.1 Obligatory Instrumental Rule (second version). The rule of Infinitive Formation applies to P-marker (3.79) producing (3.81).

As a result of Equi-NP Deletion and S-node Deletion, *poxož-* in (3.81) has become a constituent of NP_2 and must therefore undergo Case Marking. This is the origin of the LF in (3.37) and a confirmation of the main thesis of this study (LF=$[SF]_{NP}$). Yet the P-marker (3.81) plus the rules discussed so far will still not enable us to account for the instrumental *poxožim* (cf. *poxož-?*). NP_2, of which *poxož-* is a constituent in (3.81), received the feature [+ACC] from *xote-*. This would produce (3.37d), which is not a sentence of Russian.

A solution to this problem is suggested by a surface-structure observa-

(3.81)

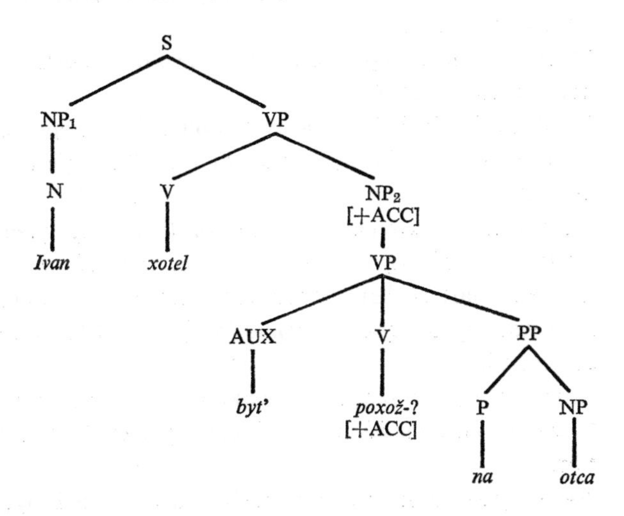

tion made independently by several different scholars working in the traditional, classificatory framework. For instance, Boguslavskyj (1964: 14) noticed that:

Pri infinitive *byt'* v sovremennom russkom jazyke kratkie formy praktičeski nevozmožny. [In modern Russian, short forms after the infinitive *byt'* are practically impossible.]

This generalization holds for both deep-structure $\underset{[+\text{ADJ}]}{\text{V}}$ (SF adjective) and derived $\underset{[+\text{ADJ}]}{\text{V}}$ (perfective passive participle (cf. §3.3.4)). The same observation has been made by Evseeva (1964:9), E. Kržižkova [= H. Křižková] (1968:219) and Ovsjaniko-Kulikovskij (1912:157-158). The general surface-structure rule that an infinitive *byt'* is not followed by a SF, but by the instrumental (i.e. the LF), is illustrated by the following sentences.

(3.82a) *Malen'kij Alëša* staralsja byt' poxožim *na otca vo vsem.*
'Little Aleša *tried to be like* (his) father in all ways.'

(3.82b) *Ja soglasilsja exat' v sledujuščee voskresen'e i* obeščal byt' gotovym *k desjati časam utra.*
'I agreed to go on the following Sunday and *promised to be ready* by ten in the morning.'

(3.82c) Zasluživaet byt' otmečennym *sredi pročego vlijanie i èstetičeskogo momenta,...*
'Among other things also the influence of the esthetic aspect *deserves to be noted...*'

(3.82d) *Vot čelovek! Vsë boitsja pomešat'*, boitsja byt' nespravedlivym.
'Here is a man! Always afraid of meddling, *afraid of being unjust.*'

(3.82e) *V štabe ne bylo uverennosti*, sposoben *li molodoj lejtenant* byt' stojkim, ubeždennym *v vsoix rešenijax komandirom.*
'At headquarters there was no certainty that the young lieutenant was *capable of being stable (and) sure* of his decisions as commander.'

(3.82f) ...ne imel udovol'stvija byt' znakomym *so svoim sosedom.*
'*...did not have the pleasure of being acquainted* with his neighbor.'

(3.82g) *Nesmotrja na postigšuju nas neudaču*, my ne mogli byt' ravnodušnymi *k krasotam prirody.*
'Regardless of the misfortune which befell us, *we could not be indifferent* to the beauties of nature.'

(3.82h) *Rovno k vos'mi časam vse v učilišče* dolžny byt' gotovymi *k priemu gostej.*
'By precesely eight o'clock everyone in the school *should be ready* for receiving the guests.'

(3.82i) *Voennye dela* prodolžali byt' očen' neutešitel'nymi.
'Military matters *continued to be very disturbing.*'

(3.82j) *Ty xotel* byt' otkrovennym, – *tak bud' otkrovenen do konca.* (Kuzmin)
'You wanted *to be frank* – so be frank to the end.'

The fact that, in the surface structure of Russian, the infinitive *byt'* is invariably followed by an instrumental can be captured by the following rule.[12]

[12] Note that *byt'* is the only infinitive in Russian to behave in this way (NB: **Ja xoču pročitat' ètoj knigoj*). This phenomenon is quite natural if we bear in mind the fact that, according to the analysis proposed in § 3.5.0, *byt'* is the only surface-structure infinitive that is not a deep-structure verb.

The Obligatory Instrumental rule can be formulated in more general terms than it is in (3.83). Speaking in surface-structure terms, not only adjectives and passive pariciples must appear in the instrumental immediately after *byt'*, but so must NOUNS.

a. *Ja vsjakomu rad byt'* drugom.

(3.83) OBLIGATORY INSTRUMENTAL RULE II

	X	— [*byt'* —	V [+ADJ] [αCASE]	— $Y]_{NP_i}$	— Z	
						Obligatory
SD:	1	2	3	4	5	⇒
SC:	1	2	3 [+INST]	4	5	

CONDITION: Term 3 is a constituent of NP_i.

Since the rule of Infinitive Formation (3.75) is directly dependent upon S-Node Deletion, term 3 of rule (3.83) will be a constituent of NP_i and, consequently, will have the case feature of NP_i ([αCASE]). Rule (3.83) CHANGES the case feature received from NP_i, no matter what it is, to [+INST]. For instance, in the derivation of (3.37), (3.83) changes V [+ADJ] [+ACC] to V [+ADJ] [+INST] (cf. (3.81) and (3.86)). In the derivation of (3.84) from (3.85), (3.83) changes V [+ADJ] [+DAT] to V [+ADJ] [+INST].

'I am glad to be a *friend* to everyone.'

b. *Čelovek dolžen byt' graždaninom prežde vsego.*
'A man ought to be a *citizen* before everything else.'

c. *Puškin byl prizvan byt'* poètom-xudožnikom *na Rusi.*
'Puškin was called to be a *poet-artist* in Russia.'

d. *Ja ne želaju byt'* raboj *nikakoj sily.*
'I do not wish to be a *slave* of any power.'

e. *Ja obeščaju byt'* xorošim ispolnitelem, *no rukovoditel' iz menja ne polučitsja.*
'I promise to be a *good person to get the job done*, but I won't become a leader.'

A more general rule could include nouns by using a variable after *byt'* (cf. *byt'*— X [αCASE]) or by having the rule change NP_i itself to [+INST], and thereby account not only for the instrumental of nouns, adjectives and passive participles, but also for the instrumental of prenominal adjective + noun, which derives from a deep-structure $[\ NP — S\ ]_{NP}$ configuration. But the adoption of a more general version of rule (3.83) would require very detailed discussions of facts not related to the topics covered in this book. (3.83) is adequate as it stands for our immediate goals. A more general rule can be worked out in future studies of Russian syntax.

The condition on (3.83) ensures that an S-node does not intervene between NP_i and term 3.

(3.84a) *Èto pomešalo emu byt' gotovym k ot''ezdu.*
'It kept him from being ready to leave.'

(3.84b) **Èto pomešalo emu byt' gotovomu k ot''ezdu.*

(3.84c) **Èto pomešalo emu byt' gotov k ot''ezdu.*

(3.85)

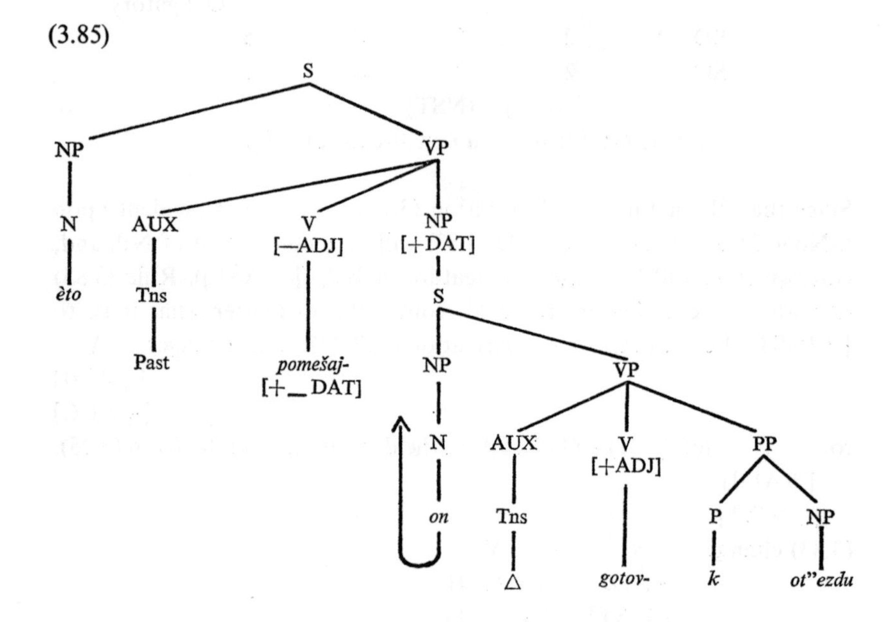

Rule (3.83) makes the prediction that VP complements ($[V — S]_{VP}$), if there are any in Russian, will have *byt'* + SF in the surface structure, since the deep-structure $\begin{matrix}V\\ [+ADJ]\end{matrix}$ will not come under NP domination in the course of the derivation. The SD of rule (3.83) specifically mentions a case feature ([αCASE]) that the SC changes to [+INST]; rule (3.83) itself does not copy [+INST] on to a markable element that is not yet marked. All the derivations that have been discussed have been NP complements ($[V — [S]_{NP}]_{VP}$).[13]

[13] Kržižkova (1968: 219) observed, along with Boguslavskij and Evseeva, that the instrumental is used almost exclusively after *byt'* (cf. examples in (3.82)). However, she explicitly points out the one important exception to this surface-structure formulation:

Tvoritel'nyj padež objazatelen, esli *byt'* + ADJ ne sočetaetsja s modal'nym glagolom ili že prilagatel'nym s modal'nym značeniem v sostave skazuemogo dvučlennogo predloženija.
[The instrumental case is obligatory if *byt'* + ADJ does not combine with a

modal verb or an adjective with modal meaning in the predicate of a two-member sentence.]

EXAMPLES:

a. *My dolžny byt' vnimatel'ny k starym ljudjam.*
'We must be kind to old people.'

b. *Naša rabota dolžna byt' zakončena kak možno skoree.*
Our work should be finished as soon as possible.'
(cf. *My dolžny zakončit' našu rabotu kak možno skoree.* 'We should finish our work as soon as possible')

c. *Èta rabota možet byt' sdelana v korotkij srok.*
'This job can be done in a short time'.
(cf. *My možem sdelat' ètu rabotu v korotkij srok.* 'We can do this job in a short time'.)

In other words, Kržižkova has noted that when the verb in the matrix sentence is a "modal" verb (*dolž #n-* 'must', *mog-* 'can'), the predicate of the embedded sentence
[+ADJ] [—ADJ]
emerges in the surface structure in the SF; when the matrix verb is not a "modal" verb, the predicate of the embedded sentence is in the instrumental (= LF) in the surface structure.

The formulation of rule (3.83) suggests an explanation for this phenomenon: if the verb in the matrix sentence has a VP complement, the surface structure will contain *byt'* + SF, since at no time in the derivation did the $\underset{[+\text{ADJ}]}{\text{V}}$ of the embedded sentence come under NP domination. It therefore seems likely that *mog-* and *dolž#n-* take VP complements.

Accordingly, the deep structure of sentence (a) is (i).

(i)

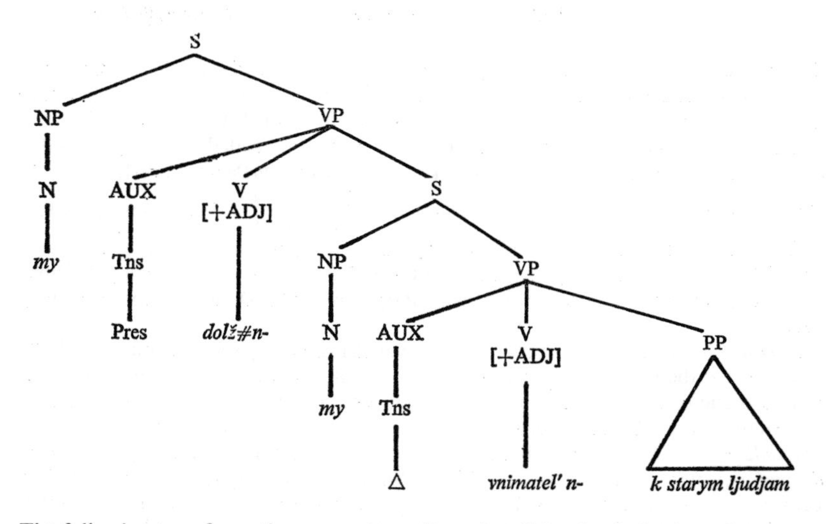

The following transformations operate on P-marker (i) in the derivation of sentence (a) (irrelevant details omitted).

3.5.2 Having introduced rule (3.83) into our grammar of Russian, it is possible to return to the derivation of (3.37). P-marker (3.81) meets the

---

Cycle I: SUBJECT-V AGREEMENT (giving *vnimatel'ny*).
Cycle II: SUBJECT-V AGREEMENT (giving *dolžny*).
EQUI-NP DELETION (deletes *my* in the embedded S).
S-NODE DELETION (deletes the embedded S-node).
INFINITIVE FORMATION (3.75) (gives *byt'* from tense-marker).

Note that the rule of Infinitive Formation (3.75) does not mention a higher NP and will therefore produce an infinitive in a reduced VP complement just as it has in reduced NP complements. The P-marker that results from Infinitive Formation does NOT meet the SD for the Obligatory Instrumental rule (3.83), since the lower verb-phrase is not a NP constituent.

The surface structure of (a) is (ii).

(ii)

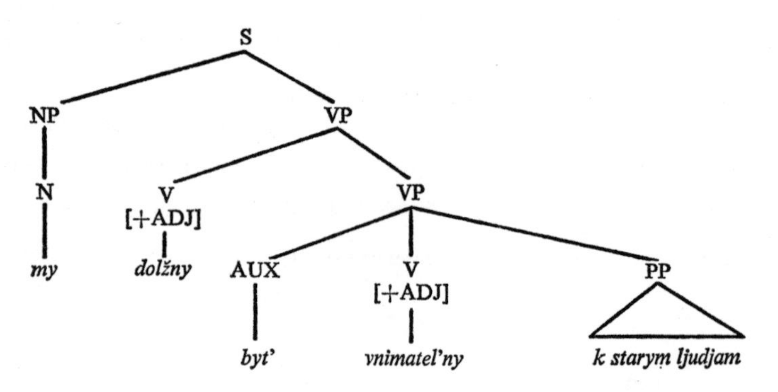

The problems that arise in accounting for properties of *mog-* and *dolž#n-* in a transformational-generative grammar of Russian are by no means solved by the above suggestions. For instance, in sentences (b) and (c) it is not at all clear whether the Passive Transformation has applied on the first cycle (i.e. in the embedded sentence) or on the second cycle (i.e. *mog-* and *dolž#n-* may themselves govern the Passive transformation). Furthermore, (3.82g) and (3.82h) are examples of $\left\{\begin{matrix} \textit{mog-} \\ \textit{dolž\#n-} \end{matrix}\right\}$ + *byt'* + instrumental. This fact may be accounted for by positing "transitive / intransitive pairs" for *mog-* and *dolž#n-*. Space does not permit a more detailed examination of these problems. C. Chvany, however, has treated them in great detail in her Ph.D. dissertation (Harvard, 1970).

It seems that there is no justification for recognizing a category or feature "modal". The fact that these Vs are felt to constitute a separate class can be accounted for by a characteristic or unique clustering of features, any one of which may belong to a V not felt to be a member of this class. For instance, besides taking VP complements, *mog-* and *dolž#n-* are both negatively marked for Relative Clause Reduction (cf. **Lektor, dolžnyj segodnja vystupit', zabolel* 'The lecturer (who is) supposed to speak today became ill'), but so is *rad-* 'glad'. "Modal" or "auxiliary" verb, like the term "long form", is a useful surface-structure term, but it does not seem to be a deep-structure category or feature.

SD of rule (3.83), since *poxož-* is a constituent of NP_2 and, therefore, has the feature [+ACC] by rule (3.24). Rule (3.83) thus applies to (3.81), giving P-marker (3.86), the correct surface structure of (3.37).

(3.86)

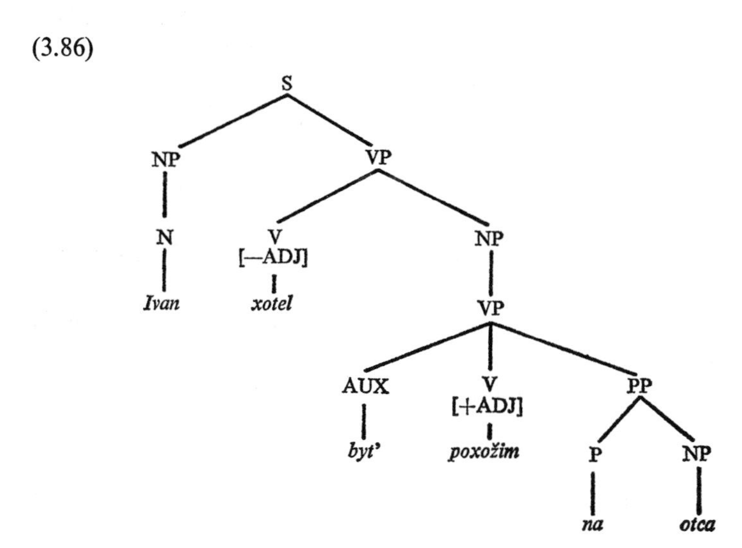

Note that once again a deep-structure $\underset{[+\text{ADJ}]}{\text{V}}$ (cf. *poxož-* in (3.78)) emerges in the surface structure as a LF (*poxožim* in (3.86)) as a direct result of being transformationally introduced into the constituency of a NP (NP_2 in (3.79)) and acquiring a case feature therein. Rule (3.83) merely CHANGED this feature to [+INST]. The derivation of the LF in (3.37) therefore is essentially the same as in all the derivations examined in §2.12 and Chapter 3: LF= $\underset{[+\text{ADJ}]}{\text{V}}$ + features acquired by Subject-V Agreement (number, person, gender, etc.) + ANY case feature.

3.5.3 Having accounted for the instrumental in (3.37) in terms of P-marker (3.81) and rule (3.83), we may now turn to sentences (3.87)-(3.89), which provide some additional evidence that our analysis of the tense-marker and Infinitive Formation (especially *byt'* from an underlying tense-marker) is correct.

(3.87a) *Ja xoču byt' priglašennym (imi) na večer.*
'I want to be invited (by them) to the party.'

(3.87b) *Ja xoču, čtoby (oni) menja priglasili na večer.*
lit. 'I want that they invite me to the party.'

(3.88a) *Ja xoču byt' informirovannym o ee priezde.*
'I want to be informed of her arrival.'

(3.88b) *Ja xoču, čtoby menja informirovali o ee priezde.*
(Izrailevič, 1955:242)
lit. 'I want that they inform me of her arrival.'

(3.89a) *Nam predstoit pročitat' Čexova po-novomu.*
'We will have to read Čexov in a new way.'

(3.89b) *Čexovu predstoit byt' pročitannym (nami) po-novomu.*
'Čexov will have to be read (by us) in a new way.'

(3.87) is of particular interest for Chapter 3 since the embedded sentence in it is identical to (3.67), the underlying P-marker of (3.65) and (3.66). (3.89) is discussed in Appendix I to Chapter 3 in connection with verbs that require a dative subject NP.

The deep structure of (3.87a) and (3.87b) is (3.90).

(3.90)

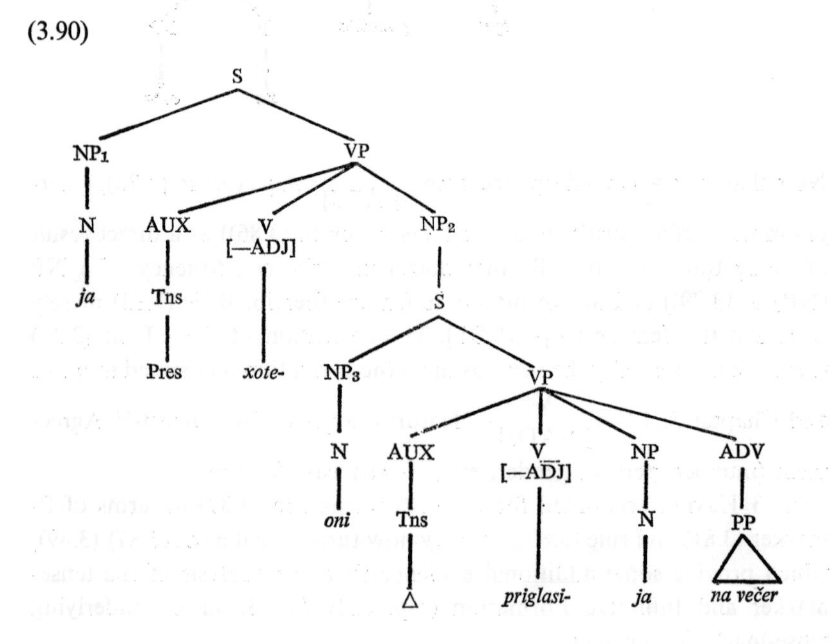

(3.87b) is derived from (3.90) as follows (details omitted):

Cycle I : SUBJECT-V AGREEMENT.
Cycle II: SUBJECT-V AGREEMENT
COMPLEMENTIZER PLACEMENT (introduces *čtoby*).

Notice that the derivation of (3.87b) does not involve the deletion of the embedded S-node and, therefore, the SD for Infinitive Formation (3.75) is not met.

(3.87a) is derived from (3.90) by the following transformations:

Cycle I: PASSIVE TRANSFORMATION.
SUBJECT-V AGREEMENT (producing *priglašen*).

The transformations in Cycle I produce the intermediate P-marker (3.91).

(3.91)

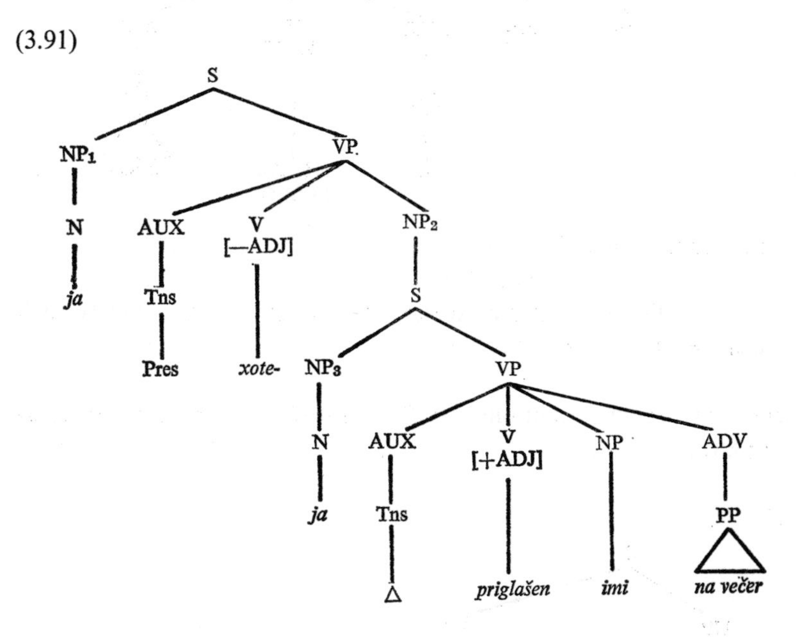

The change of the feature [—ADJ] to [+ADJ] in conjunction with the Passive transformation is discussed in §3.3.4.

Cycle II: EQUI-NP DELETION (NP_3 is deleted by NP_1)
S-NODE DELETION
AGENT DELETION

These three transformations produce the intermediate P-marker (3.92).

Cycle II (continued):
INFINITIVE FORMATION (3.75) ((3.92) meets the SD of (3.75) since there are two tense-markers in the same S. (3.75) will give *byt'*

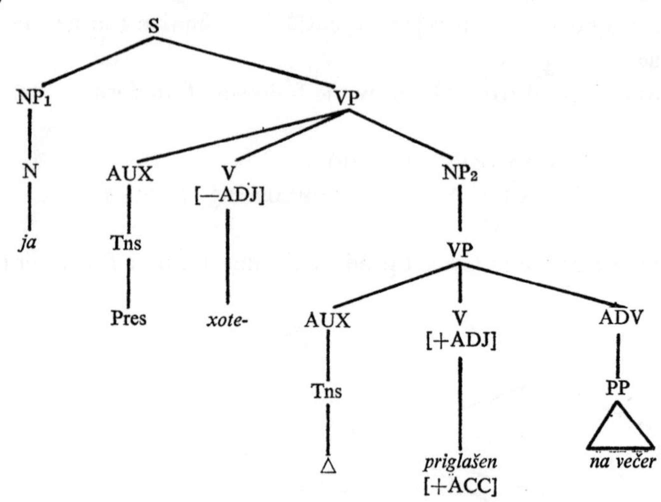

in conjunction with V).
[+ADJ]

OBLIGATORY INSTRUMENTAL TRANSFORMATION (3.83) (will change [+ACC] to [+INST]).

These last two transformations map (3.92) into (3.93), the surface structure of (3.87a).

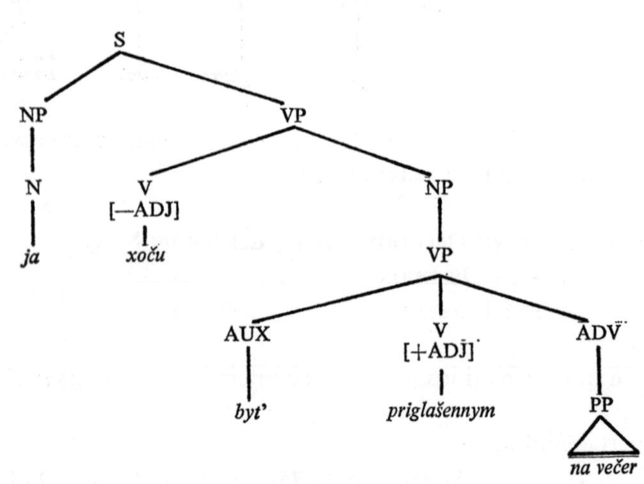

(3.87a) and (3.87b) can be derived from the same deep structure only if *byt'* in (3.87a) is analyzed as deriving from the tense-marker of the embedded sentence in the deep structure (3.90). If *byt'* is analyzed as an underlying verb, it is no longer possible to relate (3.87a) and (3.87b) by a common deep structure, since (3.87a)'s deep structure would contain a verb (*bud-*) that (3.87b)'s does not.

This is precisely the same type of argument that was employed in demonstrating the tense-marker origin of *byl* in (3.66). I repeat the sentences here again for contrast. Note that P-marker (3.67), the deep-structure of (3.65) and (3.66), is identical to the embedded S in P-marker (3.90), the deep structure of (3.87a) and (3.87b).

(3.65) *Oni priglasili menja na večer.*
(3.66) *Ja* byl *priglašen (imi) na večer.*
NB: **Ja byl priglašennym na večer.*
(3.87b) *Ja xoču, čtoby oni priglasili menja na večer.*
(3.87a) *Ja xoču* byt' *priglašennym (imi) na večer.*
NB: *Ona xočet* byt' *priglašennoj (imi) na večer.*

The tense-marker in (3.67) is spelled out by the morphophonemic rules as *byl* (cf. (3.66)) after the Passive transformation changed [—ADJ] to [+ADJ]: there was only one tense-marker in the S. The tense-marker in (3.90) is spelled out as *byt'*: there were two tense-markers in the same S and the transformation of Infinitive Formation operated.

Priglašen in (3.66) derives from the same deep-structure lexical item as *priglasili* in (3.65) in precisely the same way that *priglašennym* in (3.87a) and *priglasili* in (3.87b) have a common deep-structure source in (3.90). We get *priglašennym* in (3.87a) when the underlying *priglašen* (cf. (3.91)) is introduced into the upper NP and acquires a case feature (NB: LF=SF + case feature); the Obligatory Instrumental transformation (3.83) accounts for the instrumental.

The fact that we are able to handle the complex structures just discussed (expecially the relation: *byl priglašen / byt' priglašennym / priglasili* from an underlying Tns + *priglasi-*) in a simple and intuitively satisfying manner serves as strong evidence that the rules and assumptions presented in Chapter 3 are correct, at least in principle, and necessary in a transformational grammar of Russian.

3.6.0 THE RULE OF *byt'* DELETION. In §3.6 we will examine sentences of the type exemplified by (3.94) to (3.97) (cf. Ovsjaniko-Kulikovskij, 1912:167).

(3.94a) *On kažetsja umnym.*
'He seems (to be) smart.'

(3.94b) **On kažetsja umen.*

(3.94c) **On kažetsja umnyj.*

(3,94d) *Kažetsja, čto on umen.*
'It seems that he is smart.'

(3.95a) *Vsem kažetsja strannym (to), čto my živem v raznyx gorodax.*
'It seems strange to everyone that we live in different cities.'

(3.95b) **Vsem kažetsja stranno (to), čto my živem v raznyx gorodax.*

(3.95c) *Vsem kažetsja, čto to, čto my živem v raznyx gorodax, stranno.*

(3.95d) **Vsem kažetsja, čto to, čto my živem v raznyx gorodax, strannym.*

(3.96a) *Nam teper' kažetsja strannym, čto my živem v takom bol'šom gorode.*
'Now it seems strange to us that we live in such a large city.'

(3.96b) **Nam teper' kažetsja stranno, čto my živen v takom bol'šom gorode.*

(3.96c) *Nam teper' kažetsja strannym žit' v takom bol'šom gorode.*

(3.96d) **Nam teper' kažetsja stranno žit' v takom bol'šom gorode.*

(3.97a) *Mat' prislušivalas' k sporu... Ona bol'še ponimala Andreja, i on kazalsja ej* pravym.
'Mother listened to the argument... She understood Andrej best, and he seemed to her to be right.' (Gor'kij)

(3.97b) *Mat' prislušivalas' k sporu... Ona bol'še ponimala Andreja, i ej kazalos', čto on prav.*
'Mother listened to the argument... She understood Andrej best, and it seemed to her that he was right.'

The sentences in (3.94)-(3.97) seem to contain the same syntactic relationship between a deep-structure SF and a surface-structure LF that we have already seen in the other sentences examined in Chapter 3. This is particularly clear in (3.97), since, as was already pointed out in connection with sentences (3.1) and (3.2), *prav-* in the meaning 'right = correct' may appear only in the SF in a simple sentence. The form *pravym* in (3.97a), which has this meaning, must therefore be derived from an underlying *prav-* in precisely the same way that all the LFs treated in §2.12 and Chapter 3 are derived from underlying SFs

There is, however, one important difference, at least superficially, between the sentences in §§3.1-3.5 and those in §3.6: neither of the two proposed Obligatory Instrumental rules ((3.34) and (3.83)) seems capable of accounting for the instrumental LF in (3.94)-(3.97). In (3.94a), for instance, the instrumental *umnym* 'smart' cannot be accounted for by rule (3.34) because the configuration $[V — NP — NP]_{VP}$, specifically mentioned in the rule's SD, is not present. Rule (3.83), it seems, cannot explain the instrumental *umnym* since there is no infinitive *byt'* in (3.94a). The derivation of (3.94), however, suggests a solution to this problem.

3.6.1 The deep structure that is capable of relating *umnym* in (3.94a) and *umen* in (3.94d) is:

(3.98)

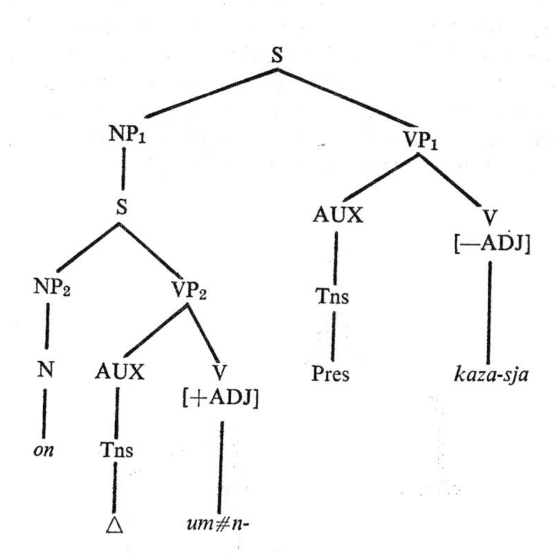

Positing a sentential subject in (3.98) not only allows us to account for the syntactic relations between (3.94a) and (3.94d); it allows us to distinguish explicitly sentences like (3.94) from sentences like (3.99) and (3.100).

(3.99a)	*On javljaetsja umnym (celovekom).*
	'He is an intelligent person'
(3.99b)	**Javljaetsja, čto on umen.*
(3.99c)	**Javljaetsja, čto on umnyj čelovek.*
(3.100a)	*On pritvorjaetsja, čto on bolen.*
	'He is pretending that he is sick.'
(3.100b)	*On pritvorjaetsja bol'nym.*
	'He is pretending (to be) sick.'
(3.100c)	**Pritvorjaetsja, čto on bolen.*

Javljaj-sja and *pritvorjaj-sja* take object complements. This fact allows us to account for the ungrammaticality of (3.99b), (3.99c) and (3.100c); *kaza-sja* takes a sentential subject, which accounts for the grammaticality of (3.94d).

(3.94d) is derived from (3.98) by Extraposition, a transformation that moves a sentential subject to the end of its matrix sentence[14] (other details of the derivation are omitted, since they contain nothing new).

[14] The rule of Extraposition seems to differ in English and Russian. In English the rule removes S from the configuration [*it* — S $]_{NP}$ and leaves behind [*it* $]_{NP}$ as the surface-structure subject (cf. *He seems to be smart* and *It seems that he is smart*). There is no evidence for an expletive *to* with verbs like *kaza-sja* in Russian (cf. **(è)to kažetsja, čto on umen*). The Russian version of Extraposition may therefore remove S from the configuration [S $]_{NP}$: the subject NP after Extraposition would no longer dominate a terminal symbol and would be automatically deleted by the convention that deletes all non-terminal nodes that do not dominate a terminal symbol. According to these considerations, the surface-structure P-marker of (3.94d) is:

(i)

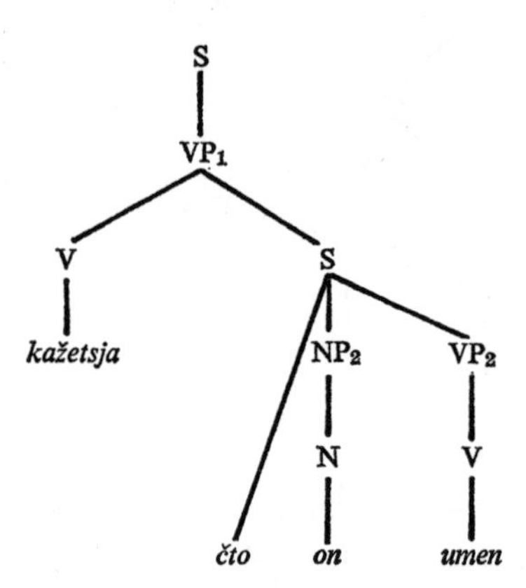

The matrix S-node does not delete because it was stated in the S-Node Deletion convention (3.15) that only an EMBEDDED S-node must be pruned. Ross excluded non-embedded S-nodes from (3.15) in order to account for imperative sentences in which the subject NP is deleted. If the version of Russian Extraposition proposed here is correct, it can serve as evidence that Ross's formulation of S-Node Deletion is correct in stipulating that only embedded S-nodes are deleted.

Our version of Extraposition in Russian has the advantage of producing a surface structure that explains why sentences like (3.94d) are traditionally felt to be "impersonal" sentences: they have no surface-structure subject NP. It may very well be possible to define the notion "impersonal sentence" in terms of the configuration [VP $]_S$ in the surface structure. This helps to isolate the central problem of impersonal sentences: namely, is the configuration [VP $]_S$ ever found in the deep structure, i.e. is S→(NP)VP a possible PS rule?

The remarks on Extraposition in Russian presented here are highly tentative. I have offered them at this time in order to demonstrate that the problem exists, and not to provide a final solution.

In The derivation of (3.94a) from the deep-structure P-marker (3.98), Subject-V Agreement applies on the first cycle, giving *um* # *n-* [+3PER] [+SING] [+MASC]. On the second cycle, the rule of Subject Raising applies. This rule raises *on* m.sg.nom. 'he', the subject of the embedded sentence, up into the matrix sentence.

In the derivation (3.94a) from (3.98) we are dealing with Subject Raising from a sentence embedded in the SUBJECT NP. In the derivation of (3.2) from (3.9), we observed Subject Raising from a sentence embedded in the OBJECT NP. Subject Raising from object position may be schematically represented by (3.101).

(3.101)

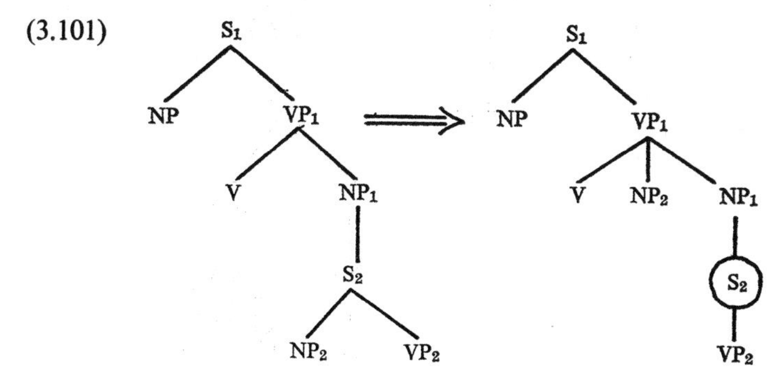

Note that NP_2, the raised subject NP of S_2, is attached to the node immediately dominating NP_1, the node in which NP_2's S is embedded. The remainder of S_2 is left behind as the last constituent of VP_1.

Subject Raising from a sentence embedded in a SUBJECT NP involves essentially the same operations as Subject Raising from a sentence embedded an in object NP:

(3.102)

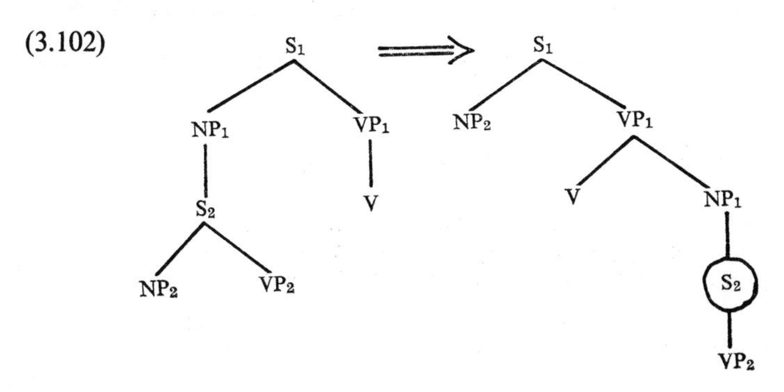

Note that NP_2, the raised subject NP of the embedded sentence, is attached to the node directly above NP_1, the node in which NP_2's S is embedded. The remainder of S_2, dominated by NP_1, is moved around VP_1 and adjoined to it as its last constituent. Observe that this is also the position of NP_1 in (3.101).[15]

Subject Raising converts (3.98), the deep structure of (3.94), into (3.103).

(3.103)

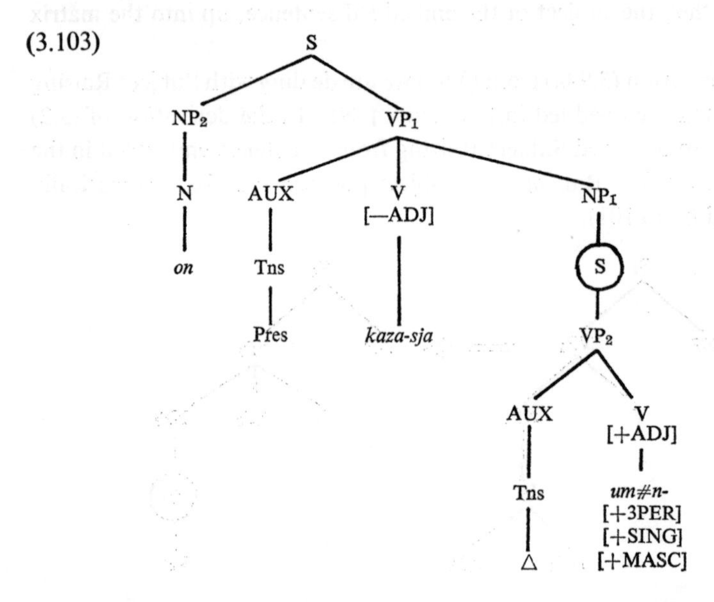

[15] The version of Subject Raising just presented is due, to a great degree, to Catherine V. Chvany.

(3.101) and (3.102) make it clear that it is possible to express Subject Raising from subject or object position in the matrix sentence by a single rule, since the transformation performs the same operations in either position:

(a) NP_2, the subject of the embedded sentence, is moved up into the matrix sentence and adjoined to the node immediately dominating the NP in which the sentence of which NP_2 was subject is embedded. In (3.101) this node is VP_1; in (3.102) it is S_1.

(b) The remainder of S_2 (dominated by NP_1) is adjoined to the matrix VP as its last constituent.

Based on these facts, the rule of Subject Raising in Russian may be tentatively formulated as follows:

SUBJECT RAISING

X — [NP_2 — VP_2 $]_{NP_1}$ — Y — VP_1 — Z Optional

SD: 1 2 3 4 5 6 ⇒

SC: (a) Adjoin 2 to the node dominating NP_1.

(b) Adjoin 3 (= [VP_2 $]_{NP_1}$) to the end of VP_1.

CONDITION: VP_1 and NP_1 are in the same simple sentence.

In Subject Raising from object position (cf. (3.101)), the seond part of the SC applies vacuously, since 3 is already the last constituent of VP_1.

After S-Node Deletion prunes the embedded S-node, *um # n-* is a constituent of NP_1 and, accordingly, receives its case feature (nominative?) by rule (3.24). This is the origin of the surface-structure LF. The resulting P-marker meets the SD for Infinitive Formation (3.75), which changes the embedded tense-marker to *byt'* (more precisely, to its prephonological form). This P-marker meets the SD for the Obligatory Instrumental transformation (3.83), which produces P-marker (3.104). Other details are omitted.

(3.104)

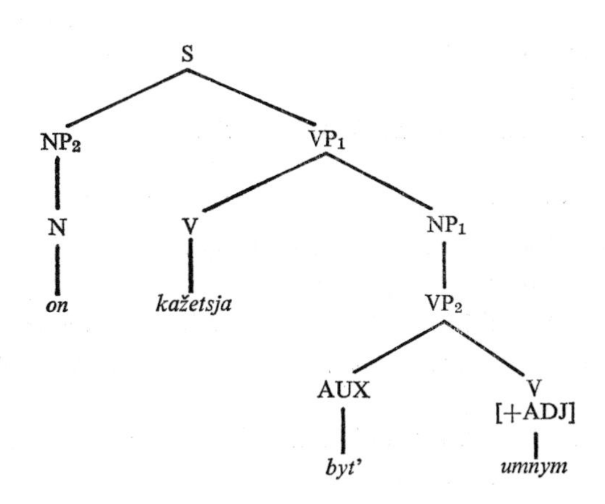

P-marker (3.104) enables us to account for the instrumental *umnym* in (3.94a) in precisely the same way that we accounted for it in §3.5.1 (cf. sentences in (3.82)). However, P-marker (3.104) is not the surface structure of any sentence possible in modern Russian.

Sentences like (3.105), of which (3.104) is the final derived P-marker, were possible at the end of the eighteenth century (cf. §3.6.2).

(3.105) **On kažetsja byt' umnym.*
'He seems to be smart.'

Sentence (3.94a) can be derived from (3.98) with (3.104) as an intermediate P-marker by the application of one final transformation: *byt'*-Deletion. It is generally recognized that a *to be*-Deletion rule is required by the grammar of English, but in English it is optional (cf. *He seems (to be) intelligent*). The equivalent rule in Russian is obligatory: when the matrix verb permits *byt'*-Deletion, it must be applied. This accounts for the nonoccurrence of sentences like (3.105): *kaza-sja* governs *byt'*-Deletion. *Seem* in English also governs *to be*-Deletion, but the rule is optional.

Okazyvaj-sja, priznaj-, javljaj-sja, and *sčitaj-* govern *byt'*-Deletion; *prodolžaj-, xote-, staraj-sja, obeščaj-*, etc. do not (cf. (3.82)). There seem to be no instances of a matrix V [+ADJ] governing *byt'*-Deletion. The rule of *byt'*-Deletion is tentatively stated in (3.106).

(3.106) RULE OF *byt'*-DELETION

	X —	[V —	byt' —	Y]$_{VP}$ —	Z	
						Obligatory
SD:	1	2	3	4	5	⇒
SC:	1	2	ø	4	5	

CONDITION: 2 is marked for *byt'*-Deletion

The Obligatory Instrumental rule (3.83) in conjunction with the rule of *byt'*-Deletion (3.106) allows us to make a significant generalization about Russian: the instrumental in sentences like *On xočet byt' poleznym nam* 'He wants to be useful to us' and *On xotel kazat'sja umnym i interesnym* 'He wanted to seem smart and interesting' can be accounted for by the same rule.

The final derived P-marker underlying (3.94a) is (3.107), which is derived from (3.104) by *byt'*-Deletion.

(3.107)

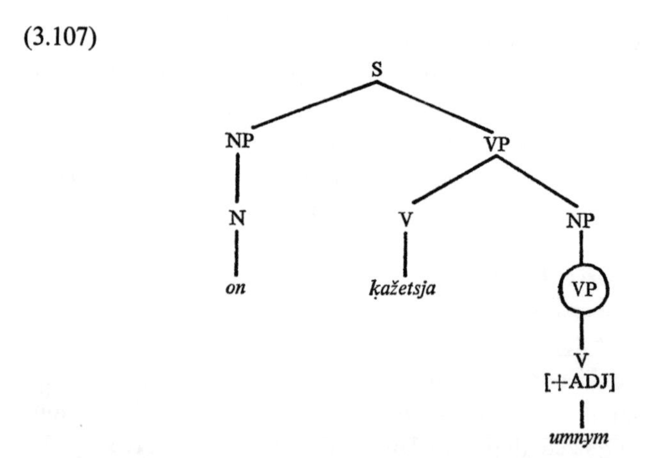

The derivation of sentences like (3.94a) provides us with another instance of a deep-structure SF emerging as a surface-structure LF as the result of introducing the SF into a NP, where it acquired a case feature. More

specifically, as a result of Subject-V Agreement, *um # n-* picked up the features [+3PER], [+SING], and [+MASC). If no other features were added in the course of the derivation, this would give a SF *(umën)* (cf. (3.94d)). However, *um # n* was introduced into a NP as the result of
[+3PER]
[+SING]
[+MASC]
Subject Raising and S-Node Deletion, and, accordingly, acquired a case feature by (3.24). This case feature was changed to [+ INST] by (3.83). *um #n* emerges as the LF *(umnym)*.
[+3PER]
[+SING]
[+MASC]
[+INST]

3.6.2 In order to account for (3.94a) in the simplest, most general manner, we have posited an intermediate P-marker (3.104) which, if interpreted as a final derived P-marker, would underlie the ungrammatical (3.105).

The positing of abstract, underlying structures that reveal the regularities of and the relations between otherwise irregular or unrelated surface phenomena is an accepted practice in linguistic science. We need not necessarily identify our deep or intermediate structures with observable surface structures in order to justify them. Thus the correctness of (3.104) as an intermediate P-marker in the derivation of (3.94a) does not depend on whether a sentence like (3.105) has ever existed in Russian. It depends only on whether (3.104) allows us to make a significant generalization about Russian without complicating the grammar at some other point.

Yet it is interesting to note that structures like (3.104), the postulation of which was motivated by purely synchronic considerations, were able to occur as surface structures in Russian as recently as the beginning of the nineteenth century. Sentences like (3.108) to (3.112) were considered quite normal at the end of the eighteenth century ((3.108)-(3.112) from Vinogradov and Švedova (eds.), 1964:116ff.).

(3.108) *I* kazalis' *oni* byt' *oxotnymi k provožaniju nas na goru.*
'And they seemed *to be* willing to lead us to the mountain.'

(3.109) *Ženščina...*kazalas' byt' *otčajannoju žizni.*
'The woman...seemed *to be* despairing of life.'

(3.110) *Suprug s orakulom* kazalsja byt' *soglasnym.*
'(My) spouse *seemed to be* in agreement with the oracle.'

(3.111) *...a potomu i k zastupleniju ego mesta ne* priznaetsja byt' *sposobnym.*
'...and therefore (he) does not *admit being* capable of taking his place.'

(3.112) *...o takom čeloveke, kotoryj sčital sebja* byt' *sčastlivym.*
'...about such a man who considered himself *to be* happy.'

3.6.3 DISCUSSION OF SENTENCE (3.95). The sentences in (3.95) can be accounted for by various combinations of transformational rules that have already been introduced. The deep structure of (3.95) is (3.113); details not of immediate interest are omitted.

(3.113)

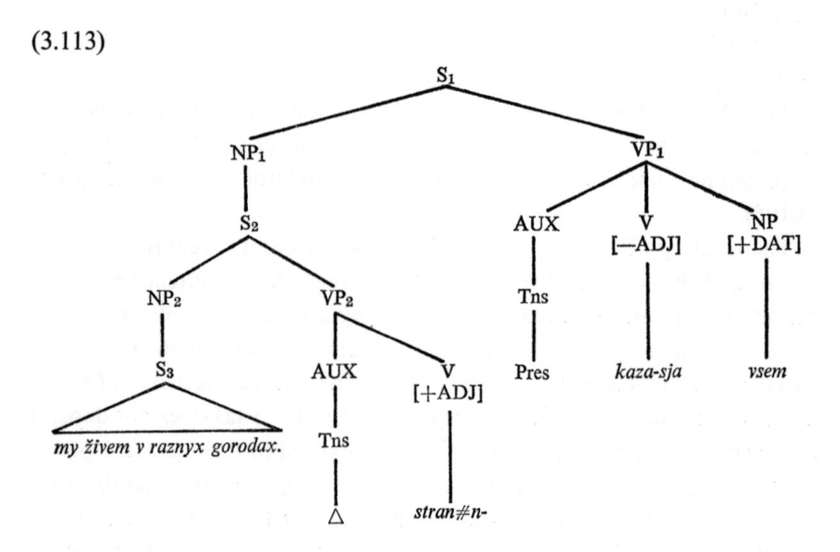

S_3 is processed on the first cycle. Details are omitted.

S_2 is processed on the second cycle. The subject of S_2 is $[S_3]_{NP_2}$ and the Subject-V Agreement transformation results in *stran # n-* [+3PER] [+SING] [+NEUT] (*stranno*). The third-person neuter singular is the unmarked form of person, number, and gender (cf. Kržižkova, 1968:212) and is invariably the result in Russian when Subject-V Agreement applies to a subject that does not possess the inherent features of gender, number, and person. Additional examples of this phenomena are given in (3.114).

(3.114a) *Kogda by ja ni vernulsja v rodnoj gorod, v rodnoj dom, surovoe "nu, rasskazyvaj" neizmenno ždalo menja.* (Kaverin)
'Whenever I returned to my home town, to my home, a stern "well, tell us all about it" invariably awaited me.'

(3.114b) *Tvoe beskonečnoe "ustal" mne uže nadoelo.*
'I've had enough of your endless "I'm tired".'

(3.114c) *Vstretit' blizkogo čeloveka vsegda prijatno.*
'To meet someone close is always pleasant.'

The subject of S_2 in (3.113) is a sentence (S_3) and, since a sentence does not possess inherent features of gender, number, or person, Subject-V Agreement results in *stranno*.

Stranno in (3.95) is thus not an adverb, as a number of linguists have maintained; it is a V ($\underset{[+ADJ]}{V}$) which has undergone Subject-V Agreement with a "non-agreeable" subject (cf. §3.3.3 for a discussion of adverbs in *-o* and "predicate adjectives" in *-o*).

(3.95c) is derived from (3.113) by Extraposition: S_2, the subject of S_1, is moved to the end of S_1 in the third cycle. *Stranno*, the main V of S_2, does not become a LF because the S-node of S_2 is not pruned in the course of the derivation of (3.95c) (compare with (3.95a)).

(3.95a) is derived from (3.113) by Subject Raising on the third cycle. The subject of S_2, $[S_3]_{NP_2}$, is raised up into the subject position of S_1; the remainder of S_2 is adjoined to VP_1 as its last constituent. This instance of the rule of Subject Raising differs from the others we have encountered only in that the raised subject NP in (3.95a) has a sentence embedded in it. Subject Raising converts P-marker (3.113) to (3.115). Details omitted.

After S-Node Deletion prunes S_2, (3.115) meets the SD of Infinitive Formation (3.75) and, sequentially, of the Obligatory Instrumental rule II (3.83). These rules map P-marker (3.115) into P-marker (3.116). Note that deep-structure *stran # n-* in (3.95a) emerges as a surface-structure LF (*strannym*) as a result of S-Node Deletion and Case Marking. This did not take place in the derivation of (3.95c) and, predictably, its surface structure contains a SF (*stranno*).

Subject-V Agreement (giving *kažetsja*, the third-person neuter singular (cf. *stranno* in the derivation of (3.95c))) and *byt'*-Deletion (3.106) convert (3.116) into (3.117), the surface structure of (3.95a).

(3.115)

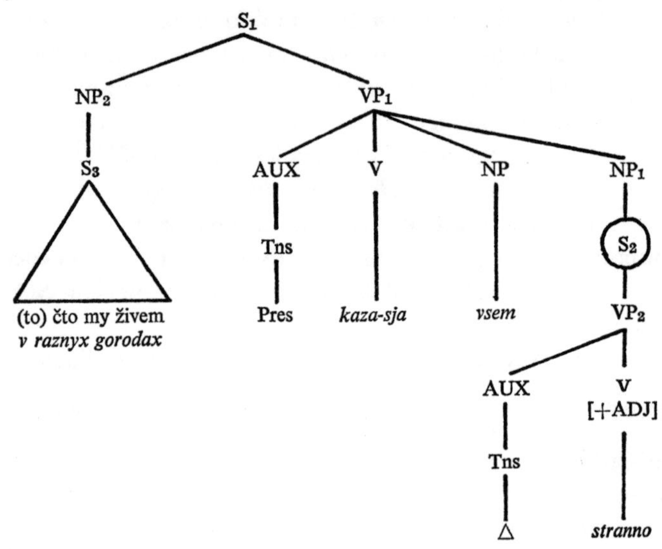

(3.116)

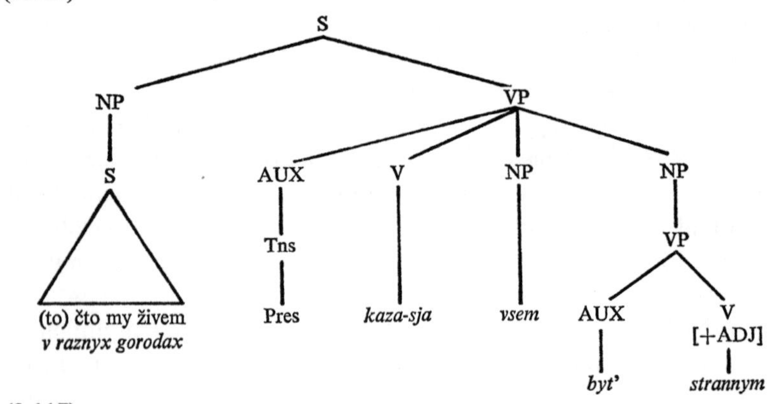

(3.117)

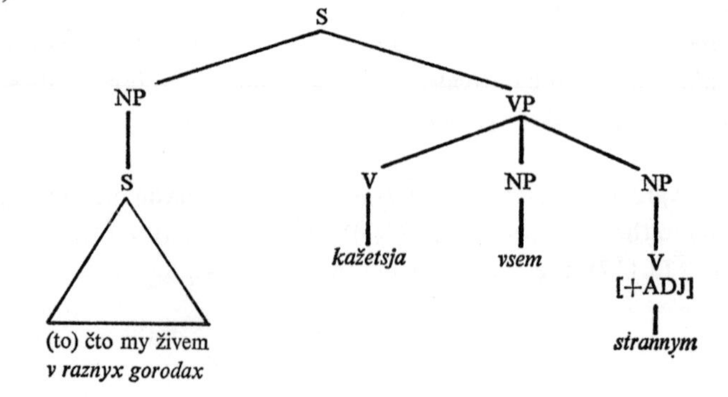

In Russian, word order at the level of surface structure does not seem to be a function of the transformational rules.

The grammar of Russian may therefore need post-transformational rules that move surface-structure constituents and do not alter agreement or case (cf. Chomsky, 1965:220-221). Paragraph 3.8.1 contains a discussion of one of the factors that determine word order in Russian.

3.6.4 OBLIGATORY INSTRUMENTAL RULE I AND II. P-marker (3.115) contains the derived configuration $[V — NP — NP]_{VP}$ and thus meets the SD for the Obligatory Instrumental rule I (3.34). The derivations studied in Chapter 3, however, have made it quite clear that rule (3.34) is inadequate and must be abandoned in favor of rule (3.83). One reason is that rule (3.83) can apply in every derivation in which (3.34) can apply (cf. (3.95a)), but there are a great many derivations where the reverse is not true. For instance, in the derivation of (3.94a) only (3.83) can account for the instrumental *umnym* since the configuration $[V — NP — NP]_{VP}$ is absent (cf. (3.87), (3.82), (3.37), etc., for derivations where (3.34) cannot account for the instrumental). There are no instances when (3.34) can apply and (3.83) cannot.

(3.34) seems incorrect for another reason. As stated, it will convert a sentence like (3.118a) into the ungrammatical (3.118b).

(3.118a) *Ja dal ej knigu.*
'I gave her a book.'
(3.118b) **Ja dal ej knigoj.*

Obligatory Instrumental rule (3.83) is the simpler, more general rule and is therefore to be preferred to (3.34). I can find no justification for retaining rule (3.34) in the grammar of Russian.

3.7 EXAMPLES (3.1) AND (3.2). The derivations and transformations presented in §§3.2-3.6 require that we return to examples (3.1) and (3.2) which are crucial to our explication of the transformational relationship between the SF and LF. Chapter 3 has been essentially an extended discussion of these two sentences.

(3.1) *Oni sčitali, čto oni pravy.*
(3.2) *Oni sčitali sebja pravymi.*

(3.119) is the deep structure of (3.1) and (3.2).

Sentence (3.1) is derived from P-marker (3.119) by the following transformations:

(3.119)

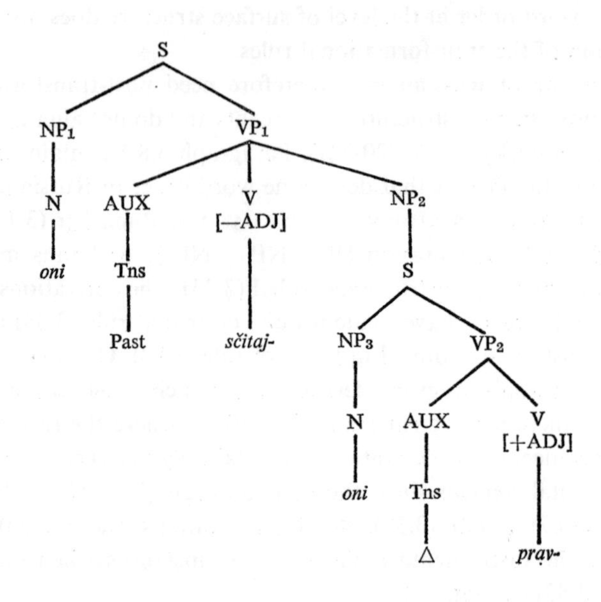

Cycle I: SUBJECT-V AGREEMENT, which gives *prav-* [+3PER] [+PLUR] (= *pravy*)

Cycle II: SUBJECT-V AGREEMENT (*sčitali*)
COMPLEMENTIZER PLACEMENT (*čto*)

(3.1) contains a SF because the embedded S-node is not deleted and, consequently, $\underset{[+ADJ]}{\mathrm{V}}$ never comes under NP domination. (3.10) is the final derived P-marker of (3.1).

Sentence (3.2) is derived from P-marker (3.119) by the following rules:

Cycle I: SUBJECT-V AGREEMENT, which gives *prav-* [+3PER] [+PLUR]

Cycle II: SUBJECT-V AGREEMENT, which gives *sčitali*.
SUBJECT RAISING, which raises the subject NP (NP_3) of the embedded sentence up into direct object position in the matrix sentence.
REFLEXIVIZATION, which changes the raised subject (*oni*) into *sebja* after it received the feature [+ACC] as the derived direct object of *sčitaj-*.

S-NODE DELETION, which deletes the embedded S-node by (3.15).

CASE MARKING (3.24), which gives *prav-* (= LF).
[+3PER]
[+PLUR]
[+ACC]

INFINITIVE FORMATION (3.75), which gives *byt'* from the Tense-marker.

OBLIGATORY INSTRUMENTAL TRANSFORMATION (3.83), which changes the case feature acquired by *prav-* into [+INST].

These second-cycle rules map P-marker (3.119) into the intermediate P-marker (3.120) (cf. (3.112)).

(3.120)

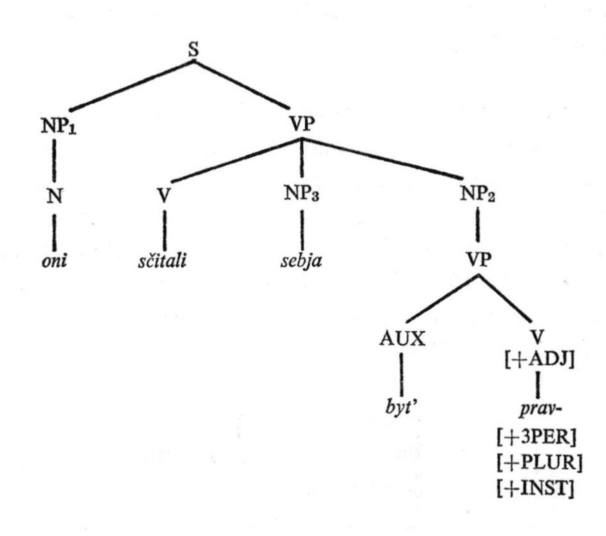

byt'-DELETION (3.106), which deletes *byt'* and produces (3.121), the final derived P-marker of (3.2).

The derivation of (3.1) and (3.2) clearly demonstrates that the difference between the SF *pravy* (*prav-* [+3PER] [+PLUR]) and the LF *pravymi* (*prav-* [+3PER] [+PLUR] [+INST]) is a case feature acquired as the result of S-Node Deletion and Case Marking. The transformation that occasions S-Node Deletion and the case feature

(3.121)

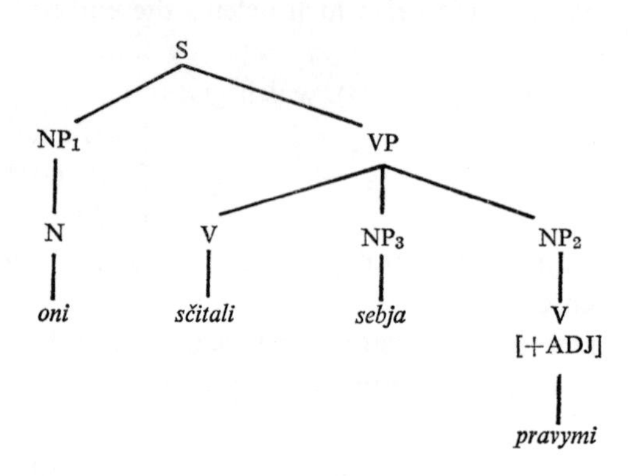

that is acquired by V [+ADJ] vary from derivation to derivation. The invariant in derivation of a LF from a SF is acquisition of ANY case feature ([αCASE]) by the latter.

3.8.0 SLOŽNOE SOSTAVNOE SKAZUEMOE SMEŠANNOGO TIPA [The complex compound mixed predicate]. The analyses presented in §3.8 are intended as additional evidence that the transformational rules and relations presented in §§3.1-3.7 are correct. The type of syntactic structure treated in §3.8 is schematically presented in (3.122); concrete examples are given in (3.123g), (3.139), (3.140), (3.159), (3.162), and (3.163). These structures are traditionally called *složnoe sostavnoe skazuemoe smešannogo tipa* (cf. Galkina-Fedoruk, 1957:178).

(3.122) $$\textit{Ona}\begin{Bmatrix}\textit{sčitaet}\\ \\ \textit{naxodit}\\ \vdots\end{Bmatrix}\begin{Bmatrix}\textit{važnym}\\ \textit{nužnym}\\ \textit{neobxodimym}\\ \textit{celesoobraznym}\\ \textit{razumnym}\\ \vdots\end{Bmatrix}\begin{Bmatrix}\text{infinitive phrase}\\ \\ \textit{čto(by)} + \text{S}\end{Bmatrix}$$

The sentences in (3.123) will serve to illustrate the relations we wish to explicate.

(3.123a) *Ej nužna èta kniga.*
'She needs this book.'

(3.123b) *Ej* {**nužnoe* / *nužno* / **bylo nužnym*} *pročitat' ètu knigu.*
'She needs to read this book.'

(3.123c) *Ona sčitaet, čto nam nužno pročitat' ètu knigu.*
'She considers that it is necessary for us to read this book.'

(3.123d) **Ona sčitaet nam nužnym pročitat' ètu knigu.*

(3.123e) **Ona sčitaet nužnym nam pročitat' ètu knigu.*

(3.123f) *Ona sčitaet nužnym, čtoby my pročitali ètu knigu.*
'She considers it necessary that we read this book.'

(3.123g) *Ona sčitaet nužnym pročitat' ètu knigu.*
'She considers it necessary to read this book.'

(3.123h) **Ona sčitaet nužnym sebe pročitat' ètu knigu.*

(3.123i) **Ona sčitaet nužnym nam, čtoby my pročitali ètu knigu.*

(3.123j) **Ona sčitaet, čto nam nužno, čtoby my pročitali ètu knigu.*

3.8.1 WORD ORDER AND CONSTITUENT COMPLEXITY. Before discussing the derivations of the sentences in (3.123), it is necessary to say a few words about surface-structure word order in Russian.

Word order in English serves primarily to reflect deep structure grammatical relations at the level of surface structure. Case serves this function in Russian, thus permitting the juxtaposition of surface-structure constituents to serve other ends. In Chapter 2 it was noted that word order in Russian serves an anaphoric function.

There is another factor determining Russian word order that is of immediate concern in accounting for the sentences in (3.123).

Consider sentences (3.124) and (3.125); their word order is neutral or unmarked.

(3.124) *Ivan sčitaet teoriju ošibočnoj.*
'Ivan considers the theory mistaken.'

(3.125) *Ivan sčitaet ošibočnoj teoriju, kotoraja utverždaet, čto* + S.
'Ivan considers mistaken the theory that maintains that....'

The word order in (3.124) and (3.125) depends upon "constituent complexity" (for a discussion of the difficulties of this concept of complexity, cf. Ross, 1969:291-292) and is a purely surface-structure consideration: it is not a projection of the deep-structure order of elements and not the order produced by the rules of the transformational component. (3.124) and (3.125) have essentially the identical derivation. The difference in word order ("constituent order" would be a more accurate term) can be explained entirely in terms of the complexity of the NP dominating *teorija*: in (3.125) it contains a relative clause and in (3.124) it does not. The difference in word order is a matter of acceptability, not grammaticality, since the same sentences with the NPs juxtaposed are grammatical, but not preferred (the word order is marked).

(3.124a) (?) *Ivan sčitaet ošibočnoj teoriju.*
(3.125a) (?) *Ivan sčitaet teoriju, kotoraja utverždaet, čto..., ošibočnoj.*

The deep structure of (3.124) and (3.124a) is (3.126):

(3.126)

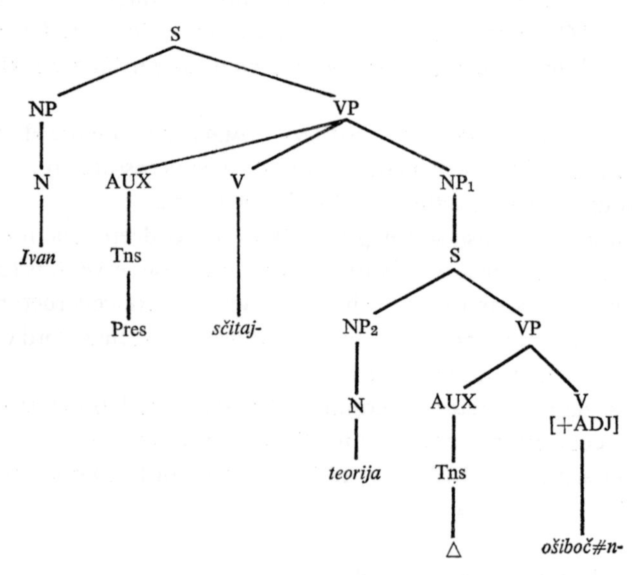

(3.127), the surface structure of (3.124) and (3.124a), is derived from (3.126) by Subject Raising (other transformations involved in the derivation of (3.124) have been discussed in detail and will not be specifically mentioned in subsequent derivations).

(3.126) and (3.127) show that the neutral constituent order in sentence (3.124) (NP_2—NP_1) coincides with the constituent order produced by the rules of the transformational component.

(3.128) is the deep structure of (3.125); (3.129) is the final derived P-marker of (3.125), i.e. the P-marker produced by the last transformational

(3.127)

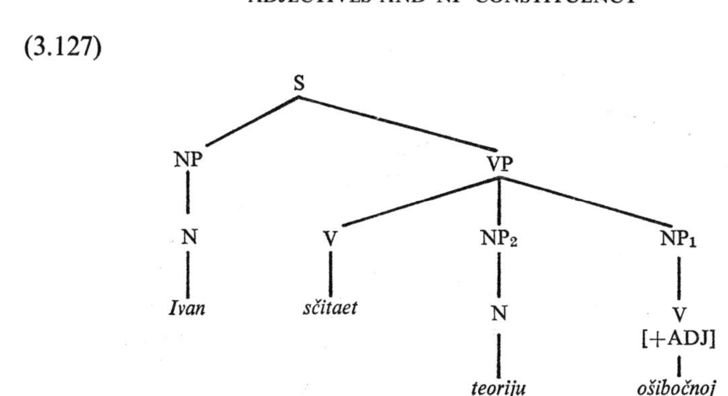

rule to operate in the derivation of (3.125). Note that the transformations employed in the derivation of (3.125) are the same as those employed in (3.124): Subject Raising moves NP_2 up into direct object position in the matrix sentence. NP_2 in (3.124) is "simple" ($[N]_{NP_2}$), while NP_2 in (3.125) is "complex" ($[NP — S]_{NP_2}$).

(3.128)

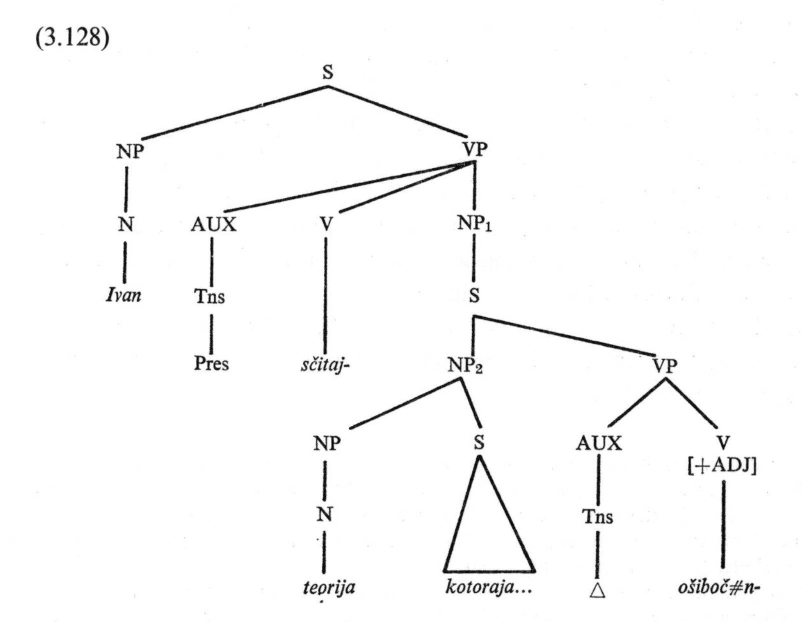

The neutral constituent order in (3.125) is $NP_1 — NP_2$, but the constituent order produced by the transformational rules is $NP_2 — NP_1$, the marked order of (3.125a). (3.125) is derived from (3.129) by a "constituent-order" rule that juxtaposes NP_2 and NP_1. These rules operate after the

(3.129)

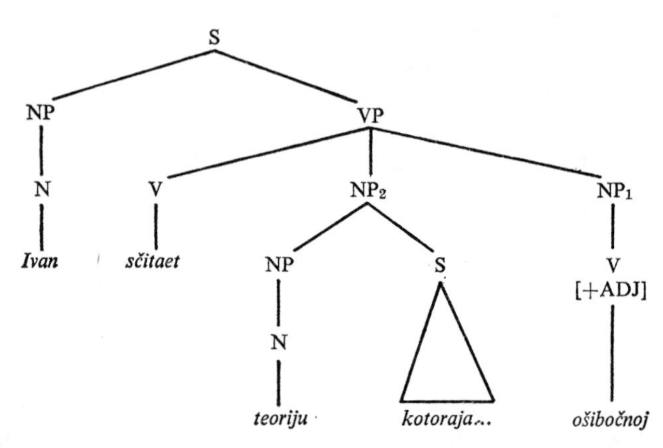

rules of the transformational component proper and do not change grammatical relations, agreement, etc. (cf. Chomsky, 1965:220-221).

Since the deep structure and derivation of (3.124) and (3.125) are identical except for the relative clause in NP_2, it is reasonable to assume that it is the complexity of NP_2 alone that is responsible for the difference in constituent order between (3.124) and (3.125).

It would therefore be a mistake for a linguist to try to build surface-structure word order into the transformational component of a transformational-generative grammar of Russian. This observation may be stated in another, more useful way: a sequence of transformational rules may not be adjudged incorrect because it does not result in the most neutral order of surface-structure constituents.[16]

3.8.2 DERIVATION OF THE SENTENCES IN (3.123). An explanation of the relations that obtain in (3.123) depends on our interpretation of the lexical item *nuž # n-* 'necessary'.

[16] The derivation of (a) *On sčitaet ee umnoj* 'He considers her intelligent' from an underlying (b) *On sčitaet* [*ona umna*]$_{NP}$ is identical to the derivation of (3.124) and (3.125), yet the juxtaposition of the NPs in the final derived P-marker in this instance results in an ungrammatical sentence ((c) **On sčitaet umnoj ee*), not one of decreased acceptability (cf. (3.124a) and (3.125a)).

This phenomenon is undoubtedly related to the ungrammaticality of sentences containing a pronoun with a preposed modifier (reduced relative clause): (d) **Ja uvidel krasivuju ee* 'I saw a pretty her'. The non-ocurrence of sentences like (d), if taken as an isolated case, may be explained by a restriction on Modifier Shift such as: a reduced relative cannot be moved around a pronoun. In sentence (c), however, *umnoj* is not a modifier of *ee*. The fact that (c) is ungrammatical makes it seem likely that we are dealing with a wider, more general restriction, perhaps one involving the impossibility of any transformational rule moving any constituent around a pronoun.

(3.130) is the deep structure of (3.123a); note that *nuž # n-* takes a dative object and a nominative subject (cf. Appendix I to Chapter 3 for a discussion of verbs that require "oblique" subjects).

(3.123a) *Ej nužna èta kniga.*

(3.130)

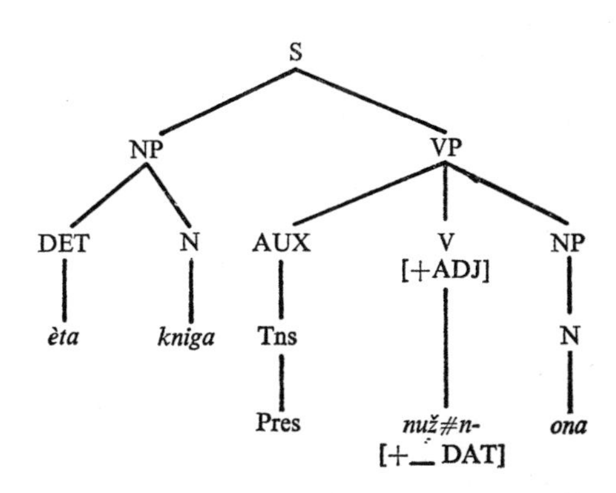

3.8.3 THE DERIVATION OF (3.123b) AND EQUI-NP DELETION. The "logical" or "understood" subject of *pročitat'* in (3.123b) is unambiguously *ej*. This fact can be captured by positing (3.131) as the deep structure of (3.123b).

(3.123b) *Ej nužno pročitat' ètu knigu.*

(3.131)

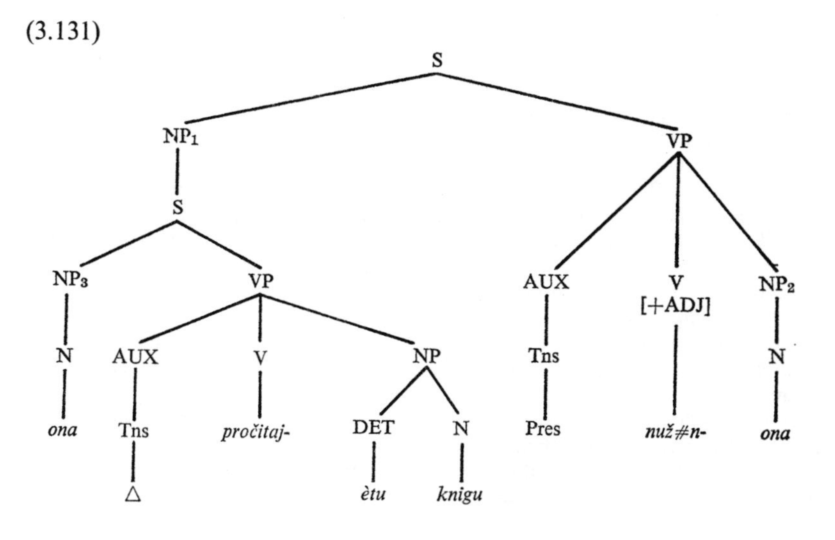

One immediate advantage of (3.131) is that it allows us to posit in our lexicon only one lexical item *nuž # n-* for (3.123a), a "personal" sentence, and for (3.123b), traditionally called an "impersonal" sentence. It brings out the fact that the only structural difference between the two sentences is that (3.123b) contains a sentential subject.[17]

[17] We are treating *nužna* in §3.8.2 and *nužno* in §3.8.3 as the same lexical item. There is at least one possible alternative analysis which treats them as two different lexical items: *nužna* in (3.123a) is transitive (i.e. it takes a dative object), while *nužno* in (3.123b) is intransitive and takes a dative SUBJECT. According to this alternative analysis, the deep structure of (3.123b) is as follows:

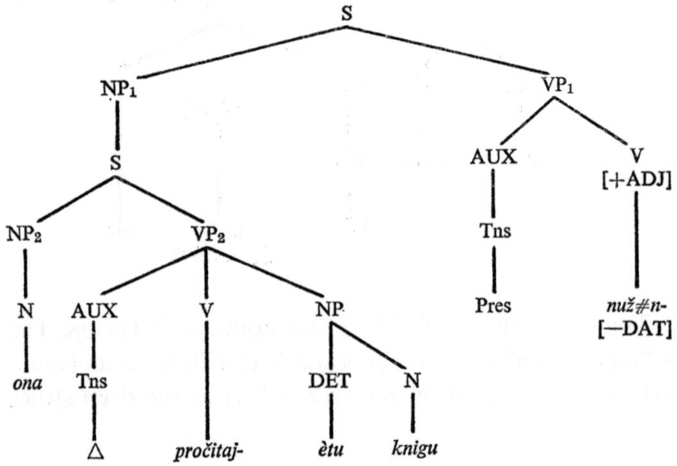

The rule of Subject Raising would move NP_2 up into matrix subject position, where it is marked [+DAT]; the remainder of the embedded sentence is adjoined to VP_1 as its last constituent (cf. §3.6.1 and footnote 3.15). The *-o* in *nužno* is the result of Subject-V Agreement with an oblique subject (cf. §3.6.3).

This "two-item" analysis of *nuž#n-* has one immediate advantage: the transformational rules produce the most neutral constituent order. However, it was pointed out in §3.8.1 that this fact alone is insufficient evidence for accepting or rejecting a given analysis. A disadvantage of the "two-item" interpretation of *nuž#n-* is that it does not capture the intuitive knowledge that "it is necessary for *her* (not someone else) that *she* read the book". Thus if the "two-item" analysis of *nuž#n-* is accepted, it becomes a difficult problem to assign a deep structure to a sentence like *Ej nužno, čtoby my priexali v tri časa* 'It is neccessary to her that we come at three' (NB: **Ej nužno, čtoby ona priexala v tri časa* (when *ej* = *ona*) vs. *Ej nužno priexat' v tri časa* 'She needs to come at three'. This is the same phenomenon as *Ona xočet, čtoby my priexali v tri časa* 'She wants us to come at three' vs. **Ona xočet, čtoby ona priexala v tri časa* 'She wants her to come at three.' vs *Ona xočet priexat' v tri časa* 'She wants to come at three'. Equi-NP Deletion is the key to these relations, not Subject Raising, which is required by the "two-item" analysis).

In view of these facts we will use the "one-item" analysis of *nuž#n-* employed in §3.8.2 and §3.8.3. It must be emphasized, however, that the question of which alternative is correct is still open. I do not choose to pursue it here, since it does not bear directly on the relation of the LF and the SF, the main point of §3.8.

Among the transformations employed in the derivation of (3.132), the final derived P-marker of (3.123b), from (3.131) are:

EQUI-NP DELETION, which deletes NP_3, the subject of the embedded sentence, under identity to NP_2.

SUBJECT-V AGREEMENT (on the second cycle), which gives *nužno*. This is always the result of Subject-V Agreement when the subject is an embedded sentence (for details cf. §3.6.3).

(3.132)

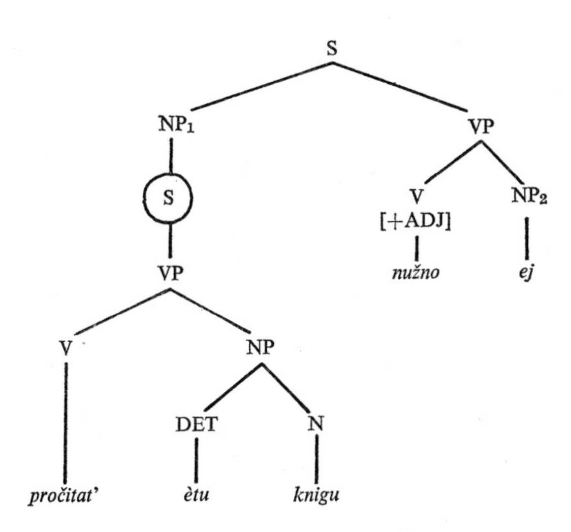

The neutral word order for (3.123b) is derived from (3.132) by the constituent order rules discussed in §3.8.1.

In all the instances of Equi-NP Deletion discussed so far the coreferential NP in the matrix sentence has been in subject position. In (3.123b), it is in object position.

J. R. Ross (1969:289) has adduced possible evidence that Equi-NP Deletion from object position is needed in English grammar.[18] He discussed the following sentences.

(3.133a) *To report the incident was wise of John.*

(3.133b) *It was wise of John to report the incident.*

[18] In "Summary of Rules of English Syntax" (MIT, 24 November 1967), the condition on the Equi-NP Deletion rule merely states that the NP to be deleted must be "identical with the nearest NP in the sentence being processed". Nothing is said about the position (subject or object) of the NP in the sentence being processed.

According to Ross, (3.133a) and (3.133b) derive from the same deep structure, which is reproduced here as (3.134).[19]

(3.134)

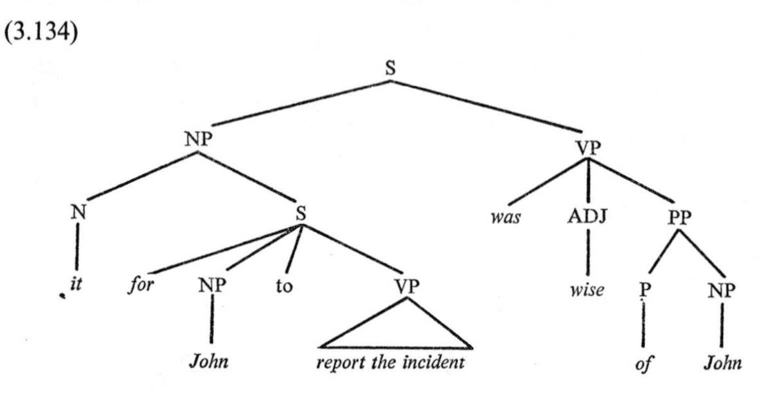

Both the sentences in (3.133) are derived from (3.134) "by a rule which deletes the subject NP of the embedded sentence, subject to the condition that it be identical to the NP in the prepositional phrase....". This rule is clearly Equi-NP Deletion. Notice that the deep structure of (3.123b) is very similar to the deep structure (3.134).

Sentence (3.123b) cannot be said to be an "impersonal" sentence in the same way that (3.135) is impersonal.

(3.135) *(Na ulice) temneet.*
'It is getting dark (out).'

Sentence (3.135) contains the configuration $[VP]_S$; (3.123b) maintains the configuration $[NP — VP]_S$ throughout its derivation (cf. footnote 3.14 for some further remarks on impersonal sentences).

3.8.4 THE DERIVATION OF SENTENCE (3.123g). The discussion of *nuž # n-* in sentences (3.123a) and (3.123b) enables us to discuss (3.123g), the syntactic structure that is the focal point of §3.8. Sentence (3.123g) contains a *složnoe sostavnoe skazuemoe smešannogo tipa* (cf. §3.8.0).

(3.123g) *Ona sčitaet nužnym pročitat' ètu knigu.*
'She considers it necessary to read this book.'

[19] It must be noted that (3.133a) is unacceptable or only marginally acceptable to some English speakers.

NB: $$\textit{*Ona sčitaet} \left\{ \begin{matrix} \textit{nužnoj} \\ \textit{nužno} \\ \textit{nužna} \\ \textit{nužnoe} \end{matrix} \right\} \textit{pročitat' ètu knigu.}$$

At first glance (3.123g) presents no problems: it appears to be a sentence like (3.123b) embedded in the object NP of a sentence whose main V is *sčitaj-*. In other words, (3.123g) appears to be a simple combination of two structures that have already been analyzed: a sentence like (3.123b) embedded in the object NP of a sentence like (3.2) (cf. §3.7 for a discussion of sentences containing *sčitaj-* + $[S]_{NP}$). Sentences like (3.123c) and (3.123f) support this view.

(3.123c) *Ona sčitaet, čto nam nužno pročitat' ètu knigu.*
'She considers that it is necessary for us to read this book.'

(3.123f) *Ona sčitaet nužnym, čtoby my pročitali ètu knigu.*
'She considers it necessary that we read this book.'

In accordance with these considerations, the deep structure of (3.123g) may be assumed to be (3.136).

(3.136)

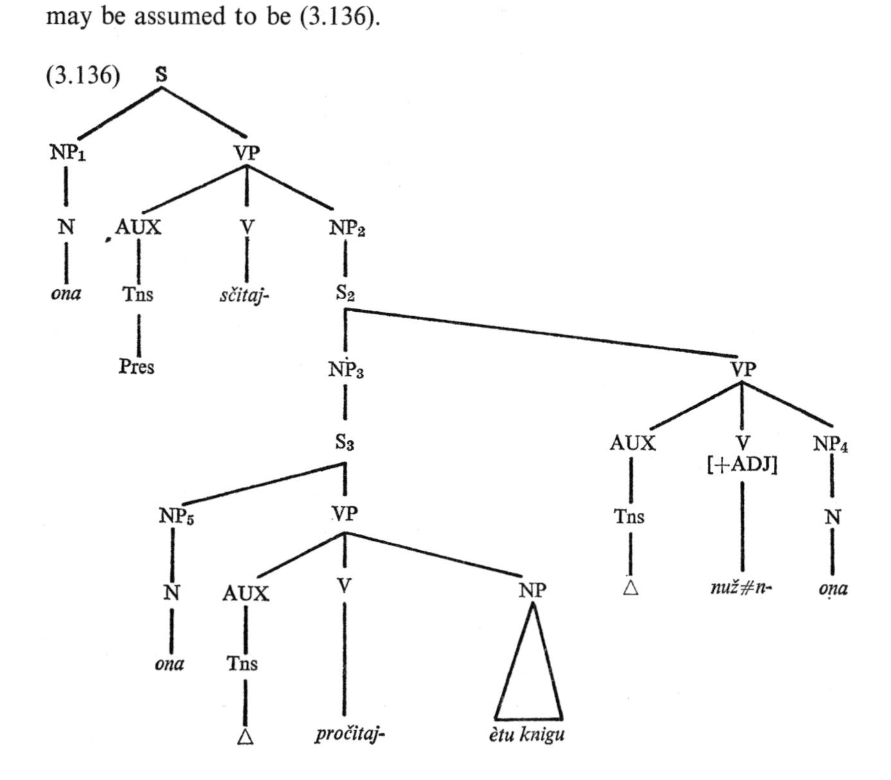

The following transformations apply to (3.136); details are omitted.

EQUI-NP DELETION (Cycle II): NP_5 in S_3 is deleted under identity to NP_4 in S_2. Equi-NP Deletion is followed by S-Node Deletion and Infinitive Formation (3.75). These transformations map (3.136) into the intermediate P-marker (3.137).

(3.137)

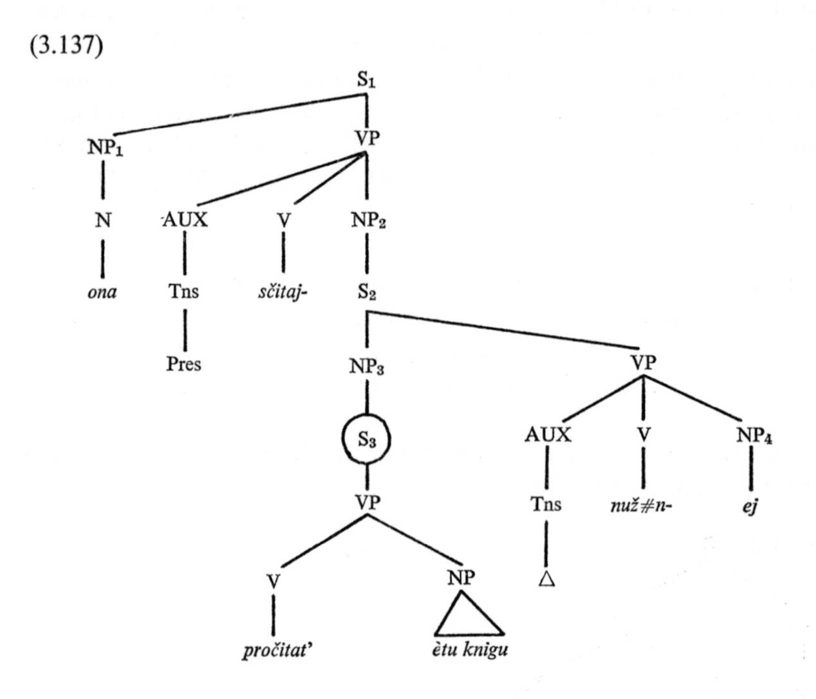

SUBJECT-V AGREEMENT (Cycle II): gives *nužno* from *nuž # n-*, since the subject of S_2 has no inherent features of gender, number, and person (cf. §3.6.3). Note that S_2, if not embedded in S_1, would be *Ej nužno pročitat' ètu knigu*, sentence (3.123b). It is this *nužno* that some Soviet linguists call an adverb.

SUBJECT RAISING (Cycle III), which moves NP_3 up into object position in S_1. Note that the SD of the Subject Raising transformation (cf. footnote 3.15) merely specifies that the subject of NP an embedded sentence be raised up into the next highest sentence; no mention is made of what the raised NP dominates. In the derivation of (3.2) it dominates only a N; in (3.137) it dominates an entire VP (*pročitat' ètu knigu*).

Subject Raising results in S-Node Deletion (S_2), which in turn results in Reflexivization (*ej→sebe*). The resulting P-marker meets the SD for Infinitive Formation (giving *byt'* from the tense-marker) and, sequentially, for the Obligatory Instrumental transformation (3.83), giving *nužnym* from *nužno*. This may serve as evidence that *nužno* in (3.123b) is not an adverb as well as providing another example of a LF (*nužnym*) being derived from a SF (*nužno*). *Byt'*-Deletion then operates, producing the final derived P-marker (3.138).

(3.138)

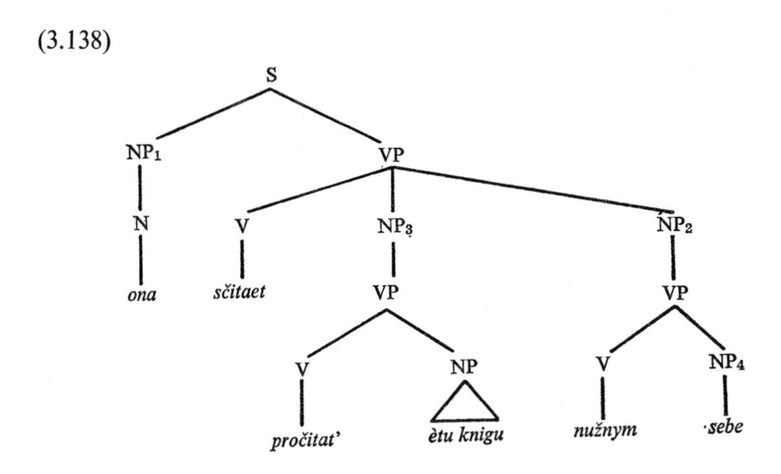

However, (3.138) is the final derived P-marker for sentence (3.123h), which is not a grammatical sentence of Russian.

(3.123h) *Ona sčitaet nužnym sebe pročitat' ètu knigu.

Sentence (3.123h) is adjudged grammatical by native speakers only if *sebe* is interpreted as the indirect object of *pročitat'* (cf. 'She considers it necessary to read the book to herself'). It is invariably adjudged ungrammatical when *sebe* is interpreted as the object of *nužnym* (cf. lit. 'She considers it necessary for herself to read this book').

Note that it would be possible to derive (3.123g) from (3.138) if *sčitaj-* governed the rule of Equi-NP Deletion: NP_4, the object of *nuž # n-*, is identical (before Case Marking) to NP_1, the subject of the matrix sentence. Equi-NP Deletion would delete NP_4, thereby deriving (3.123g) from (3.138). However, it was pointed out in §3.1.0 that the lexical item *sčitaj-* does not govern the rule of Equi-NP Deletion (cf. sentence (3.11)).

The facts presented above make it clear that (3.136) is not the deep structure of (3.123g). (3.136) is not a well-formed deep structure and, consequently, there is no combination of transformations in Russian grammar that can derive an occurring surface structure from it. (3.136) must be rejected as the deep structure of (3.123g) for still another reason: *ona*, the subject of the matrix sentence, is not necessarily identical to the "understood" subject or object of the (reduced) constituent sentence. According to the deep structure (3.136), *ona* should be the unambiguous subject of *nuž # n-* just as it is in (3.123b) (cf. §3.8.3). The correct deep structure of (3.123g) must account for this fact.

The ambiguity of (3.123g) is a crucial consideration. Even if sentences like (3.123h) were possible, it would still be necessary to account for the ambiguity of sentences like (3.123g): the matrix subject *ona* can be but is not necessarily the "logical" or "understood" subject of *pročitat'* or the object of *nužnym*. The type of ambiguity found in (3.123g) is perhaps more clearly illustrated by example (3.139).

(3.139) *Ja sčitaju važnym načat' peregovory nemedlenno.*
'I consider it important to begin the negotiations at once.'

It is not necessarily the case that *ja*, the matrix subject, is the one who is to begin the negotiations or that it is important to "*ja*" that the negotiations begin at once. If the ambiguity in these sentences is not always felt, this is because the context and the lexical items usually preclude all but one reading. This is particularly clear in the case of sentence (3.140).

(3.140) *Mnogie iz nas sočli trudnym otvetit' na vaš vopros srazu.*
'Many of us considered it difficult to answer your question straight off.'

These sentences are nevertheless ambiguous. One of the readings of *The lamb is too hot to eat* may not be obvious, but the sentence is still ambiguous.

Sentences like (3.123g) can be accounted for most satisfactorily if the most deeply embedded sentence in each deep structure has an UNSPECIFIED SUBJECT that is deleted in the course of the derivation by an obligatory transformation (cf. Chomsky, 1965:105; 222: "Δ is an unspecified element that will be deleted by an obligatory transformation"; R. Rothstein, 1966:49ff.).

Deep structures containing unspecified subjects are needed in the grammar of Russian independently of sentences like (3.123g) in order to account for "impersonal" sentences like (3.141) and (3.142).

(3.141) *Nužno byt' ostorožnym pri perexode čerez ulicu.*

'One should be careful when crossing the street.'
'One should be careful when one crosses the street.'

(3.142) *Nužno vsegda deržat' svoe slovo.*
'One should always keep one's word.'
'One should always keep his word.'

In the deep structure of (3.141) and (3.142), *nuž # n-* has a sentential subject ($[S]_{NP}$) with an unspecified subject.[20]

The rule that deletes the unspecified subject has a far wider range of application in Russian than the cognate rule in English does, and it is therefore responsible for a great many surface structures in Russian that are impossible in English. This is illustrated by the following sentences.

(3.143a) *Kapitan prikazal razgruzit' paroxod.*
'The captain ordered the ship unloaded.'
lit. 'The captain ordered to unload the ship.'

(3.143b) *Kapitan prikazal matrosam razgruzit' paroxod.*
'The captain ordered the sailors to unload the ship.'

(3.144a) *Ona poprosila prinesti stakan vody.*
lit. 'She asked to bring a glass of water.'

(3.144b) *Ona poprosila syna prinesti stakan vody.*
'She asked (her) son to bring a glass of water.'

(3.145) *Začem vy pozvoljaete sebja duračit'*?[21]
*'Why do you allow to fool yourself?'
'Why do you allow people to fool {you / *yourself}?'
'Why do you allow {*you / yourself} to be fooled?'

(3.146) *Ja ne pozvolju govorit' s soboju takim obrazom.*
'I will not allow (anyone) to speak to *me* like this.'

(3.147) *On prikazal ubit' svoju lošad'.*
'He ordered his horse killed.'

The deep structures of (3.143a) and (3.143b) are identical except for the subject NP of the embedded sentence: in (3.143b) it is a lexical noun

[20] Notice the "infinitives" *byt' ostorožnym* from an underlying Tns + *ostorož#n-* in (3.141) and *deržat'* from Tns + *derža-* in (3.142).

[21] *Sebja*, which refers to *vy*, is unambiguously the direct object of *duračit'*, since *pozvoljaj-* governs the dative. See R. Rothstein, "Reflexive 'Reflexive' Verbs", in *SEEJ*.

(*matrosy*), while in (3.143a) it is an unspecified subject (Δ). To avoid needless repetition, the deep structure of (3.143a) and (3.143b) are given together:

(3.148)

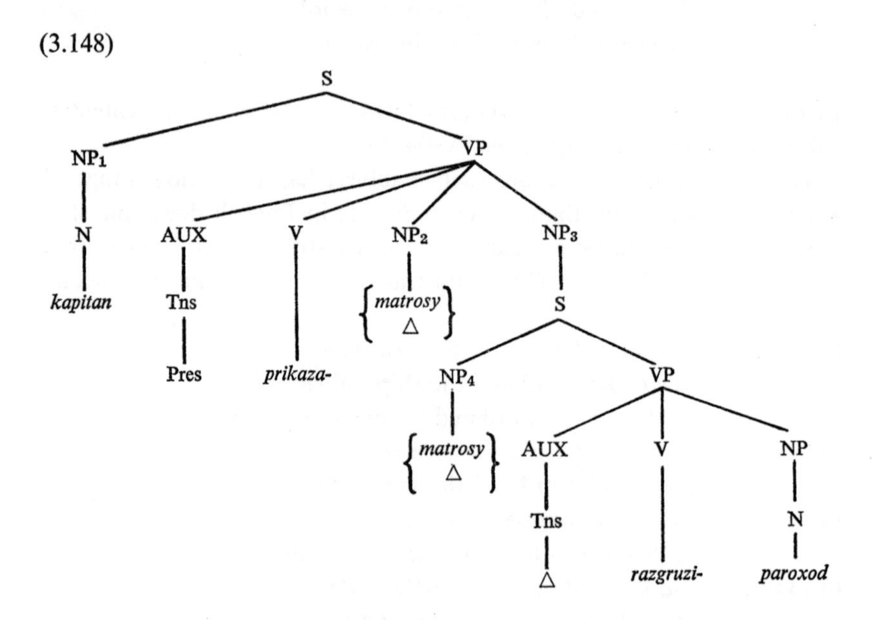

(3.143) is derived from (3.148) by the following transformations (details are omitted): Equi-NP Deletion deletes NP_4 under identity to NP_2. S-Node Deletion and Infinitive Formation follow. In the derivation of (3.143a), an obligatory transformation deletes the unspecified $[\Delta]_{NP_2}$.

Sentence (3.143) was derived from a deep-structure $[V—NP—[S]_{NP}]_{VP}$ (cf. (3.148)) by Equi-NP Deletion rather than from a deep-structure $[V—[S]_{NP}]_{VP}$ by the optional rule of Subject Raising in order to account for the non-occurrence of sentences like (3.149).

(3.149) **Kapitan prikazal paroxodu byt' razgružennym (kem-n.).*
'The captain ordered the ship (to be) unloaded (by someone).'

Sentences (3.143)-(3.147) illustrate that Russian admits surface structures in which the deep-structure subject of an infinitive complement may be deleted if it is unspecified. The English glosses in (3.143)-(3.147) demonstrate that this type of surface structure is not possible in English.

3.8.5 The derivation of sentence (3.123g) continued. (3.123g) is merely a particular case of a sentence whose deep structure contains an embedded sentence with an unspecified subject that is obligatorily deleted. This accounts for the ambiguity noted above (cf. (3.139)); whether or not the unspecified constituent subject is interpreted as being the same as the matrix subject is wholly dependent on the context.

Accordingly, the deep structure of (3.123g) is (3.150).

(3.123g) *Ona sčitaet nužnym pročitat' ètu knigu.*
'She considers it necessary to read this book.'

(3.150)

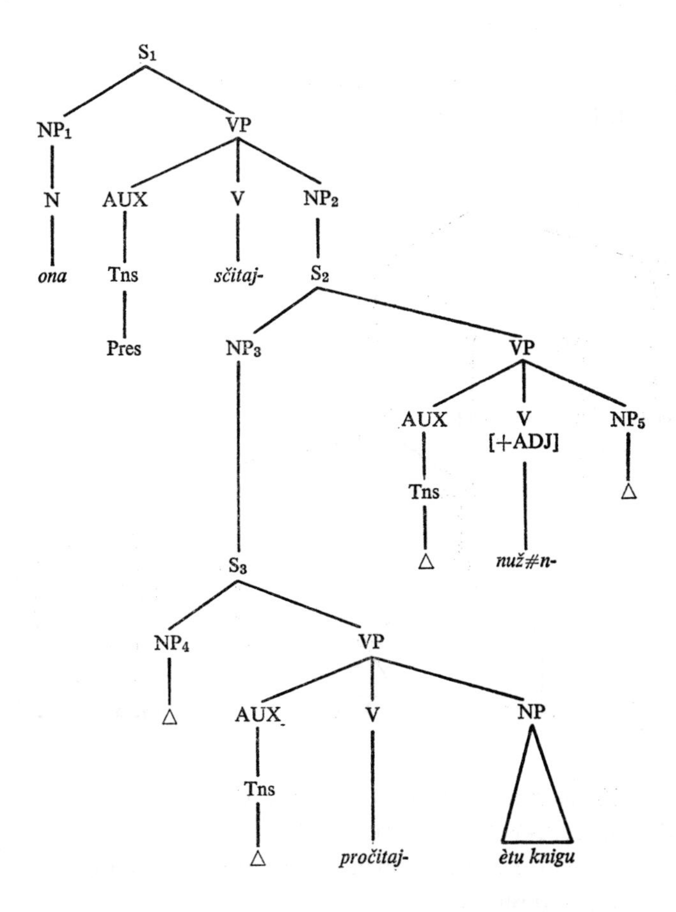

The following transformations are employed in the derivation of (3.123g) from (3.150); irrelevant details are omitted.

Cycle II: SUBJECT-V AGREEMENT, which results in *nuž # n-* [+3PER] [+SING] [+NEUT] *Nužno* is used in the intermediate P-marker as a shorthand notation.

EQUI-NP DELETION, which deletes NP_4 under identity to NP_5 (cf. §3.8.4 for a discussion of Equi-NP Deletion from object position).

S-NODE DELETION (3.15), which deletes the embedded node S_3.

INFINITIVE FORMATION (3.75), which produces *pročitat'* from Tns + *pročitaj-*.

The application of these transformations produces the intermediate P-marker (3.151) from (3.150).

(3.151)

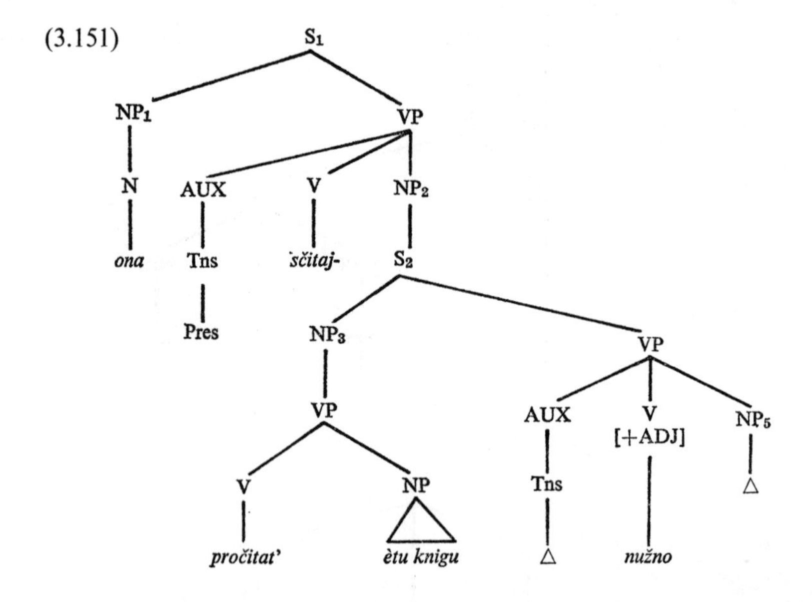

UNSPECIFIED-SUBJECT DELETION, which deletes NP_5.

Cycle III: SUBJECT-V AGREEMENT, which gives *sčitaet*.

SUBJECT RAISING, which raises NP_3, the subject of S_2, into object position in S_1.

S-NODE DELETION (3.15), which deletes the embedded node S_2.

CASE MARKING (3.24), which copies the case feature of NP_2 on to *nuž # n-*.

INFINITIVE FORMATION (3.75), which produces *byt'* from Tns + V
[+ADJ]·
OBLIGATORY INSTRUMENTAL TRANSFORMATION (3.83), which changes the case feature acquired by *nuž # n-* to [+INST]:
nuž # n- (= LF *nužnym*).
[+3PER]
[+SING]
[+NEUT]
[+INST]
byt'-DELETION (3.106), which deletes the infinitive *byt'*.

These rules derive the final derived P-marker of (3.123g):

(3.152)

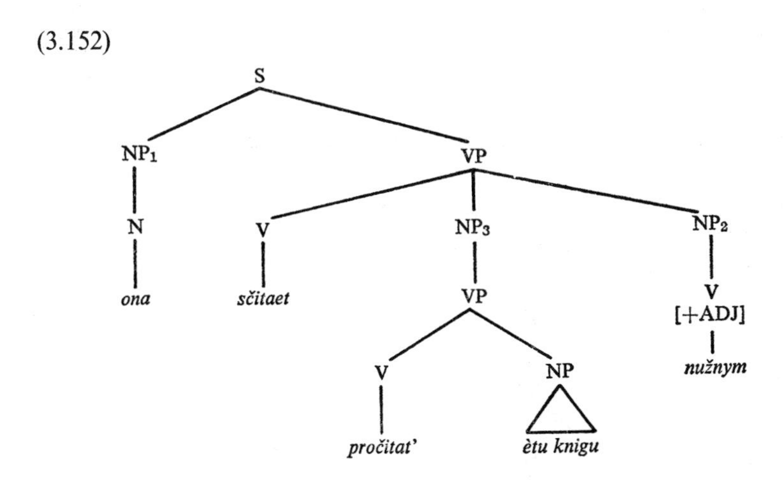

(3.152) underlies (?)*Ona sčitaet* [*pročitat' ètu knigu*]$_{NP_3}$ [*nužnym*]$_{NP_2}$. NP_3, which has a VP embedded in it, is more complex than NP_2 and, according to the principles discussed in §3.8.1, a Constituent Order rule will juxtapose them. This is the last rule in the derivation of (3.123g): *Ona sčitaet* [*nužnym*]$_{NP_2}$ [*pročitat' ètu knigu*]$_{NP_3}$. In the derivation of (3.2) (cf. §3.7), on the other hand, Subject Raising produces the derived configuration [V—NP—NP]$_{VP}$ just as it does in (3.123g), but since the NPs are of equal complexity in (3.2), the Constituent Order rule that shifts the more complex NP to the end of its VP does not operate. The derivation of (3.123g) provides additional evidence that the rules of the transformational component in Russian do not derive the most neutral order of surface-structure constituents.

In this section we have demonstrated that the LF *nuž # n-* [+3PER] [+SING] [+NEUT] [+INST] (= *nužnym*) is derived from the SF *nuž #n-* [+PER] [+SING] [+NEUT] (=*nužno*), which is itself derived by Subject-V Agreement from an underlying *nuž # n-*. Furthermore, the proposed derivations explain explicitly why Russian has *Ona sčitaet nužnym pročitat' ètu knigu* and not **Ona sčitaet nužnoj pročitat' ètu knigu* or **Oni sčitajut nužnymi pročitat' ètu knigu* at the same time that it has *Ona kažetsja umnoj* and not **Ona kažetsja umnym* or **Oni kažutsja umnym.*

3.8.6 SENTENCES (3.123c), (3.123d), (3.123e) and (3.123h).

(3.123c) *Ona sčitaet, čto nam nužno pročitat' ètu knigu.*

The grammaticality of (3.123c) demonstrates that the sentence embedded in the subject NP of *nuž # n-* need not necessarily contain an unspecified subject. The deep structure of (3.123c) is (3.153).

(3.153)

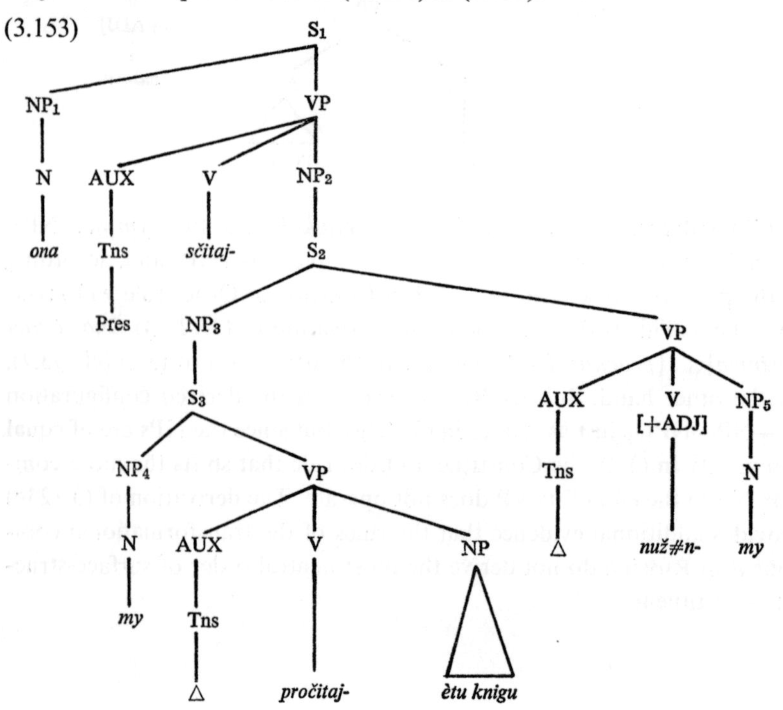

(3.154), the final derived P-marker in the derivation of (3.123c), is derived from (3.153) by the following transformations (all but the most essential transformations have been omitted to avoid repetition):

Cycle II: SUBJECT-V AGREEMENT, which gives *nužno*, since the subject of S_2 is $[S_3]_{NP_3}$.
EQUI-NP DELETION, which deletes NP_4, the subject NP of S_3, under identity to NP_5, the object of *nuž* # *n*-. It is in this capacity that NP_5 is marked [+DAT].
COMPLEMENTIZER PLACEMENT, which places *čto* before S_2.

(3.154)

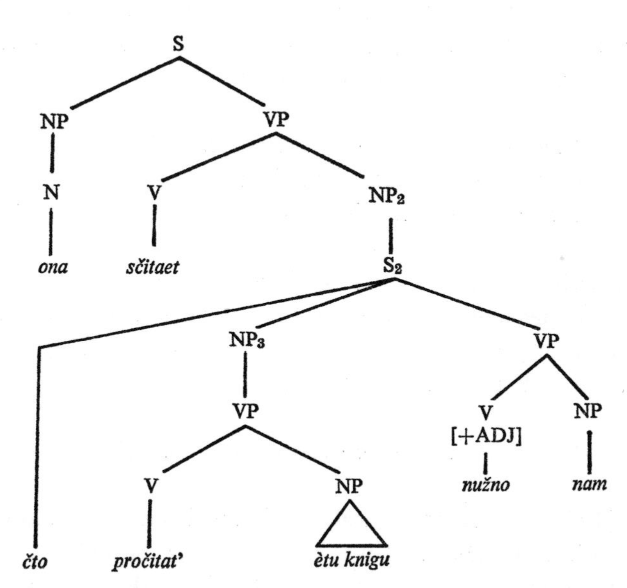

Note that (3.123c) contains the SF *nužno* in its surface structure because the embedded S_2-node is not pruned in the course of the derivation: *nužno* is, consequently, never a NP constituent and never picks up a case feature. Compare the derivation of (3.123c) with that of (3.123g) in §3.8.5. In the latter case, *nužno* is introduced into NP constituency, with the result that (3.123g) contains a LF (*nužnym*) in its surface structure. The derivation of (3.123c) supports our contention that the LF is always derived from a SF.

That (3.153) is indeed the correct deep structure of (3.123c) is clear from the fact it predicts the ungrammaticality of (3.123i) and (3.123j).

(3.123i) **Ona sčitaet nužnym nam, čtoby my pročitali ètu knigu.*

(3.123j) **Ona sčitaet, čto nam nužno, čtoby my pročitali ètu knigu.*

(3.123i) and (3.123j) are both derived from deep structure (3.153) if Equi-NP Deletion, which is an obligatory transformation, is not applied. (3.123i) differs from (3.123j) in that Subject Raising, which is optional, has applied in its derivation. The grammar of Russian must explicitly account for all grammatical sentences and not generate ungrammatical ones. (3.153) accounts for (3.123c) and, in addition, blocks (3.123i) and (3.123j) without needlessly complicating the grammar: (3.153) plus the fact Equi-NP Deletion is obligatory is all the information that is necessary. To put it in slightly different terms, positing (3.153) as the deep structure of (3.123c) permits us to capture a significant generalization about Russian grammar: (3.123i) and (3.123j) are to be adjudged ungrammatical for the same reason that (3.155a) is ungrammatical.

(3.155a) **Ona xočet, čtoby ona pročitala ètu knigu.*
lit. 'She wants that she reads this book.'
(3.155b) *Ona xočet pročitat' ètu knigu.*

(3.123c) is derived from (3.153) by Subject-V Agreement, Equi-NP Deletion, and Complementizer Placement (other details omitted). If the rule of Subject Raising is applied (raising NP_3 into S_1, cf. (3.153)) instead of Complementizer Placement, the result is (3.123e).

(3.123e) **Ona sčitaet nužnym nam pročitat' ètu knigu.*

Sentence (3.123e) is ungrammatical only if *nam* is interpreted as the deep structure object of *nužnym*. If it is interpreted as the indirect object of *pročitat'*, the sentence is grammatical. (3.123d) has the same deep structure and transformations as (3.123e); they differ only in word order.

Sentence (3.123e) brings us back to the problem that arose in §3.8.4 in conjunction with the ungrammaticality of (3.123h). Both sentences seem to be ungrammatical for the same reason and must be blocked.

The ungrammaticality of (3.123e), unlike that of (3.123i) and (3.123j), cannot be accounted for in terms of (3.153) plus the violation of an obligatory transformation: Equi-NP Deletion did operate in the derivation of (3.123e) and Subject Raising is OPTIONAL. In other words, given deep structure (3.153) and the rules discussed so far, there is no way to block (3.123e) from being freely derived. This makes it clear that some constraint must be added to the grammar of Russian in order to account for the non-occurrence of sentences like (3.123e) and (3.123h). Let us examine the exact nature of this constraint.

3.8.6.1 Whatever it is that blocks sentences like (3.123e) and (3.123h), it does not involve a restriction on [*nuž # n-* — $\genfrac{}{}{0pt}{}{\text{NP}}{[+\text{DAT}]}$]$_{VP}$ being introduced into the constituency of a matrix NP as a result of S-Node Deletion, since (3.156a) is a perfectly good sentence of Russian. The deep structure of (3.156) is (3.157).

(3.156a) *Oni sčitajut ee nužnoj obščestvu.*
'They consider her (to be) necessary to society.'

(3.156b) **Oni sčitajut ee nužnym obščestvu.*

(3.156c) *Oni sčitajut, čto ona nužna obščestvu.*
'They consider that she is necessary to society.'

(3.157)

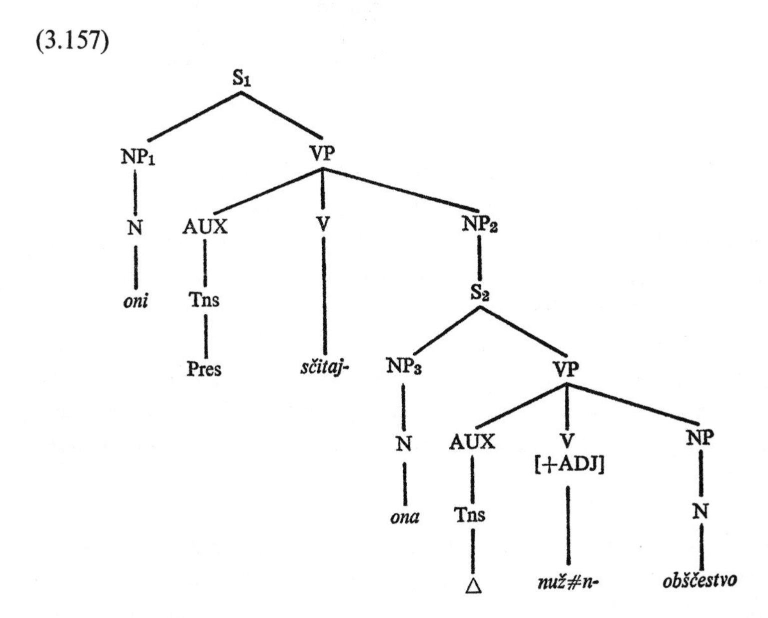

(3.156c) is derived from (3.157) by Subject-V Agreement and Complementizer Placement. (3.156c) has a SF (*nužna*) in its surface structure because node S_2 is not deleted.

Among other transformations, (3.156a) is derived from (3.157) by Subject-V Agreement (giving *nužna*) and Subject Raising (NP_3 is raised into S_1; the LF *nužnoj* is derived from *nužna* just as in the derivation of sentence (3.2) from (3.119)). The most neutral constituent order coincides with the order determined by the transformational component rules, since NP_2 is more complex than NP_3. The surface structure of (3.156a) is (3.158).

(3.158)

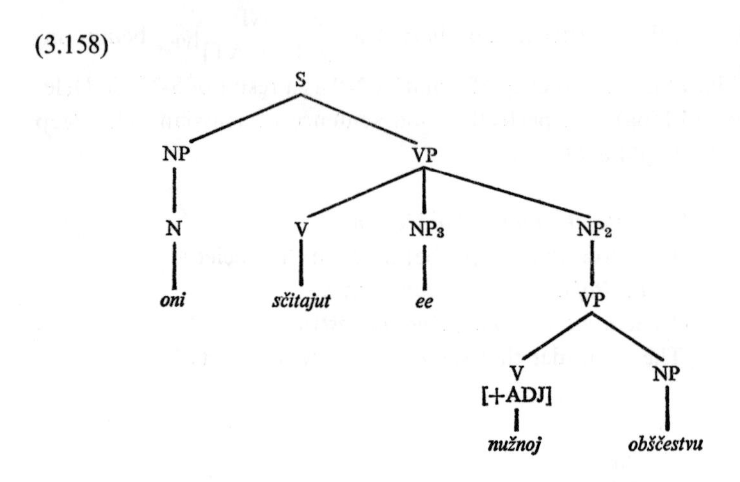

3.8.6.2 Nor can the constraint that must block sentences like (3.123e) and (123h) involve the complexity of the subject NP that is moved up into object position in the matrix sentence by Subject Raising, since sentences like (3.159) are perfectly grammatical sentences of Russian.

(3.159) *Ja naxožu strannym, čto on ne prišel.*
'I find it strange that he did not come.'

(3.160) is the deep structure of (3.159) and (3.161) is its surface structure. NP_3, which is the NP moved up into S_1 by the rule of Subject Raising, has S_3 embedded in it. The complexity of NP_3 does not make (3.159) ungrammatical.

Since NP_3 is more complex than NP_2, it is moved to the end of its VP in accordance with the Constituent Order rules discussed in §3.8.1. This gives $[V—NP_2—NP_3]_{VP}$, which is the correct constituent order of (3.159). Compare the order of constituents in (3.156a) and (3.159).

3.8.6.3 A simple subject NP may be raised when its V is transitive (cf. (3.156a) in §3.8.6.1 and *Vse ljudi sčitajut ee neobxodimoj dlja sebja* (Platonov)) or intransitive (cf. (3.2) in §3.7). A complex subject NP may be raised when its V is intransitive (cf. §3.8.6.2). In order to block sentences like (3.123e) and (3.123h), the grammar of Russian must be constrained so as

(3.160)

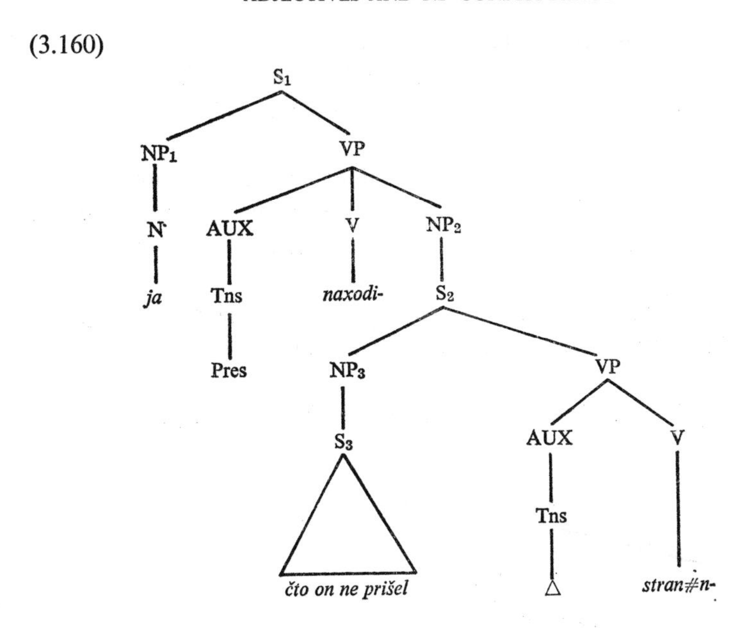

(3.161)

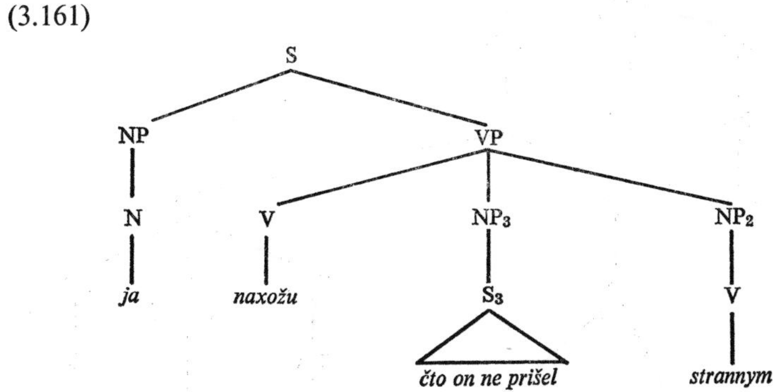

to prevent the optional rule of Subject Raising from raising a complex subject NP when its V governs an oblique NP. In other words, Vs like *nuž # n-*, *neobxodim-*, *verojat # n-*, etc., allow their complex subject NP to be raised provided that they do not govern an oblique NP at the moment when the rule of Subject Raising is applied. This is illustrated by the following examples.

(3.162) *Oni sčitali ves'ma verojatnym, čto zima budet dlinnoj i surovoj.* 'They considered it probable that winter would be long and hard.'

(3.163) *Ja sčitaju pravil'nym otkazat'sja ot poezdki.*

'I consider it right to refuse to go on the trip.'

(3.164) *Ja sčitaju neobxodimym podoždat' neskol'ko dnej.*
'I consider it necessary to wait a few days.'

(3.123e) and (3.123h) violate this constraint and are therefore ungrammatical. In (3.123e), $[VP]_{NP_3}$ is raised while *nužno* governs *nam* (cf. (3.153)-(3.154)). In (3.123h), $[VP]_{NP_3}$ is raised while *nužnym* governs *sebe* (cf. (3.136)-(3.138)).

(3.123f) does not violate this constraint and, consequently, it is grammatical. The deep structure of (3.123f) is (3.165).

(3.123f) *Ona sčitaet nužnym, čtoby my pročitali ètu knigu.*

(3.165)

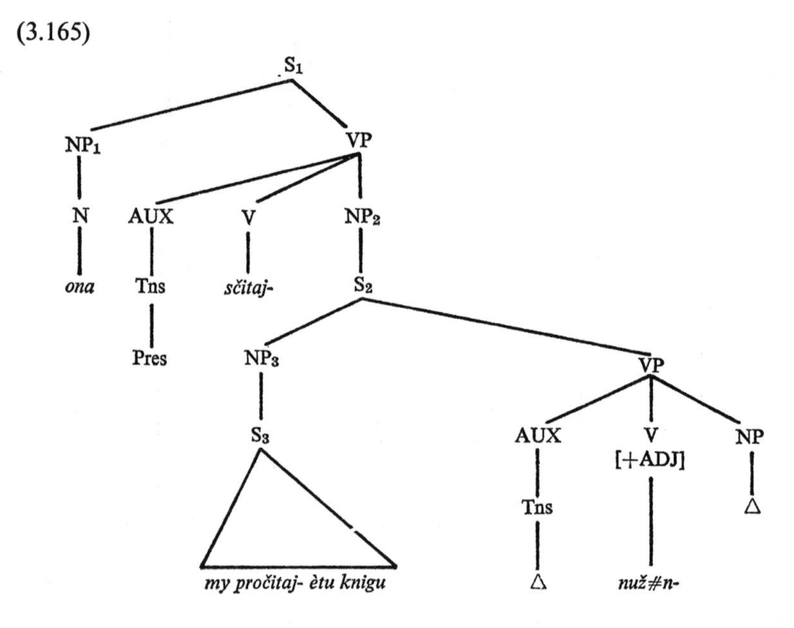

On Cycle II $[\Delta]_{NP}$ is obligatorily deleted (cf. §3.8.4) so that on Cycle III, when $[S_3]_{NP_3}$ is raised, *nuž # n-* no longer governs an oblique (Dative) NP and therefore does not violate the constraint that accounts for the ungrammaticality of (3.123e) and (3.123h). The surface structure of (3.123f) is (3.166). Note once again that the surface structure LF (*nužnym*) is derived from a SF as a result of acquisition of a case feature upon introduction into a higher NP.

Since $[S]_{NP_3}$ is more complex than $[V]_{NP_2}$, it is moved to the end of its VP, giving (3.123f).

(3.166)

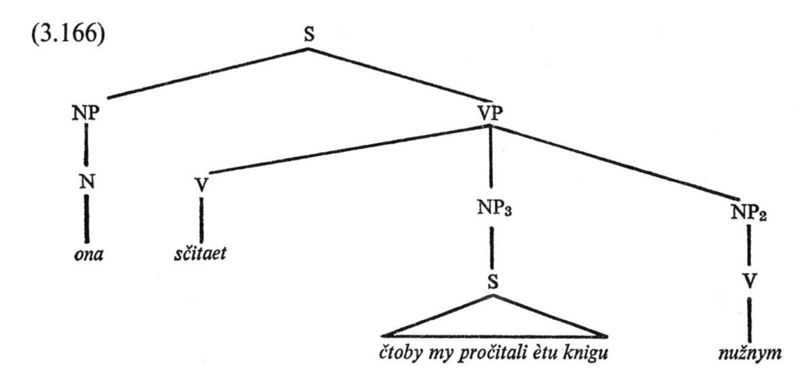

It is too early to evaluate this constraint with respect to either Russian grammar or the theory of grammar. Future research is required to determine how important it is in Russian and whether it operates in other languages. What appears to be a variant of this constraint is discussed in Chapter 4 in conjunction with the question as to why predicate LFs cannot take a complement.

3.8.7 SUMMARY OF §3.8. The sentences discussed in §3.8 (cf. (3.123a)-(3.123j)) turn out to have basically the same syntactic relations that we observed in sentences (3.1) and (3.2) (cf. §3.7). The only significant difference is that in (3.123) the NP which is moved (optionally) up into the next highest sentence was complex (in (3.2) it was "simple": $[N]_{NP}$) and the $\underset{[+ADJ]}{V}$ was transitive (*prav-* in (3.2) does not govern a NP). The complications that result from a raised complex subject NP and a transitive V, while of general interest in the study of Russian syntax, must not obscure the main point of §3.8: a surface-structure LF is derived from a deeper SF which has acquired a case feature.

3.9 SUMMARY OF CHAPTER 3 AND INTRODUCTION TO CHAPTER 4. In §2.12 it was suggested that a SF is a lexical $\underset{[+ADJ]}{V}$ that has undergone Subject-V Agreement and a LF is a SF that has acquired a case feature when it is introduced into a NP. Chapter 3 provided a great deal of evidence supporting this derivational relationship and, furthermore, it demonstrated that ANY transformation that leads to S-Node Deletion will give rise to surface-structure LFs. In §2.12 the only transformation resulting in S-Node Deletion discussed was Relative Clause Reduction. In Chapter 3 we discussed Equi-NP Deletion and Subject Raising, both of which result only in the LF INSTRUMENTAL.

In §2.12 it was pointed out that as a result of the sequence Relative Clause Reduction, S-Node Deletion, and Case Marking, the SF may acquire ANY case feature, including [+INST]:

NOM	*devuška*		*krasivaja devuška*
GEN	*devuški*		*krasivoj devuški*
DAT	*devuške*	, *kotoraja krasiva* ⇒	*krasivoj devuške*
ACC	*devušku*		*krasivuju devušku*
INST	*devuškoj*		*krasivoj devuškoj*
	.		.
	.		.
	.		.

These facts allow us to make an extremely important observation: IN MODERN RUSSIAN, A LF IN ANY CASE BUT THE INSTRUMENTAL IS DERIVED BY THE RELATIVE CLAUSE REDUCTION SEQUENCE OF TRANSFORMATIONS. An instrumental LF, however, has two sources: (i) Relative Clause Reduction, when the higher NP has the feature [+INST] or (ii) the Obligatory Instrumental transformation (3.83), which is occasioned by either Equi-NP Deletion or Subject Raising. Relative Clause Reduction does not invariably give an instrumental LF because, unlike Equi-NP Deletion and Subject Raising, it deletes the tense-marker of the embedded sentence along with the NP dominating *kotor-*.

The fact that the LF nominative is unambiguously the result of Relative Clause Reduction will prove to be very important in Chapter 4 where LF in the predicate is discussed. If the generalization that the LF is derived from the SF is to hold for all sentences of Russian, then it must be demonstrated that the LF in sentences like (3.167a) and (3.168a) is also derived.

(3.167a) *Elka byla vysokaja.*
'The fir was tall.'
(3.167b) *Elka byla vysoka.*
(3.168a) *Reka spokojnaja.*
'The river is calm.'
(3.168b) *Reka spokojna.*

The LF in the predicate introduces a number of problems. For instance, in §2.12 it was mentioned that the LF and SF are in complementary distribution with respect to NP constituency, yet they co-occur in sentence pairs like (3.167). This means that we must either prove that the LF in

(3.167a) and (3.168a) are dominated by NPs or abandon our claim that LFs are derived from SFs. In Chapter 4 we will try to substantiate the claim that the surface structure of (3.167a) is (3.169); it has already been established that the surface structure of sentences like (3.167b) is (3.170).

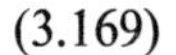
(3.169)

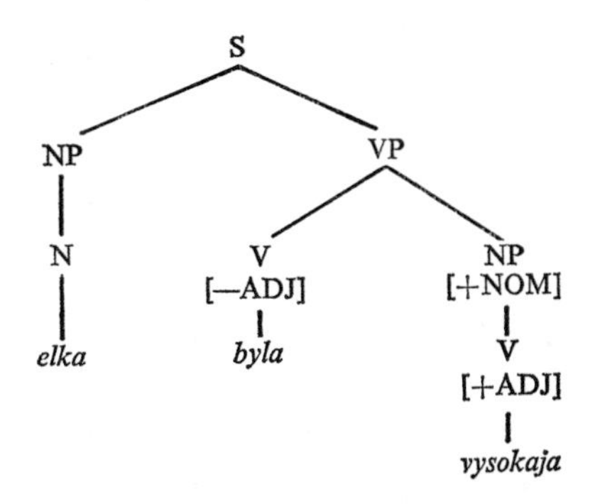

(3.170)

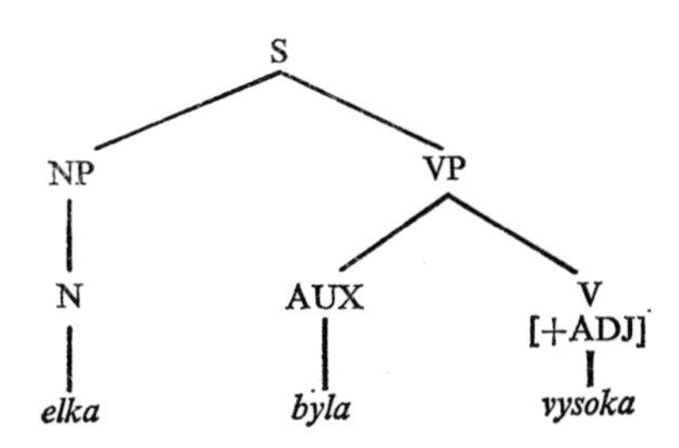

In Chapters 1-3, it was shown that the LF, unlike the SF, does not behave syntactically like a V. In Chapter 4 it will be shown that this is due mainly to the fact the LF is dominated by a NP (the SF is not). In traditional terms, the LF is a predicate nominal and has almost the same surface structure as (3.171).

(3.171) *Ona byla učitel'nica*
'She was a teacher'

The first part of Chapter 1 presented several compelling arguments for not allowing the ADJ to be an expansion of the NP. More evidence is given for this in Chapter 4.

Accordingly, if the LF is dominated by a NP in the surface structure predicate, as it is everywhere else, and, in addition, it cannot be a deep-

(3.172)

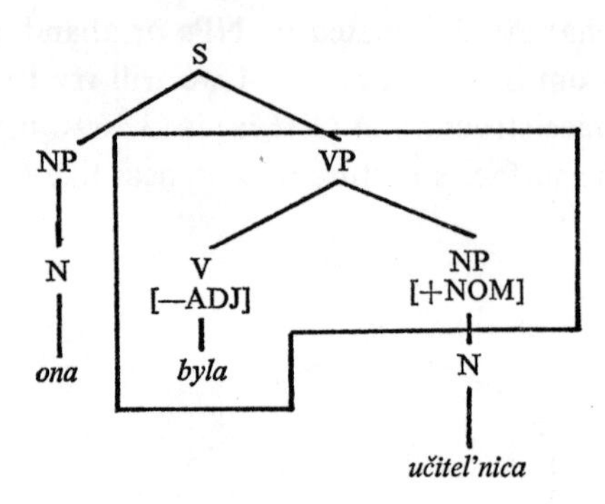

structure NP constituent, then it follows that the surface-structure configuration $[[LF]_{NP}]_{VP}$ is derived transformationally.

It will be proposed in Chapter 4 that at the level of deep structure the surface-structure predicate LF is a relative clause configuration. Accordngly, the P-marker underlying (3.167a) is (3.173).

i

(3.173)

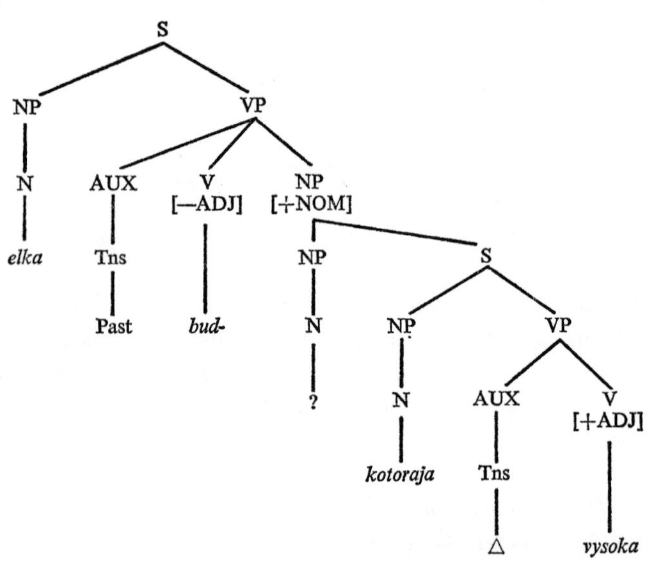

The antecedent of the relative clause embedded in the VP, designated in (3.173) for the time being as "?", is discussed in Chapter 4. Evidence will be presented that it is either identical to the subject (*elka* here) or its semantic features are contained in the subject .

Relative Clause Reduction, S-Node Deletion, and Case Marking convert P-marker (3.173) into P-marker (3.174). This is precisely the way the LF was derived in §2.12.

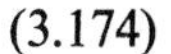

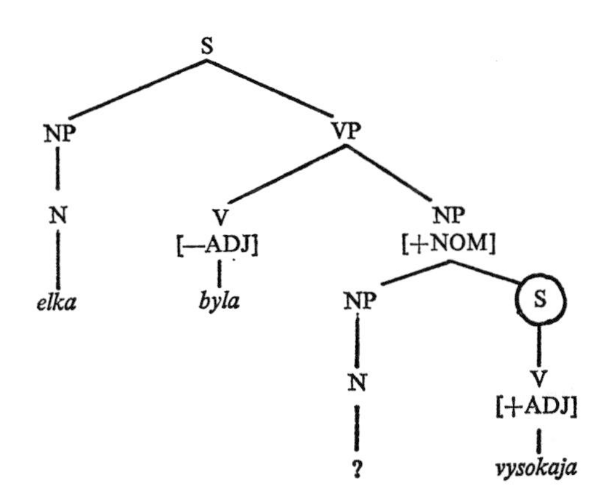

(3.174) is mapped into (3.175), the final derived P-marker of (3.167a), by a transformational rule that deletes the reduced relative clause antecedent under certain well-defined conditions. This rule of Antecedent Deletion (cf. §4.6) is optional; its non-application to reduced relative clauses in predicate position is responsible for sentences like (3.176) and (3.177).

(3.176) *Net, ona ne ošiblas' v nem, on čelovek dostojnyj velikoj ljubvi.*
'No, she was not mistaken in him. He is a person worthy of great love.' (Kočetov)

(3.177) *Otec Maksima Gor'kogo byl čelovek sposobnyj.*
'Maksim Gor'kij's father was a capable person.'

The surface structure of (3.167a) is (3.175) (= (3.169)).

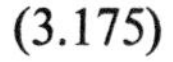

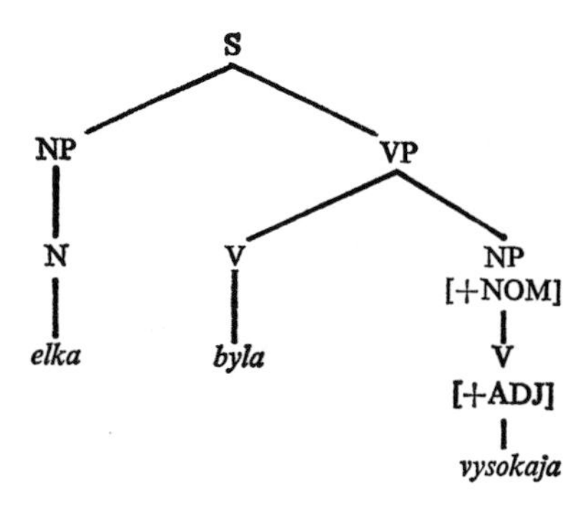

The derivation of (3.167a) demonstrates that the LF in predicate position is what traditional grammar calls a headless reduced relative clause.

Active participles in the predicate are derived in precisely the same way as LF "adjectives" (recall that in §2.12 it was pointed out that the LF (*vysokaja*) is the active participle of the SF (*vysoka*)). (3.178) contains some examples of active participles in the predicate.

(3.178a) *Moroznyj vozdux op'janjajuščij, žizn' prosto prekrasna.*
'Frosty air is intoxicating, life is simply beautiful.'

(3.178b) *Staroe, beloe lico glavnokomandujuščego bylo ne takoe ulybajuščeesja, kak včera, a, skoree, strogoe i toržestvennoe.*
(L. Tolstoj)
'The old, white face of the commander-in-chief was not so smiling as yesterday but, rather, stern and triumphant.'

(3.178c) ..., *vse dviženija ee byli padajuščie.*
'..., all her movements were falling.' (L. Tolstoj)

The derivation of predicate LFs proposed above automatically accounts for the fact that active participles of $\underset{[-\text{ADJ}]}{\text{V}}$ are always in the LF: they are derived from relative clauses and are consequently always dominated by a NP in the surface structure. From this it is clear that a LF is any markable element that is dominated in the surface structure by a NP in which it has acquired a case feature. What seem to be SF active participles in the predicate are in fact not active participles; they are lexical $\underset{[+\text{ADJ}]}{\text{V}}$s. Sentence (3.179) is an example of this phenomenon (cf. Ickovič, 1968:22).

(3.179) *Spiski produktivnyx modelej i neproduktivnyx form isčerpivajušči.*
'The lists of productive patterns and unproductive forms are exhaustive.'

The rule of Antecedent Deletion is not an ad hoc rule that has been added to the grammar of Russian merely to account for the LF in the predicate. It is needed at other points in the grammar and is thus independently motivated. The rule of Antecedent Deletion is needed to derive the (b) sentences from the deep structures underlying the (a) sentences in the following examples.

(3.180a) *Tem, kto želaet bolee osnovatel'no poznakomit'sja s ètim voprosom, prednaznačen naučnyj doklad.*
'A scientific report has been earmarked for those who want to familiarize themselves more fully with this question.'

(3.180b) *Želajuščim bolee osnovatel'no poznakomit'sja s ètim voprosom, prednaznačen naučnyj doklad.*

(3.180c) **Tem želajuščim bolee osnovatel'no poznakomit'sja s ètim voprosom, prednaznačen naučnyj doklad.*

(3.181a) *To, čto ja pročital, nadolgo soxranilos' v moej pamjati.*
'What I read long remained in my memory.'

(3.181b) *Pročitannoe mnoju nadolgo soxranilos' v moej pamjati.*

(3.181c) **To pročitannoe mnoju nadolgo soxranilos' v moej pamjati.*

The participles in (3.180) and (3.181) are derived by Relative Clause Reduction and Antecedent Deletion. Condensations of this sort are, in fact, quite common in Russian. They are responsible for what is traditionally called "substantivization of adjectives"; *sčastlivye* 'happy $\left\{\begin{array}{l}\text{people}\\ \text{ones}\end{array}\right\}$,' is a "substantivized adjective" and is derived by Relative Clause Reduction and Antecedent Deletion from the deep structure underlying (3.182a).

3.182a) [$\left\{\begin{array}{l}\textit{te}\\ \textit{ljudi}\\ \Delta\end{array}\right\}$, *kotorye sčastlivy,*]$_{NP}$ *ne nabljudajut vremja.*
'Those / people who are happy don't notice the time.'

(3.182b) [*Sčastlivye*]$_{NP}$ *ne nabljudajut vremja.*
'Happy (people) don't notice the time.'

These facts make it seem quite probable that the LF in the predicate is just a special case of this sequence of transformations.

This derivation of the LF in the predicate not only allows us to account for all LFs in the same way (LF = SF + case feature), but, as will be shown in Chapter 4, it also allows us to account for the semantic difference between the LF and the SF in predicate position, a classic problem of Russian linguistics.

The relative-clause origin of the predicate LF outlined above has another advantage: it allows us to account for the predicate instrumental LF in a simple manner. Unlike the sentences examined in §3.1-3.8, where the instrumental was produced by the Obligatory Instrumental rule (3.83), the instrumental LF in these sentences is optional (cf. (3.183)) and, therefore, not produced by rule (3.83).

(3.183) *Elka byla vysokoj.*

Any NP after *byl* or *budet* may optionally be placed in the instrumental regardless of what is embedded in it.[22] Thus the fact that a predicate LF is dominated by a NP allows us to mark both predicate nouns and adjectives [+INST] by the same transformation.

That an instrumental LF in the predicate is a nominative LF which has been marked [+INST] is clear from the fact that the nominative LF and the instrumental LF in the predicative have identical restrictions: the instrumental LF may not appear in just those sentences in which the nominative LF may not appear. If the instrumental LF in these sentences were viewed as being derived from a SF by the Obligatory Instrumental rule, this identity of restriction could not be accounted for. (3.184) and (3.185) are examples of two types of sentences in which the nominative LF and the instrumental LF share restrictions; more details will be given in Chapter 4.

(3.184a) *Govorit' s nim bylo trudno.*
'It was difficult to speak with him.'
(3.184b) **Govorit' s nim bylo trudnoe.*
(3.184c) **Govorit' s nim bylo trudnym.*
(3.185a) *On byl poxož na otca.*
'He resembled his father.'
(3.185b) **On byl poxožij na otca.*
(3.185c) **On byl poxožim na otca.*

This solution for the "predicate instrumental" problem has one immediate advantage. It permits us to show that there is no "three-way opposition in the nominal predicate" (*Elka byla vysoka* vs. *Elka byla vysokaja* vs. *Elka byla vysokoj*). This superficial three-way opposition is actually two binary oppositions:

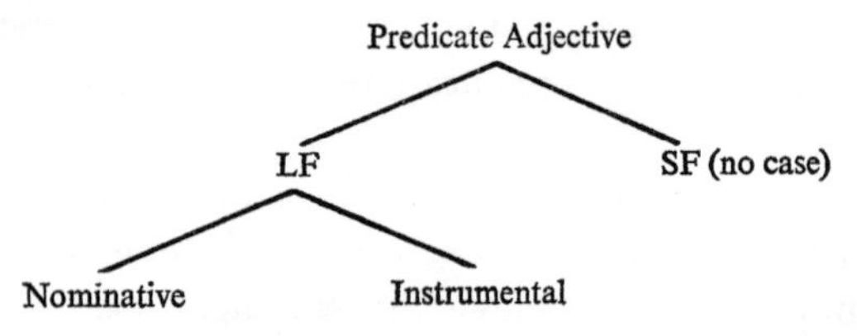

[22] I have avoided touching on the status of the semantic difference between the nominative and instrumental after *bud-* because it is not relevant to the main point of Chapter 3. An interesting discussion of this problem is found in A. A. Kam ynina, 1958

3.10 Appendix to Chapter 3: Some observations on Case in a Transformational-Generative Grammar of Russian

3.10.1 Case is a device in the grammar of Russian which conserves deep-structure grammatical relations that have been otherwise obscured or distorted by the operation of the transformational rules. This same function is fulfilled in English to some extent by word order.

This study of Russian syntax has led to a rather unexpected conclusion about the assignment of case. Although a great deal more research is necessary, it seems at this point that case features are assigned to NPs by means of "government" only. A NP in a P-marker receives a case feature by virtue of its being in the environment of a P or V. For instance, a NP will be marked [+DAT] in the environment of *nuž # n-* [+— DAT] (cf. §3.8) and [+GEN] in the environment of *dostoj # n-* [+— GEN]. What case a given V or preposition "governs" is part of its inherent lexical information. Once a NP receives a case feature from a V or P, this feature is distributed to all the NP's markable constituents by the rule of Case Marking (cf. (3.24)).

Crucial to the acceptance of this generalization is recognition of the fact a V governs not only the case of its object NP, but the case of its subject NP as well. Most Vs require a nominative subject, but, as (3.186) will demonstrate, there are a number of Vs in Russian that require an oblique subject NP in the dative.[23]

(3.186a) *Nam predstoit pročitat' Čexova po-novomu.*
'We have to read Čexov from a new point of view.'

(3.186b) *Čexovu predstoit* byt' *pročitannym (nami) po-novomu.*
'Čexov has to be read (by us) from a new point of view.'

(3.187) is the deep structure of (3.186a) and (3.186b).

(3.186a) is derived from (3.187) by the following transformational rules; irrelevant details have been omitted. Note that no new rules are required by our grammar of Russian in order to derive (3.186).

[23] (3.186a) and (3.186b) were suggested to me by *Blizko to vremja, kogda Čexovu predstoit byt' pročitannym po-novomu* 'The time is near when Čexov [dat.] must be read [inst.] in a new way' (Xodasevič). Both (3.186a) and (3.186b) were adjudged fully grammatical by several informants. Note that these two sentences are crucial to our claim that *byt'* in sentences containing a past passive participle derives from a tense-marker and that the instrumental of the past passive participle is derived by rule (3.83). Compare (3.186) with the sentences in §3.5.

(3.187)

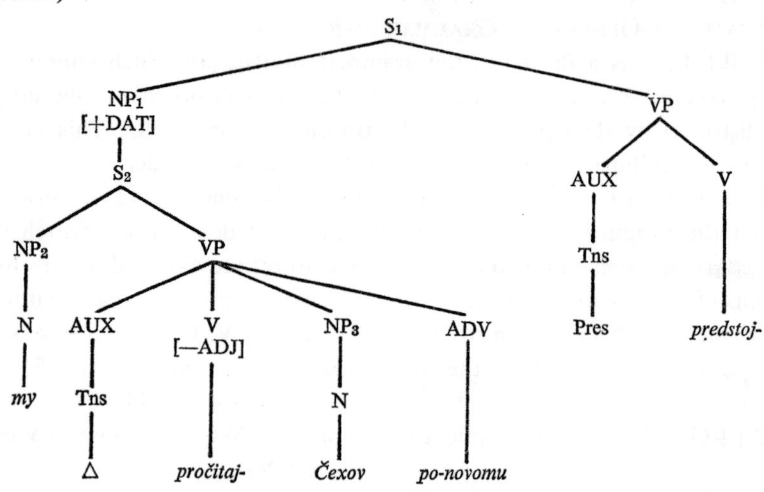

Cycle II: SUBJECT RAISING, which raises NP_2, the subject NP of the embedded sentence, into subject position in S_1 where it is marked [+DAT] in the environment ___*predstoj-*. The remainder of S_2 is adjoined to the matrix VP as its last constituent (cf. footnote 3.15).

S-NODE DELETION, which deletes node S_2, since it no longer dominates both NP and VP.

INFINITIVE FORMATION, which gives *pročitat'* from the deep-structure Tns + *pročitaj-*.

SUBJECT-V AGREEMENT, which gives *predstoit*, the third person singular (neuter). This is always the result when the V undergoes agreement with an oblique NP (cf. §3.6.3).

These transformations map deep structure P-marker (3.187) into (3.188), the surface structure of (3.186a).

(3.186b) is derived from (3.187) by the following transformations:

Cycle I: PASSIVE TRANSFORMATION, which interchanges NP_3 and NP_2, making NP_3 the subject of S_2. The feature [—ADJ] on *pročitaj-* is changed to [+ADJ] (cf. §3.3.4).

Cycle II: SUBJECT RAISING, which raises NP_3, the DERIVED subject NP of the embedded sentence, into subject position in S_1 where it is marked [+DAT] (*Čexovu*) in the environment ___*predstoj-*. The remainder of S_2 is adjoined to the matrix VP as its last constituent.

(3.188)

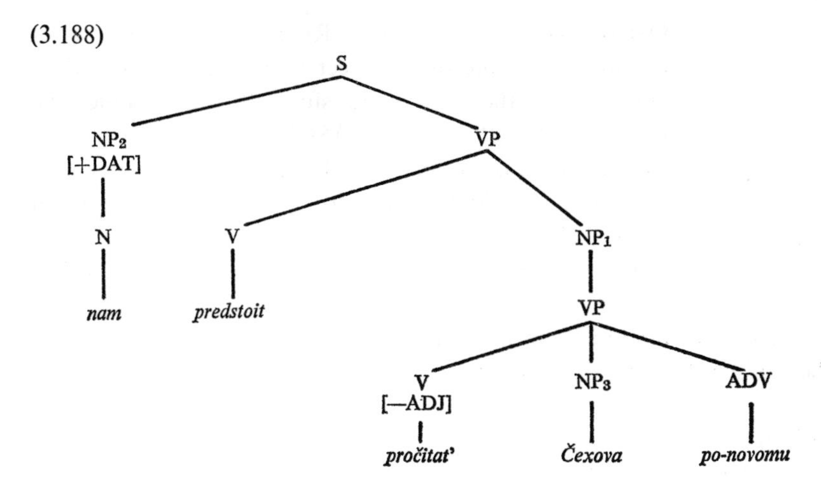

These transformations map deep structure (3.187) into the intermediate P-marker (3.189).

(3.189)

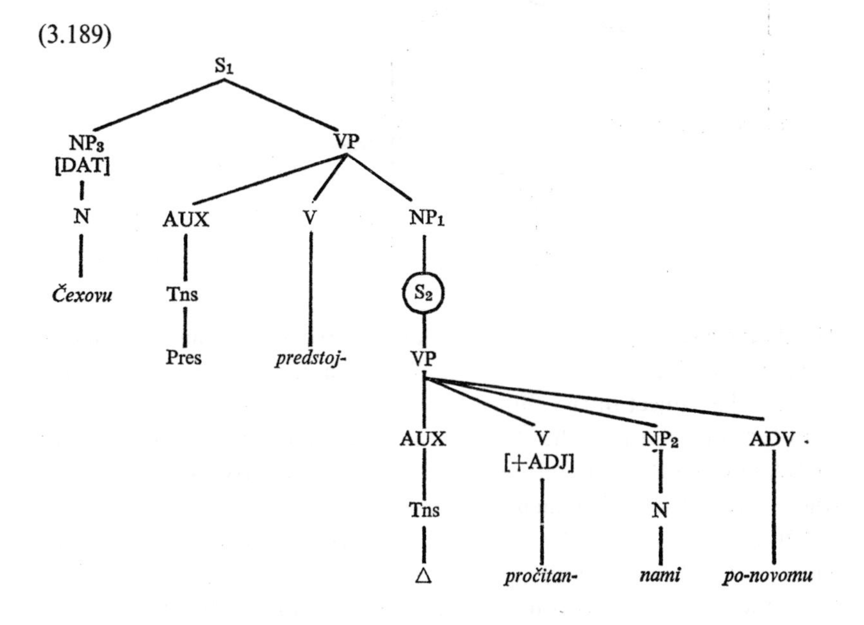

S-Node Deletion, which deletes S_2.
Case Marking, which copies the case feature of NP_1 onto *pročitan-* (giving a LF).
Infinitive Formation (3.75), which gives *byt'* from the tense-marker in S_2 (cf. §3.5.0).

OBLIGATORY INSTRUMENTAL RULE (3.83), which gives *pročitannym*. Note that Subject-V Agreement on Cycle I applies after the Passive transformation and copies the features of [+SING], [+MASC], etc. from the derived subject *Čexov* on to *pročitan-*. These Subject-V Agreement features along with [+INST] from (3.83) explain the origin of the LF *pročitannym*.
SUBJECT-V AGREEMENT, which gives *predstoit* (cf. §3.6.3).

These transformations map intermediate P-marker (3.189) into (3.190), the surface structure of (3.186b).

(3.190)

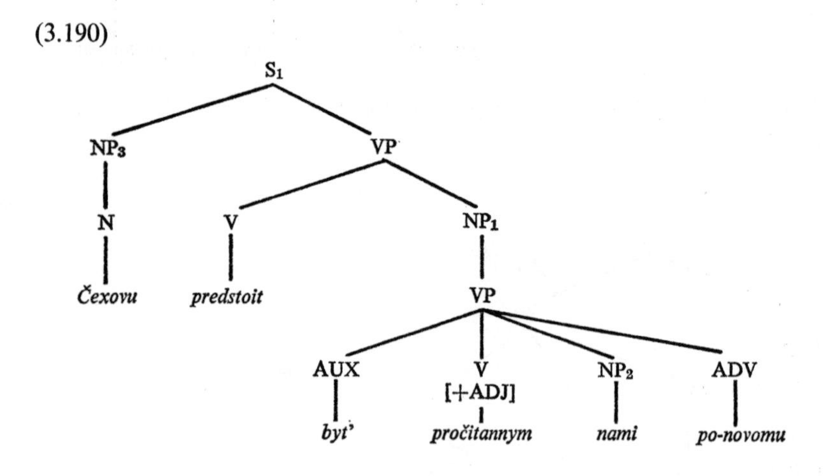

The dative *nam* in (3.186a) and *Čexovu* (3.186b) can be explained in terms of a common deep structure only if *predstoj-* is assumed to require a dative subject; the subject of the embedded sentence, *my* in (3.186a) and *Čexov* in (3.186b) (derived by the Passive transformation), receives the feature [+DAT] when Subject Raising moves it up into matrix subject position where it is in the environment ___ *predstoj-*.

3.10.2 AGREEMENT IN CASE. The Case Marking transformation (3.24), which copies the case feature acquired by a NP through "government" on to all the markable constituents of this NP, requires that we reevaluate the traditional view of agreement.

Subject-V Agreement copies certain inherent features (gender, number, person, and perhaps other features like [+animate]) from the subject N on to the V (without regard to whether it bears the feature [+ADJ] or [—ADJ]). The SF may be defined as a lexical item (*um # n-*, *nuž # n-*, etc.)

plus only the features acquired by the Subject-V Agreement transformation. In a similar manner, what is traditionally called the "finite form of the verb" is the result of the Subject-V Agreement transformation copying the inherent features (number, person, etc.) of the subject N on to a lexical or "underlying" $\underset{[-\text{ADJ}]}{\text{V}}$ stem (cf. *čitaj-*, *nës-*, *skaza-*, etc.) (cf. footnote 3.11). It is extremely important to bear in mind that the Subject-V Agreement transformation does NOT copy the case feature of the subject N on to the V, even if that feature is [+NOM]; a case feature is not an inherent feature of a N.

A markable item (N or $\underset{[+\text{ADJ}]}{\text{V}}$) receives a case feature only when it is a NP constituent, deep-structure or derived, by rule (3.24), Case Marking. Since a N is invariably the expansion of NP, it will always be a NP constituent in a given P-marker and, therefore, it will always have a case feature. I know of no transformation that moves a N out of a NP. In other words, a surface-structure N is always dominated by a NP. Since a $\underset{[+\text{ADJ}]}{\text{V}}$ is invariably the expansion of VP (cf. Chapter 1), it may emerge as a NP constituent only as the direct or indirect result of the operation of the rules of the transformational component. A SF (lexical item + features acquired by Subject-V Agreement) that receives a case feature upon introduction into NP constituency emerges from the phonological component as a LF. These relations are summarized by (3.191).

(3.191)

SF	LF	
um#n-	*um#n-*	Lexicon
[NUMB] [GEND] [PERS] ———	[NUMB] [GEND] [PERS] [αCASE]	Features added to the lexicon item by transformation.
umen *umna* . . .	*umnyj* *umnomu* . . .	Interpretation of the lexicon item + features by the phonological component.

The facts just presented make it clear that we cannot speak of agreement in case in the same way that we can speak of agreement in, say, number. The Subject-V Agreement transformation copies the feature of number from a lexical item in which this feature is inherent (N) on to a lexical item in which it is not (V). This kind of feature copying is the essence of "syntactic" agreement and I propose to limit the definition of AGREEMENT to this. Therefore there is no agreement in case in this sense. Constituents of the same NP do not agree in case, since a case feature is not copied by transformation from a lexical item in which it is inherent on to one in which it is not. Each NP constituent receives its case feature (by (3.24)) from above, i.e. from the dominating NP. In other words, constituents of the same NP COINCIDE in case, they do not "agree" in case. Two lexical items may be said to agree only if inherent features of one are copied on to the other by a transformation. Thus a prenominal adjective does not agree with its head noun in case; it coincides with it by virtue of the fact that they are in the same NP (cf. Chapter 1). There is no agreement in case in Russian if we accept the explicit definition of AGREEMENT just offered.

Given the fact that prenominal adjectives derive from deep-structure relative clauses and given the narrowed definition of AGREEMENT, another interesting fact emerges: a prenominal adjective does not agree with its head noun in gender or number either. The prenominal adjective acquires these features by SUBJECT-V AGREEMENT when it is still the main $\underset{[+\text{ADJ}]}{\text{V}}$ in the embedded relative clause, before Relative Clause Reduction, S-Node Deletion, Case Marking, and Modifier Shift make it a "prenominal adjective". Of course, the subject of the embedded sentence in a relative clause configuration must be identical to the head noun, thus ensuring that the prenominal adjective always coincides with the head noun in number and gender. Thus a prenominal adjective does not agree with its head noun in case, number, or gender, in terms of the new definition of AGREEMENT.

It seems at this juncture that a transformational grammar of Russian can account for all surface-structure "Agreement" phenomena by various combinations of two transformations: Subject-V Agreement, which copies the features of number, gender, and person from the subject N to the V and Case Marking, which copies the feature of case from the dominating NP on to its constituents. This observation has an important corollary: THERE IS NO AGREEMENT IN CASE BETWEEN THE SUBJECT AND THE PREDICATE IN A SENTENCE OF RUSSIAN. More specifically, there is no transformation that copies the case feature from a subject NP on to a [... NP]$_{VP}$, regardless of what is contained in the "predicate" NP. We are thus claiming that in (3.192a) *Puškin* and *predstavitel'* do not agree in case, just as they do not agree in number, gender, or person; they COINCIDE in case (cf. (3.192b)), number, gender, and person.

(3.192a) *Puškin byl naibolee jarkij predstavitel' svoej èpoxi.*
'Puškin was the most brilliant representative of his era.'
(3.192b) *Puškin byl naibolee jarkim predstavitelem svoej èpoxi.*

The view of agreement just presented makes another, more important claim, the significance of which will become apparent in Chapter 4: A PREDICATE ADJECTIVE IN THE LF DOES NOT AGREE IN CASE WITH THE SUBJECT NP, contrary to traditional Russian grammars (cf. Gvozdev, II, 1961:76). Since the SF undergoes only Subject-V Agreement, it agrees with the subject in number, gender, and person, but not in case (cf. §2.11). Thus in (3.193a), *devočka* does not agree with *bol'naja* (or *slabaja*) in case (cf. (3.193b)) or in number, gender, and person.

(3.193a) *Devočka byla bol'naja, slabaja.*
'The girl was sick (and) weak.'
(3.193b) *V detsve ona byla bol'noj, slaboj, no potom ej pomogla fizkul'tura.*
'In (her) childhood she was sick (and) weak, but later physical education helped her.'

Recall that a LF in the predicate derives from a deep-structure relative clause configuration, i.e. it is a headless reduced relative clause, and it is consequently dominated in the surface structure by a NP (cf. §3.9). This is why a predicate N and a predicate LF behave in a similar way with respect to agreement: they are both dominated by NPs and both have essentially the same surface structure (cf. (3.169) and (3.172)); the Subject-V Agreement transformation copies the features of number, gender, and person on to the V (*bud-*), not on to its complement NP.

3.10.3 CASE MARKING AND VALENCE. J. R. Ross (1967:81ff.) has noted what he considers a flaw in his own formulation of Case Marking (cf. (3.24)). (3.195) is derived from (3.194) by Relative Clause Reduction, which deletes *quae est* 'who is', and by S-Node Deletion.

(3.194) *Puer amat puellam quae est similis deae.*
'The boy loves a girl who is similar to a goddess.'

(3.195) *Puer amat puellam similem deae.*
'The boy loves a girl (who is) similar to a goddess.'

S-Node Deletion has the effect of making *similis* f.sg.nom. a constituent of the same NP that dominates *puellam* (acc.). Since this NP is [+ACC] (it is the direct object of *amat*), Case Marking copies [+ACC] on to *similis*, giving *similem* (cf. (3.195)).

Ross was bothered by this problem: if *similis* (nom.) becomes *similem* (acc.) by Case Marking upon introduction into $\underset{[+\text{ACC}]}{\text{NP}}$, why does *deae* (dat.) not become *deam* (acc.) and give (3.196), since it too becomes a constituent of $\underset{[+\text{ACC}]}{\text{NP}}$ after S-Node Deletion.

(3.196) **Puer amat puellam similem deam.*

Ross proposed altering the rule of Case Marking to account for the fact that sentences like (3.196) are not produced. I submit that the parallel problem in Russian shows that rule (3.24) is valid as stated.

How is it that (3.197c), which has *bogine* (dat.), is grammatical and (3.197d), which has *boginju* (acc.), is ungrammatical?

(3.197a) *Mal'čik ljubit devušku, kotoraja podobna bogine.*
'The boy loves a girl who is similar to a goddess.'
(3.197b) **Mal'čik ljubit devušku, kotoraja podobnaja bogine.*
(3.197c) *Mal'čik ljubit devušku, podobnuju bogine.*
(3.197d) **Mal'čik ljubit devušku, podobnuju boginju.*
(3.197e) *Mal'čik ljubit podobnuju bogine devušku.*

The deep structure of (3.197) is (3.198); irrelevant details are omitted.

(3.197a) is derived from (3.198) by the following transformations:

Cycle I: SUBJECT-V AGREEMENT, which copies the inherent features of *devuška* (NP_3) on to *podob # n-*, giving *podob # n-*
[+SING]
[+FEM]
[+3PER]
(= *podobna*). Note that *podob # n-* has NOT received a case feature.

(3.198)

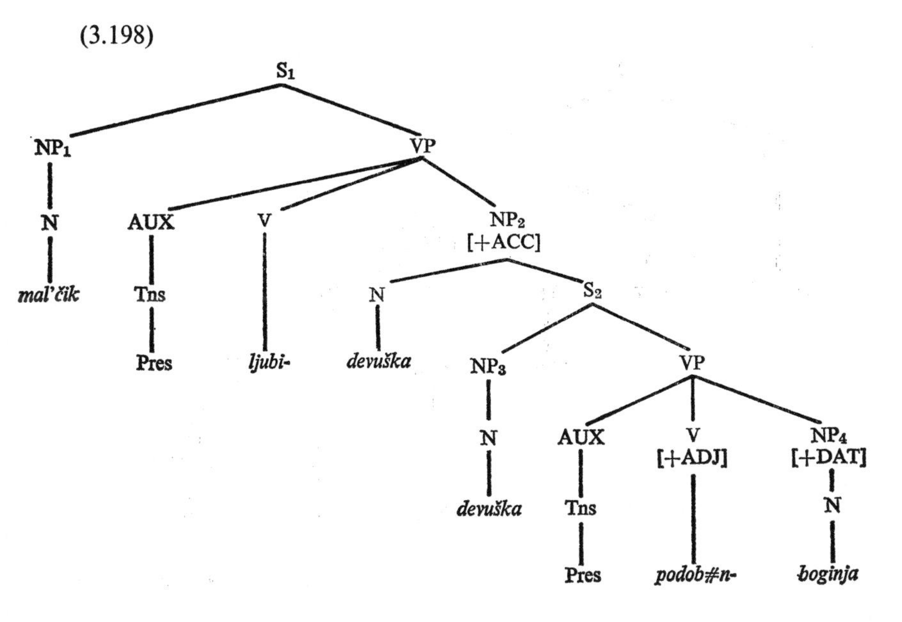

Cycle II: RELATIVE CLAUSE FORMATION, which changes *devuška in* S_2 to *kotoraja.*

SUBJECT-V AGREEMENT, which gives *ljubit.*

Note that NP_2 is marked [+ACC] because it is governed by *ljubi*____ [+ACC] and NP_4 is marked [+DAT] because it is governed by *podob # n* ____[+DAT]. Case Marking then gives *devušku* (in S_1) and *bogine* (cf. §3.10.1). These transformations map (3.198) into (3.199), the surface structure of (3.197a).

(3.197a) contains a SF (*podobna*) in its surface structure because the node S_2 is not deleted in the course of the derivation and, consequently, Case Marking is not able to copy the case feature [+ACC] from NP_2 on to *podob # n-*.
[+FEM]
[+SING]
[+3PER]

(3.197c) is derived from (3.198) by the following transformations:

Cycle I: SUBJECT-V AGREEMENT, giving *podob # n-* (*podobna*).
[+FEM]
[+SING]
[+3PER]

CASE MARKING, which copies the feature [+DAT], received

(3.199)

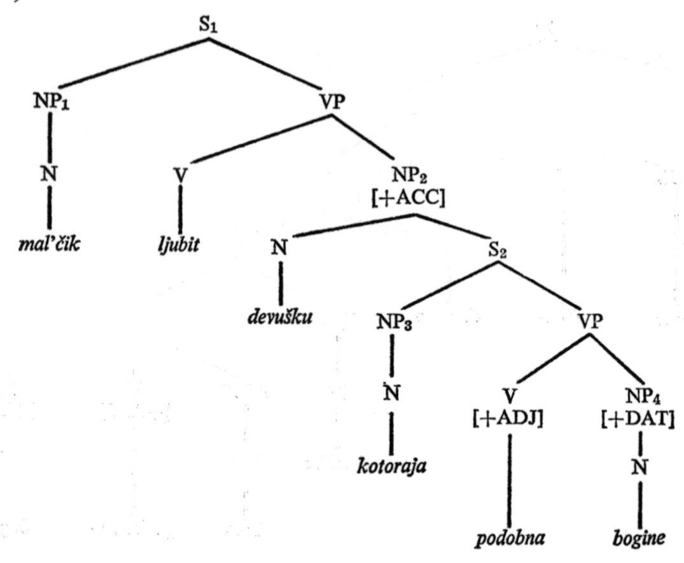

by NP_4 in the environment *podob # n*___[+DAT], on to *boginja*, giving *bogine*.

Cycle II: Relative Clause Formation, which gives *kotoraja*.
Case Marking, which gives *devušku*.
Subject-V Agreement, which gives *ljubit*.
Relative Clause Reduction, which deletes *kotoraja* + Tns in S_2.
S-Node Deletion, which deletes the node S_2.

These transformations map (3.198) into the intermediate P-marker (3.200).

After S-Node Deletion deletes the node S_2, both *podob # n-* and *bogine*
[+FEM]
[+SING]
[+3PER]
become constituents or elements of NP_2 [+ACC] and the rule of Case Marking (3.24) must operate (*devušku* (acc) is also an element of NP_2). Recall that Ross describes Case Marking as a transformation that marks every markable element of a NP except elements dominated by a S (cf. (3.24), Ross, 1969:293).

At the moment when Case Marking copies the feature [+ACC] from

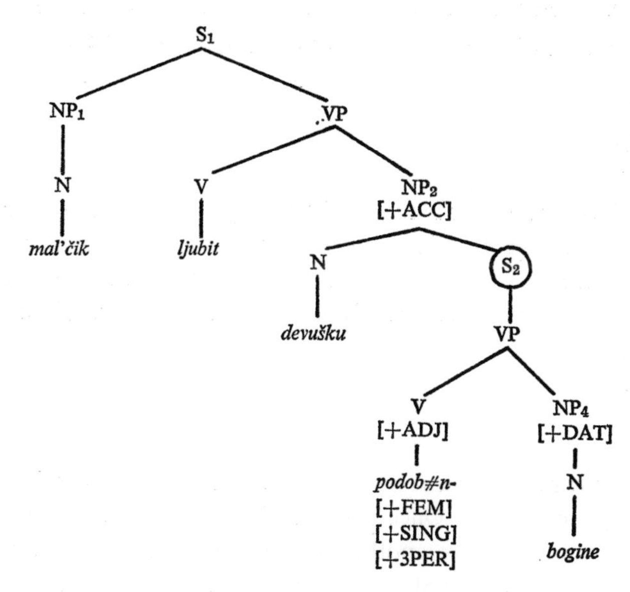

NP_2 on to the elements of NP_2, *podob # n-* has not yet received a case
[+FEM]
[+SING]
[+3PER]
and, therefore, IS NOT IN THE NOMINATIVE CASE. At this moment, *bogine* has already received the feature [+DAT] on Cycle I. Thus we see that Case Marking in this derivation does not change [+NOM] to [+ACC], while not changing [+DAT] to [+ACC]. What in fact happens is that Case Marking copies the feature [+ACC] from NP_2 on to those elements of NP_2 which have not previously received a case feature; *bogine* (dat), which received the feature [+DAT] on Cycle I, cannot receive [+ACC] when *podob # n-* does and, consequently, (3.197d) is avoided.
[+FEM]
[+SING]
[+3PER]

Ross ran into difficulty in his analysis of (3.194) and (3.195) not because his formulation of Case Marking was wrong, but because of his loose definition of what a "markable element" is. In the Russian version, *podob # n-* is a markable element: it is able to receive a case feature, but
[+FEM]
[+SING]
[+3PER]

has not yet received one. Thus when Case Marking operates on NP_2, *podob # n-* (= *podobnuju*) is produced. *Boginja* is a markable element in
[+FEM]
[+SING]
[+3PER]
[+ACC]
(3.198); thus it receives the feature [+DAT] when Case Marking applies to NP_4, giving *bogine*. When *bogine* becomes a constituent of NP_2, it already has a case feature and is no longer "markable". By the same token *podob # n-* is no longer a markable element. In other words, I am propos-
[+FEM]
[+SING]
[+3PER]
[+ACC]
ing that a markable element is a word that can receive a case feature, but has not yet received it. Once a markable element has acquired a case feature, it cannot receive another. Certain transformations are able to CHANGE an already acquired case feature (cf. (3.83)), but the Case Marking transformation (3.24) is not one of these; it can only bring a case feature to a markable element that does not have one. Speaking metaphorically, we may claim that markable elements are univalent. The key to the solution of the problem of Case Marking is recognition of the fact that the SF is not in the nominative (or any other) case.[24]

The surface structure of (3.197c) is (3.201).

(3.201)

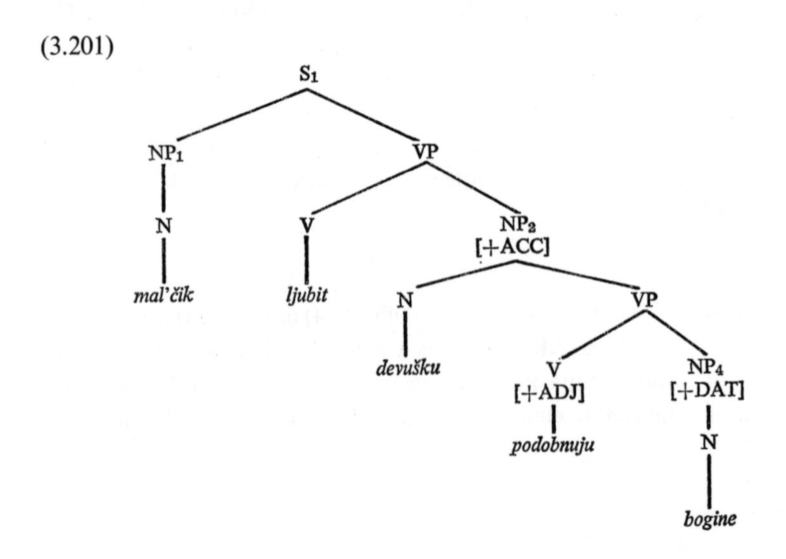

Sentence (3.197c) contains a LF (*podobnuju*) because S-Node Deletion caused a SF (*podobna*) to be introduced into NP_2 where it acquired the feature [+ACC]. A comparison of the derivations of (3.197a) and (3.197c) demonstrates once again that a LF is a SF that has acquired a case feature.

Sentence (3.197e) is derived from (3.201) by the rule of Modifier Shift, which moves a reduced relative clause ([*podobnuju bogine*]$_{VP}$) around its head noun (*devušku*).

[24] These considerations surely hold for Latin as well.

4

PREDICATE ADJECTIVES

4.1 The evidence presented in §2.12 and Chapter 3 makes it quite clear that in the sentences analyzed the LF is a SF that has acquired a case feature.

One more major type of surface structure containing a LF remains to be analyzed: the LF in predicate position preceded by the "copula" *byl, budet*, ... (from here on we will refer to this type of predicate as the "predicate LF"). In §3.9 it was hypothesized that the predicate LF is derived from a SF ($\underset{[+ADJ]}{V}$ + Subject-V Agreement) which is the predicate of a deep-structure relative clause (cf. (3.173), the deep structure of (3.167a)). If this hypothesis can be substantiated, we will be justified in claiming that any LF, regardless of its syntactic function or position, is derived from a deep-structure $\underset{[+ADJ]}{V}$ that has been introduced into a NP. This is an extremely important generalization about modern Russian, and it is the main purpose of this book to demonstrate its validity (cf. Summary of §2.12).

In Chapter 4 I will now present evidence of several different kinds that the predicate LF is derived from a deep-structure $\underset{[+ADJ]}{V}$ which is the main V of a relative clause ([*bud-* [NP — S]$_{NP}$]$_{VP}$).

In §4.2 three possible derivations of the predicate LF NOT involving a deep-structure relative clause will be proposed. Each one will be shown to be incorrect. This indirect or negative evidence helps make a very strong argument for the relative-clause origin of the predicate LF.

The proposed relative-clause origin of the predicate LF enables us to account explicitly for a number of INTUITIVE STATEMENTS made by Russian grammarians. Since the chief goal of a transformational-generative grammar is to account explicitly for a speaker's intuitive knowledge of his language, this material, which will be presented in §4.3, is of particular importance.

In §4.4 it will be demonstrated that the SEMANTIC PROPERTIES of the predicate LF can be fully explained in terms of an underlying relative clause configuration ($[NP — S]_{NP}$). Note that since the semantic interpretation of a sentence depends on its deep-structure P-marker only, our proposal that the predicate LF is a headless reduced relative clause predicts that the predicate LF will have essentially the same semantic interpretation as a restrictive relative clause contained in a "*bud-*" predicate ($[$*bud-* $[NP — S]_{NP}]_{VP}$).

Paragraph 4.5 will deal with the FORMAL SYNTACTIC PROPERTIES of sentences containing a predicate LF. It will be demonstrated that the syntactic behavior of these sentences can be EXPLAINED only by assuming that the predicate LF derives from a deeper relative clause. Our strongest arguments are to be found in §4.5.

After the evidence of §§4.2-4.5 is presented, the Antecedent Deletion transformation (cf. §3.9) will be discussed. This transformation is of central interest not only because it enables us to derive predicate LFs from underlying relative clauses, but also because it provides us with the mechanism for blocking the derivation of sentences containing a predicate LF with a complement. More specifically, the ungrammaticality of sentence (4.1c) is to be explained in terms of a condition on the Antecedent Deletion transformation (cf. §4.6).

(4.1a) *Ivan Ivanovič dostoen uvaženija.*
'Ivan Ivanovič is worthy of respect.'

(4.1b) *Ivan Ivanovič–čelovek dostojnyj uvaženija.*
'Ivan Ivanovič is a man worthy of respect.'

(4.1c) **Ivan Ivanovič dostojnyj uvaženija.*

Chapter 4 is for all practical purposes an extension of Chapter 3: its purpose is to investigate yet another type of surface structure containing a LF and to offer evidence that it too has been derived from a deeper SF ($\underset{[+ADJ]}{V}$ + features acquired by Subject-V Agreement). Now, the position after the "copula" *byl, budet,* ... has been singled out by Russian grammarians for a discussion of the relation between the LF and the SF because it is the only position in which they co-occur (cf. (3.167) and (3.168)). Thus determining the syntactic and semantic properties of the predicate LF is one of the classic problems of traditional Russian grammar. For this reason it deserves special attention and a separate chapter.

In Chapter 3 it was noted that the LF and SF are in complementary distribution. The fact that they co-occur in predicate position does not constitute counterevidence to this claim. The LF and the SF are in complementary distribution WITH RESPECT TO NP CONSTITUENCY, not with respect to superficial "syntactic position" or "syntactic frames". The LF is always a NP constituent in the surface structure (cf. (3.175)) and the SF never is. Thus the SF and LF can co-occur in the predicate for the same reason that a verb and a predicate noun (cf. (3.172)) can: the SF is a V (cf. Chapter 2) and the LF is a predicate nominal (it derives from a deep-structure [*bud-* — NP]$_{VP}$). Therefore, once it is realized that the SF is a V and the predicate LF derives from a deep-structure relative clause, it becomes perfectly clear that the relation between the SF and LF in the predicate is no different from the relation between the SF and LF elsewhere.

4.2 THREE DERIVATIONS OF THE PREDICATE LF NOT INVOLVING A RELATIVE CLAUSE. This section will examine three possible derivations and show each to be incorrect either because it fails to account for certain phenomena or because it complicates the grammar without a "compensatory" gain in explanatory power.

4.2.1 It might be suggested that the LF is introduced in the Base component by the sequence of expansions given in (4.2).

(4.2a) S → NP + VP

(4.2b) NP → DET + N

(4.2c) VP → ADJ

(4.2d) ADJ → $\begin{Bmatrix} \text{SF} \\ \text{LF} \end{Bmatrix}$

(4.2) will generate sentences like (4.3) and (4.4) with surface structures (4.5) and (4.6) respectively.

(4.3) *Èta devuška umna.*
'This girl is smart.'

(4.4) *Èta devuška umnaja.*

Note that implicit in (4.2) is the assumption that the LF in the predicate is not a derived surface-structure constituent but is present in the deep structure.

A number of serious disadvantages in this proposal (see §4.2.1.1, §4.2.1.2 and §4.2.1.3) furnish the basis for rejecting (4.2).

4.2.1.1 If the base rule ADJ → $\begin{Bmatrix} \text{SF} \\ \text{LF} \end{Bmatrix}$ is accepted, we have increased

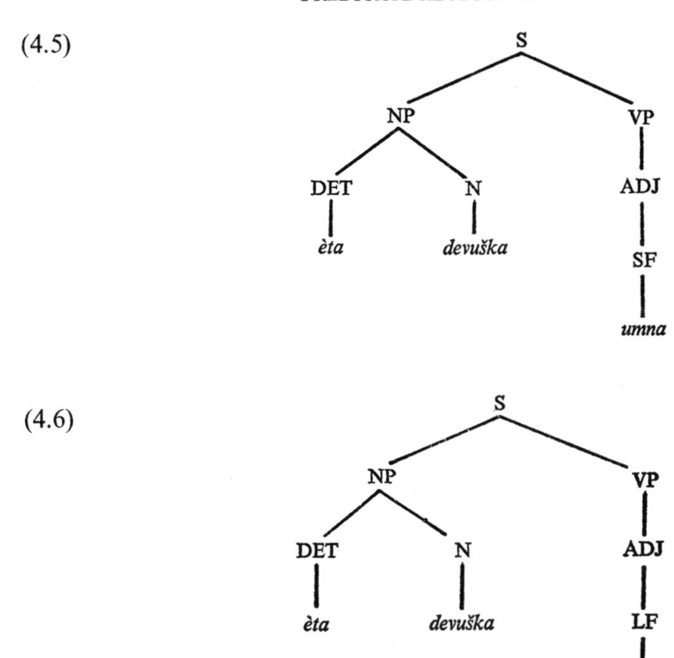

the inventory of deep-structure categories and, in effect, made the claim that the categories SF and LF have the same universal status as N, NP, V, etc. The acceptance of (4.2) also requires that we abandon the important generalization that the LF is invariably derived from the SF. In short, the adoption of the derivation proposed in (4.2) would entail an INCREASE in the complexity of the base and transformational components and a DECREASE in the explanatory power of the grammar as a whole.

If, however, we incorporate the proposals made in Chapters 1-3, including the relative-clause origin of the predicate LF (§3.9), into our grammar of Russian, we thereby decrease the number of deep-structure categories by three (ADJ, SF, and LF) and greatly increase the explanatory power of our grammar, since the semantic (cf. §4.4) and syntactic (cf. §4.5) properties of the predicate LF can be fully accounted for in terms of a deep-structure relative-clause configuration along with the set of independently motivated transformations that operate on relative clauses. In short, the adoption of the relative-clause origin of the predicate LF allows us to simplify our grammar and, at the same time, to increase its explanatory power.

While the above considerations are sufficient to permit us to reject (4.2) as a possible derivation of the predicate LF, there are several other reasons for rejecting (4.2).

4.2.1.2 In modern literary Russian a predicate adjective with a complement may not appear in the LF. Accordingly, the (a) sentences in (4.7) and (4.8) are ungrammatical, while the (b) sentences are perfectly grammatical.

(4.7a) **Ja na èto ne soglasnyj.*
(4.7b) *Ja na èto ne soglasen.*
'I do not agree to it.'
(4.8a) **Ona bespoščadnaja k tem, kto naxoditsja v ee vlasti.*
(4.8b) *Ona bespoščadna k tem, kto naxoditsja v ee vlasti.*
'She is merciless towards those who are in her power.'

If the deep-structure origin of the predicate LF suggested in (4.2) were adopted, the base rule ADJ $\rightarrow \begin{Bmatrix} SF \\ LF \end{Bmatrix}$ must be constrained in such a way that only the SF could be selected if ADJ had a complement. In other words, (4.2) requires that we convert our base from what is essentially a context-free phrase-structure grammar into a context-sensitive one. This radical change in the base structure of Russian seems totally unmotivated, since there is little if any empirical evidence indicating that the base rules of Russian (or any other language) must be context-sensitive (cf. Chomsky, 1965:141). Thus the acceptance of (4.2) forces us to change the very theory of our grammar without an accompanying increase in its explanatory power. Note, however, that if we accept the relative-clause origin of the predicate LF suggested in §3.9, we can explain the non-occurrence of sentences like (4.7a) and (4.8a) in terms of a condition on the independently motivated Antecedent Deletion transformation (§4.6.5).

4.2.1.3 The LF may NOT serve as the predicate of a *kotor-* (relative) clause (cf. L. A. Bulaxovskij, 1949:250); the SF can. My informants all rejected sentences like (4.9a) while accepting sentences like (4.9b).

(4.9a) (*)*Ja ljublju devušku, kotoraja krasivaja.*
(4.9b) *Ja ljublju devušku, kotoraja krasiva.*
'I love the girl who is pretty.'
(4.9c) *Ja ljublju krasivuju devušku.*
'I love the pretty girl.'

A relative clause in the deep structure is a simple sentence in a particular P-marker configuration (i.e. $[NP — S]_{NP}$). If the derivation of the LF proposed in (4.2) is accepted, the expansion ADJ $\rightarrow \begin{Bmatrix} SF \\ LF \end{Bmatrix}$ must be constrained so that ADJ $\rightarrow$ LF is not selected just in case ADJ is the predicate of a relative clause. Thus the adoption of (4.2) into our grammar of Russian requires that we make the expansion of ADJ directly dependent not only on whether the S dominating it is embedded or not, but also dependent on what kind of configuration the S is embedded in (a S embedded in a NP complement for instance can have a predicate LF: *Ja dumaju,* [*čto vaša doč' očen' skromnaja*]$_{NP}$ 'I think that your daughter is very modest'). There is absolutely no evidence that grammatical relations of this kind (cf. schematic representation in (4.10)) are possible in any natural language.

(4.10)

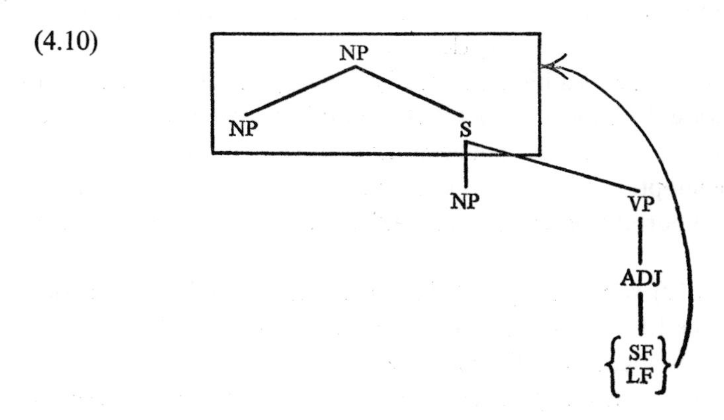

The adoption of (4.2) not only entails an extremely ad hoc constraint (cf. (4.10)), but also it fails to provide us with an explanation of WHY the LF cannot serve as the predicate of a *kotor-* clause. This phenomenon can be explained quite simply in terms of the relative-clause origin of the predicate LF: (4.9a) is unacceptable because its deep structure contains a relative clause embedded in a higher relative clause. In other words, (4.9a) has the same deep structure as (4.11) (cf. Belevickaja-Xalizeva et al.: II, 69; B. T. Panov, 1967:97; J. Ross, 1967:Chapter 2).

(4.11) (*)*Ja ljublju devušku, kotoraja krasivaja devuška.*
lit. 'I love a girl who is a pretty girl.'

4.2.1.4 The arguments presented in §§4.2.1-4.2.1.3 make it quite clear that the deep-structure origin of the predicate LF presented in (4.2) is totally incorrect.

4.2.2 A second alternative derivation of the predicate LF is this:

(4.12a) $S \rightarrow NP + VP$

(4.12b) $VP \rightarrow \begin{Bmatrix} ADJ \\ V \end{Bmatrix} + (\begin{Bmatrix} NP \\ PP \end{Bmatrix})$

(4.12c) $NP \rightarrow (ADJ) + N$

Line (b) will generate a surface-structure SF ($VP \rightarrow ADJ + (\begin{Bmatrix} NP \\ PP \end{Bmatrix})$), since ADJ does not come under the domination of a NP at any point in the derivation. Line (b) and (c) will generate a surface-structure LF ($VP \rightarrow V + NP$; $NP \rightarrow ADJ + N$), since ADJ is dominated by a NP, from which it receives a case feature by the Case Marking transformation. The N may be transformationally deleted.

This proposal achieves a higher level of generality than (4.2) because it is able to capture the important fact that the surface-structure LF and SF are the same category at the level of deep structure ($LF = [SF]_{NP}$). However, the adoption of (4.12) into the grammar of Russian would miss a number of important generalizations and create more problems than it would solve.

4.2.2.1 If (4.12) were incorporated into a grammar of Russian, the derivation of the LF **radyj* 'glad' (and **dolžnyj* 'must') would have to be blocked at no less than TWO different points in the grammar.

First, the lexical item *rad-*'glad' has to be marked as being an exception to the rule of Relative Clause Reduction in order to prevent the P-marker underlying (4.13) from being transformed into the P-marker underlying (4.14).

(4.13) [*devuška, kotoraja rada tvoemu priezdu*]$_{NP}$
'the girl who is glad about your arrival.'

(4.14) [**devuška, radaja tvoemu priezdu*]$_{NP}$

(4.15) [*devuška, kotoraja dovol'na svoej sud'boju*]$_{NP}$
'the girl who is satisfied with her lot.'

(4.16) [*devuška, dovol'naja svoej sud'boju*]$_{NP}$
'the girl satisfied with her lot.'

(4.15) and (4.16) demonstrate that the need to mark *rad-* an exception to Relative Clause Reduction does not depend in any way on how we derive the predicate LF.

Second, if (4.12) is adopted *rad-* must be prevented from replacing the symbol ADJ only when ADJ is an expansion of NP, not when it is an expansion of VP. This must be done in order to block sentences like (4.17).

(4.17) **Ona* [*byla* [*radaja*]$_{NP}$]$_{VP}$.

This restriction is extremely ad hoc (cf. §§4.2.1.2-4.2.1.3 and the objection to context-sensitive base rules) and is required only if (4.12) is chosen as the source of the predicate LF. If, on the other hand, the relative-clause origin of the predicate LF is chosen (cf. (4.18) for a schematic deep structure) sentences like (4.17) will be blocked by the same independently motivated restriction on the reduction of a relative clause containing *rad-* that blocks surface structures like (4.14).

(4.18)

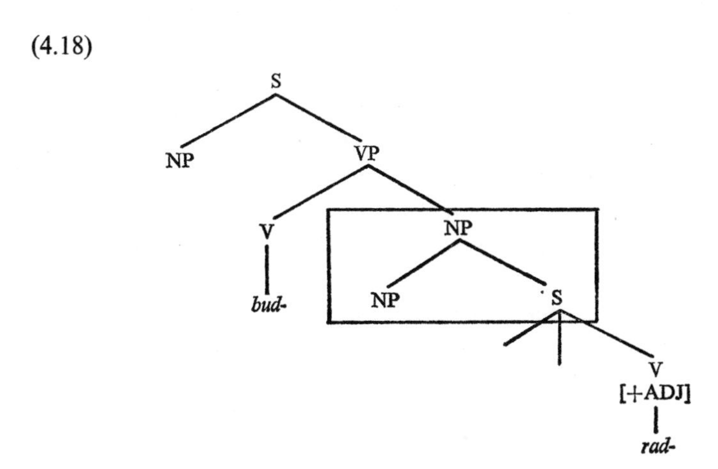

Thus the adoption of the relative-clause origin of the predicate LF greatly simplifies our grammar of Russian by eliminating the need for the ad hoc restriction described above, and, in addition, it increases the generality of our grammar by allowing us to account for the non-occurence of **radyj* at only one point (cf. §4.5.2 for additional comment on *rad-*).

4.2.2.2 Chapter 1 was devoted to adducing a considerable number of strong arguments supporting the assumption that prenominal adjectives are derived from relative clauses and, therefore, that ADJ (or $\underset{[+\text{ADJ}]}{\text{V}}$) is introduced only as an expansion of VP. If (4.12) were adopted in an attempt to account for the predicate LF, we would have to ignore all the evidence presented in Chapter 1 and abandon all the generalizations based upon it since (4.12) states that ADJ is introduced at TWO points in our base rules. The relative-clause origin of the predicate LF, on the other hand, permits our grammar to retain the generalization that ADJ is introduced at only one point in the base rules because, according to this derivation, the surface-structure predicate LF derives from the deep-structure predicate of the relative clause (SF) (cf. (4.18)), which is an expansion of VP.

It must also be mentioned that the semantic interpretation of the predicate LF cannot be accounted for in terms of the deep structure generated by (4.12) (cf. §4.4 for a more detailed discussion of the semantic properties of the predicate LF and SF).

The arguments presented in §§4.2.2-4.2.2.2 leave no doubt that (4.12) is incorrect and must be rejected.

4.2.3 ADJECTIVES AS NOUN PHRASES. The third and last derivation of the predicate LF that does not involve an underlying relative clause is a proposal based on John Ross's article "Adjectives as Noun Phrases" (Reibel and Shane, 1969), which offers several extremely stimulating proposals about the deep structure of predicate adjectives. Since Ross claims that his proposals are valid for all languages in which the predicate adjective is preceded by a copula (cf. p. 353), it is quite appropriate that they be discussed with reference to adjectives in Russian in this chapter.

Ross claims that the deep structure of (4.19) is (4.20).

(4.19) *Henry is hungry.*

(4.20)

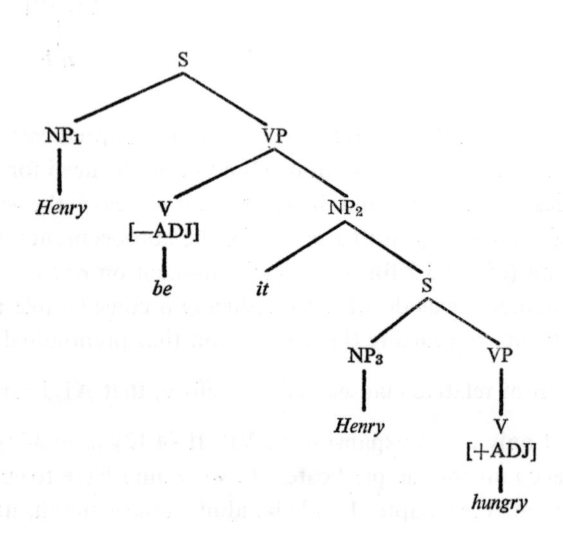

He employs the following transformations and conventions in deriving (4.19) from (4.20):

> EQUI-NP DELETION, which deletes *Henry* (NP_3), the subject of the embedded sentence.
> IT-DELETION, which deletes *it* in the configuration $[it — S]_{NP}$.
> VARIOUS AUTOMATIC CONVENTIONS OF TREE-PRUNING.

These transformations map (4.20) into (4.21), the surface structure of (4.19).

(4.21)

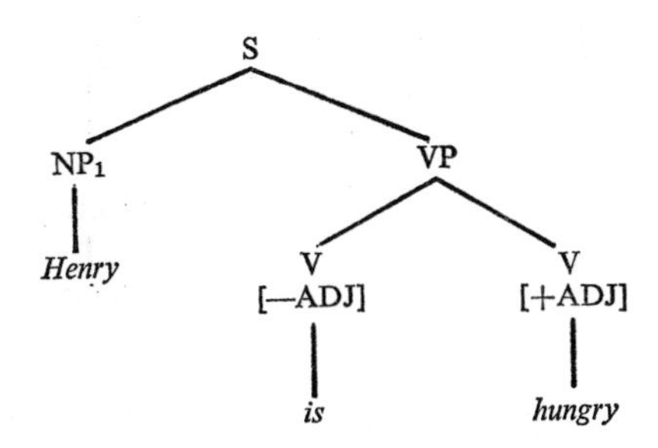

The above-mentioned transformations and conventions have deleted the following section of the deep-structure P-marker (4.20) in the derivation of (4.21).

(4.22)

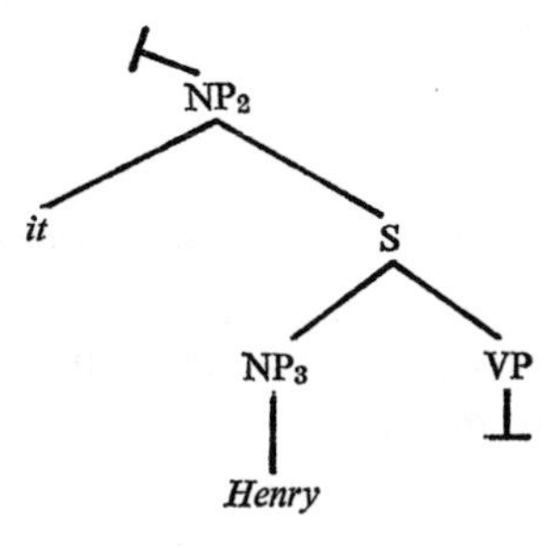

It and $[Henry]_{NP3}$ are deleted by transformation. Nodes S and VP are deleted by pruning conventions that are well motivated. However, Ross gives no justification for deleting NP_2. The conditions under which a NP node is deleted are not stipulated, and I have not been able to discover any other derivation which requires the deletion of a NP node. Note that in his earlier work (1967:101) Ross argued AGAINST NP Deletion.

For English it really seems to make no difference whether NP_2 (cf. (4.20)) is deleted or not, since the form of the adjective in English gives no indication whether the adjective in the surface structure is a NP constituent or not. In other words, there seems to be no good reason why (4.23) should not be the surface structure of (4.19) instead of (4.21).

(4.23)

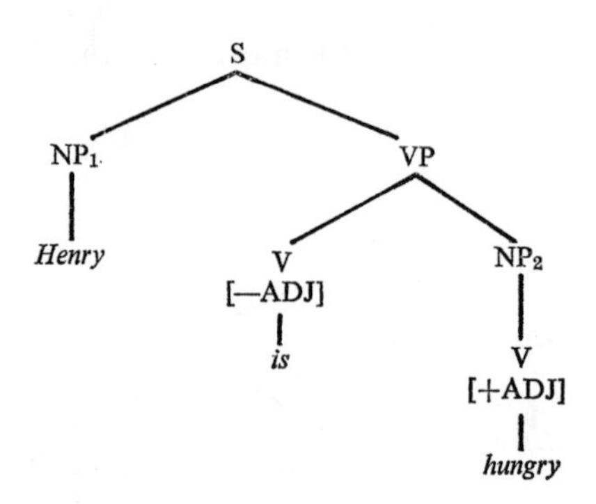

The presence or absence of NP_2, however, is of great consequence to the grammar of RUSSIAN, which requires that the surface-structure form indicate whether the adjective is a NP constituent or not (recall that $LF = [SF]_{NP}$).

In accordance with Ross's proposals, let us investigate the consequences of assuming that (4.25) is the deep structure of (4.24).

(4.24) *Ivan byl goloden.*
'Ivan was hungry.'

The following transformations apply to (4.25), producing P-marker (4.26):

SUBJECT-V AGREEMENT (on first cycle), which copies inherent features from $[\text{Ivan}]_{NP3}$ on to *golod# n-*.
EQUI-NP DELETION, which deletes $[\text{Ivan}]_{NP3}$.
to-DELETION, which deletes $[to]_{NP2}$ (cf. §2.9).
S-NODE AND VP-NODE DELETION.

Once the embedded S-node is deleted, *goloden* (= deep-structure *golod# n-* + features acquired by Subject-V Agreement on the first cycle) receives the case feature ([+NOM]) of NP_2 by the Case Marking transformation

(4.25)

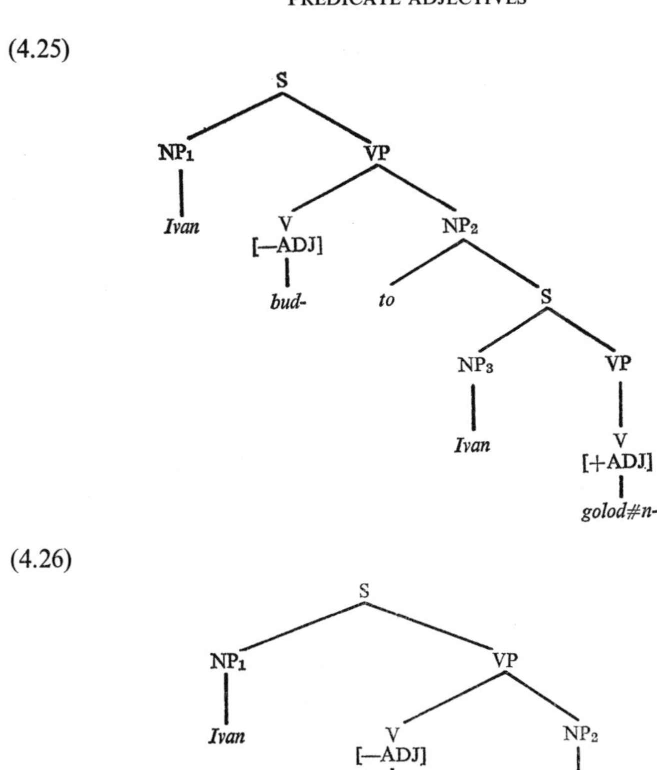

(4.26)

and therefore emerges as *golodnyj* (LF). I can see absolutely no justification in the grammar of Russian for deleting NP_2 after Case Marking (cf. §§4.3-4.6).

What is of central importance is the fact that Ross's proposal for the deep structure of the predicate adjective does not permit our grammar of Russian to generate the SF. In other words, if Ross's proposed deep structure of the adjective is incorporated into the grammar of Russian, sentences like (4.24) cannot be derived.

Sentence (4.27) could be derived from (4.25), but there would be no non-ad hoc way of preventing sentences like (4.28) and, more important, (4.25) cannot account for the semantic interpretation of (4.27) (cf. §4.4).

(4.27a) *Ivan byl golodnyj.*

'Ivan was the hungry one / Ivan was a hungry man.'

(4.27b) *Ivan byl golodnym.*

(4.28a) **Ivan byl poxožij na otca.*

(4.28b) **Ivan byl poxožim na otca.*

The evidence presented in §4.2.3 requires that we reject the proposals made in "Adjectives as Noun Phrases" and, therefore, that we question the claims of universal validity that Ross makes for deep structures like (4.20).

4.3 INTUITIVE STATEMENTS

4.3.1 One of the stated goals of a transformational-generative grammar is the expression of the native speaker's intuitive knowledge in the form of explicit rules. Therefore, if the relative-clause origin of the predicate LF proposed above is correct, it should be able to EXPLAIN certain traditional, intuitive statements made by Russian grammarians working in a non-explicit framework. I will now demonstrate that the relative-clause origin of the predicate LF DOES account explicitly for these intuitive statements. This is to be considered as further evidence that the relative-clause origin is correct.

4.3.2 Most Russian grammarians associate a LF in the predicate with a predicate noun that has been deleted. What is probably the clearest statement of this intuitive fact goes back to F. I. Buslaev (1868:II, 203).

Esli vmesto kratkogo upotrebleno v skazuemom prilagatel'noe polnoe, to ono imeet smysl opredelitel'nogo, pri kotorom opuščeno suščestvitel'noe; napr. "èti doma novye" vmesto "èti doma sut' *doma novye*".
[If instead of a short adjective a full adjective is used in the predicate, it has the meaning of an attributive adjective, where the noun has been omitted; for example, "These houses are new" instead of "These houses are *new houses*".]

Similar observations were made by A. M. Peškovskij (1938:226) in his discussion of the predicate LF (instrumental) in sentence (4.29) (emphasis is mine — L.H.B.).

(4.29) *On byl bezžalostnym.*
'He was (a) pitiless (man).'

... s formoj ètoj vsegda svjazan ottenok substantivirovanija prilagatel'nogo, tak kak poskol'ku èto prilagatel'noe predikativno, ono ne terpit pri sebe suščestvitel'nogo (inače suščestvitel'noe vzjalo by predikativnost'na sebja; *on byl bezžalostnym čelovekom*), a v to že vremja i samo ne javljaetsja podlinnym suščestvitel'nym.... Tvoritel'nyj padež est' zdes' padež upravljaemyj, tak kak on svjazan

imenno s substantivirovaniem prilagatel'nogo; prilagatel'noe stoit v tom padeže, v kotorom stojalo by suščestvitel'noe, kotoroe ono zamenjaet ("byl dobrym", potomu čto "byl dobrym čelovekom" i "dobrjakom").
[... there is always connected with this form [a predicate LF in the instrumental] the nuance of a substantivized adjective since, insofar as this adjective is predicative, it does not admit a noun with it (otherwise the noun would take on predicativity; 'He was a pitiless man.'), and at the same time is not itself a genuine noun [cf. *byl portnym* '(he) was a tailor']... The instrumental case is the governing case here since it is connected with precisely the substantivization of the adjective; the adjective appears in that case in which the noun which it replaces would appear ("(he) was good [instr.]" because "(he) was a good man [instr.]" and "(he was) a good person [instr.]").]

Similar intuitive statements are frequent in discussions of the predicate LF (cf. Bulaxovskij, 1949:251).

In these statements, the predicate LF is associated with a deleted noun with which it agrees in gender, number, and case (cf. *On byl bezžalostnym (čelovekom)* 'He was (a) pitiless (man)'). In other words, we are dealing with a deeper "adjectival phrase" ($[\text{adjective} + \text{noun}]_{NP}$), from which the "head" noun is deleted giving a surface-structure predicate LF ($[\text{adjective}]_{NP}$). However, it was demonstrated in Chapter 1 that adjective + noun constructions are derived from deep-structure relative-clause configurations by Relative Clause Reduction, S-Node Deletion, and Case Marking. Thus these intuitive statements associating the predicate LF with a deleted noun are naturally accounted for by assuming that the predicate LF derives from a deep-structure relative clause ($[NP — S]_{NP}$); and $[N — LF]_{NP}$ is therefore an intermediate structure close to the surface structure ($[LF]_{NP}$).

4.3.2.1 Russian linguistic literature abounds in intuitive statements about the nature of the predicate LF which are actually variants of the one explicated in §4.3.2. For instance, it is usually noted that the predicate LF feels like an attributive adjective (cf. the Buslaev quote in §4.3.2; V. V. Vinogradov, 1947: 268; A. A. Zaliznjak, 1967:88). The most succinct expression of this intuitive fact is provided by N. Ju. Švedova, (1952:91):

Ona [SF] možet vystupat' tol'ko v funkcii skazuemogo, èto čisto predikativnaja forma, predikativnaja sama po sebe, v to vremja kak polnaja forma grammatičeski dvuznačna, ee funkcija delitsja meždu attributivnoj i predikativnoj, i poètomu *èlement attributivnogo značenija založen v nej daže togda, kogda ona vystupaet v roli skazuemogo.*
[It [the SF] can occur only in the function of predicate; it is a purely predicative form, predicative in and of itself, while the full form is grammatically ambiguous: its function is divided between attributive and predicative, and therefore the *element of attributive meaning rests in it even when it occurs in the role of predicate.*]

This feeling that the predicate LF is an attributive adjective is quite natural if the relative-clause origin of the predicate LF is adopted: at a late stage in its derivation the predicate LF IS an "attributive adjective", if we define the term "attributive adjective" by the derived P-marker configuration $[LF — N]_{NP}$ or $[N — LF]_{NP}$. The "head noun" N is deleted by the rule of Antecedent Deletion (cf. §4.6).

4.3.2.2 Most Russian grammarians feel that the predicate LF is close to or is somehow like a predicate noun (*On takoj rassejannyj* 'He is such an absent-minded person'; *On očen' rassejan*' He is absent-minded'). This intuitive fact is usually expressed by claiming that the predicate LF is a "substantivized adjective" (cf. Peškovskij citation in §4.3.2; Vinogradov, 1947: 268; I. I. Meščaninov, 1945:129; Švedova, 1952:94; Isačenko, 1962:83). The vagueness of these statements is best exemplified by Vinogradov's:

Mne kažetsja pravil'noj mysl', čto v predikativnom značenii polnye prilagatel'nye neskol'ko substantivirujutsja; oni polučajut kakoj-to ottenok predmetnosti.
[The thought that full adjectives in the predicative meaning are somewhat substantivized seems correct to me; they receive some nuance of objectness.]

If we derive the predicate LF from an underlying relative clause configuration, these vague statements to the effect that a predicate LF feels or functions like a predicate noun can be accounted for: in the surface structure, the predicate LF IS THE CONSTITUENT OF A NP THAT DOES NOT DIRECTLY DOMINATE A N (cf. (3.173)-(3.175)); i.e. the predicate LF itself is the NP "head". The NP dominating the predicate LF in the surface structure is the higher $NP(NP_X)$ in the deep-structure relative-clause configuration ($[NP — S]_{NPX}$ and is the source of the $\underset{[+ADJ]}{V}$'s case feature.

Ovsjaniko-Kulikovskij (1912:174) notes that sentences like those in (4.30) contain LFs (instrumental) that are "close to nouns" (*približaetsja k suščestvitel'nomu*) or "substantivized" (cf. 175).

(4.30a) *Ètot postupok kažetsja mne nepravil'nym.*
'This action seems wrong to me.'

(4.30b) *Nužno byt' vežlivym.*
'One should be polite.'

(4.30c) *Vaši slova predstavljajutsja mne strannymi.*
'Your words seem strange to me.'

The derivation of sentences like those in (4.30) were analyzed in Chapter 3 where it was demonstrated that the LFs (instrumental) in these sentences are surface-structure NP constituents and that these NPs do not directly dominate a N. However, in sentences like those of (4.30) and Chapter 3, the NP that dominates the LF in the surface structure does NOT contain a (head) noun in the deep structure (cf. (3.98) and (3.107), the deep and surface structure of (3.94); cf. also §3.0). Thus the feeling that a surface-structure LF is "substantivized "or "noun-like" cannot be traced back to a deleted deep-structure N which the LF "replaces". An underlying $\underset{[+\text{ADJ}]}{\text{V}}$ is felt to be "substantivized" or "noun-like" if it is transformationally introduced into a NP that, in the surface structure, does not directly dominate a noun. Thus a "substantivized" adjective is a purely surface-structure notion: it is the derived head of a NP.

4.3.3 In §3.9 a sample derivation of a predicate LF from a deep-structure relative-clause configuration was given. The "antecedent" of the relative clause, however, was left unspecified (i.e. it was marked with a "?" (cf. (3.173)-(3.174))). The intuitive statements discussed in §4.3 enable us to fill in this missing detail. Buslaev (cf. §4.3.2) feels that *èti doma novye* 'these houses are new (ones)' is derived from the same P-marker that underlies *èti doma sut' doma novye* 'these houses are new houses'. This demonstrates that the deep-structure antecedent, which is later deleted, may be identical to the matrix subject N. Accordingly, the deep structure of *èti doma novye* is:

(4.31)

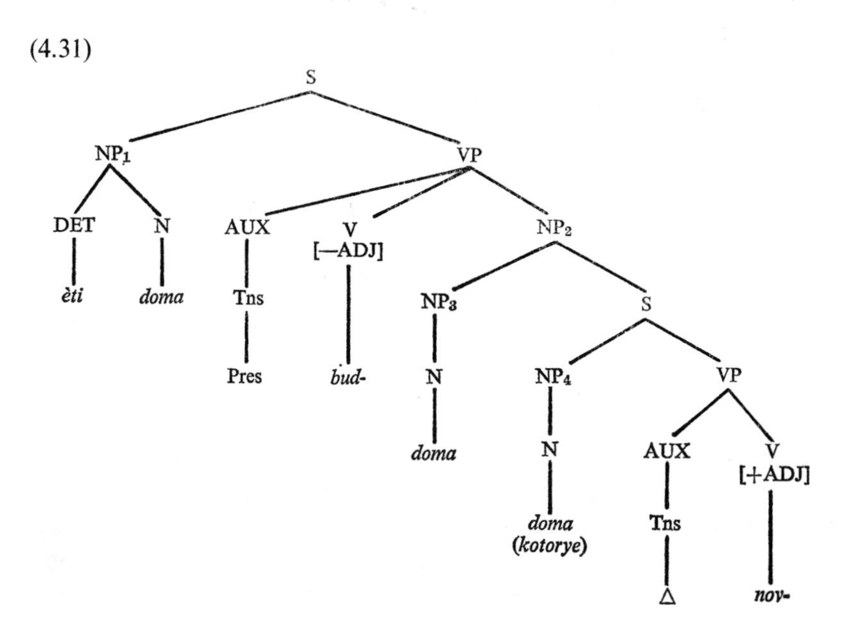

$[doma]_{NP3}$ is the deep-structure relative-clause antecedent.

Peškovskij (§4.3.2) feels that in a sentence like (4.29), *On byl bezžalostnym*, the deleted noun is *čelovek* (*On byl (čelovekom) bezžalostnym*). This feeling is shared by L. A. Bulaxovskij (1949:251):

Osobenno často polnaja forma upotrebljaetsja, kogda reč' idet o licax, i glavnym obrazom mužskogo roda *(ne dogovarivaetsja slovo "čelovek")*: "Esli ja skazal pro Vladimira, čto on *skučnyj*, to ja beru èto slovo nazad. On *prekrasnyj, čestnyj, nravstvennyj čelovek*,...." (L. Tolstoj)
[The full form is used especially often when one is speaking of persons, and mainly those of masculine gender (the word "man; person" is not included): "If I said about Vladimir that he is boring, then I take back this word. He is a fine, honest, upstanding person..."]

Accordingly, the deep structure of (4.29) is (4.32) and its surface structure is (4.33). In (4.32) the verb *bud-* governs the instrumental.

(4.32)

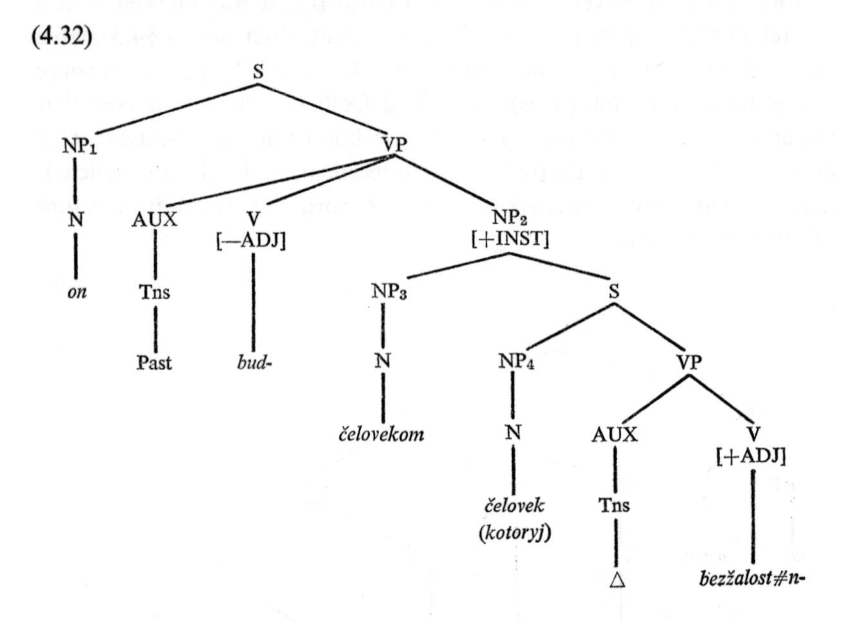

$[čelovekom]_{NP3}$ is the deep structure antecedent that is later deleted.

The above discussion brings out the important fact that the deleted deep-structure relative-clause antecedent is either identical to the matrix subject noun (NP_1 in (4.31) and (4.32)) or is a noun like *čelovek (ženščina* 'woman' *rebenok* 'child' *vešč'* 'thing' etc.; cf. §4.3.3.1). Although the antecedent *čelovek* in (4.29) is not identical to the matrix subject, it is "con-

(4.33)

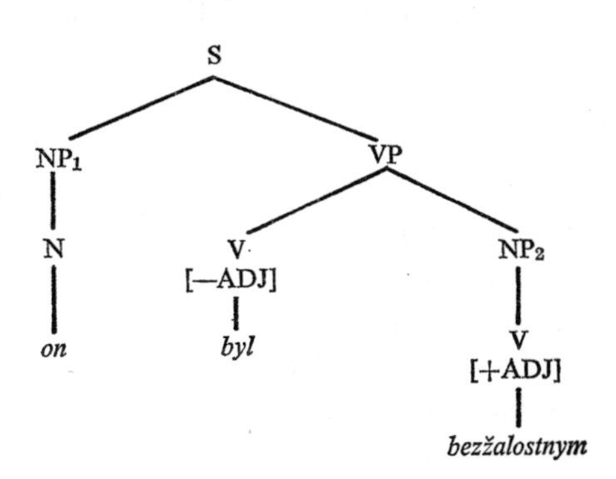

tained" in it: the set of semantic and syntactic features that make up *čelovek* is a subset of the subject noun's features. D. Bolinger (1967:20) points out that a noun like *čelovek* "represents little more than the category Human". Z. Vendler (1967:57) correctly notes that a noun like *čelovek* is merely the subject's GENUS and, therefore, is "redundant" and "easily recoverable".

Thus the deep-structure antecedent is either "contained" in the matrix subject noun or identical to it (a special case of "containment") and, therefore, it is quite easily recovered upon deletion. These notions of identity, repetition, and deletability are explicitly employed by Isačenko, (1965:I, 195) in his treatment of the relations between (4.34a) and (4.34b):

(4.34a) *Kitajskij jazyk–očen' trudnyj (jazyk).*
'The Chinese language is a very difficult language.'

(4.34b) *Kitajskij jazyk očen' trudnyj.*
'The Chinese language is (a) very difficult (one).'

Soglasno pravilam, regulirujuščim ustranenie identičnogo člena pri povtore, suščestvitel'noe (*jazyk*) opuskaetsja v atributivnoj sintagme, popavšej v poziciju skazuemogo (trudnyj jazyk →trudnyj).
[According to the rules which regulate the deletion of a repeated, identical member, a noun *(language)* is omitted in the attributive syntagm which moves into the position of the predicate *(a difficult language →difficult)*.]

In other words, a speaker of Russian will invariably associate the predicate LF with a deleted "head" noun that is either the genus of or identical to the matrix subject. This fact will prove to be of great importance in §4.4, where the semantic interpretation of the predicate LF is discussed.

4.3.3.1 Now that we have determined the nature of the antecedent that is deleted in the course of the derivation of the predicate LF from an underlying relative-clause configuration (cf. 3.173), we are able to account for the extremely revealing statements made by Russian grammarians apropos of sentences like those in (4.35).

(4.35a) *Ona ženščina neglupaja.*
'She is not a stupid woman.'

(4.35b) *On čelovek ènergičnyj.*
'He is an energetic person.'

(4.35c) *Ona devuška samostojatel'naja.*
'She is an independent girl.'

(4.35d) *Bal–vešč' xorošaja.*
'A ball is a good thing.'

(4.35e) *Net, ona ne ošiblas' v nem, on čelovek dostojnyj velikoj ljubvi.*
'No, she was not mistaken about him, he is a man worthy of great love.' (Kočetov)

From the point of view or our transformational grammar of Russian, these sentences merely contain a "semantically reduced" (cf. Bolinger, 1967:20) predicate noun modified by a reduced relative clause that has not been moved to prenominal position by the rule of Modifier Shift. Russian grammarians, however, feel that these sentences have unique syntactic properties and, accordingly, assign them the status of a separate type in their taxonomic classification (cf. Galkina-Fedoruk, 1964:II, 330). In short, they feel that sentences like those in (4.35) differ structurally from a sentence like *Puškin velikij poèt* 'Puškin is a great poet'.

It is usually stated in Russian grammars that sentences like those in (4.35) do NOT contain a predicate noun with a postnominal modifier. It is felt that the noun merely fulfills a copulative function, i.e. it merely serves to link the subject of the sentence to the PREDICATE LF. I. V. Tolstoj (1966:180) calls nouns like *čelovek*, *ženščina*, etc., in sentences like (4.35) "*svjazočnye*" *slova* (linking words); L. P. Judina et al. (1966:12) refer to them as *vspomogatel'nye suščestvitel'nye* (auxiliary or helping nouns); Isačenko (1965:195) observes that:

> Polnaja forma prilagatel'nyx, vystupaja v kačestve skazuemogo, možet soedinjat'sja s podležaščim pri pomošči suščestvitel'nyx *čelovek*, *mužčina*, *ženščina*, *devuška*, i t. p. .... V ètix slučajax priznak vyražen kak postojannyj, ne zavisjaščij ot vremeni.
>
> [The full form of adjectives occurring as a predicate can be joined to a subject by means of the nouns '*man, person*', '*man*', '*woman*', '*girl*', etc. ... In these cases the feature is expressed as a constant that does not depend on time.]

Grammatika russkogo jazyka, AN SSSR (1960: II, 419), assigns sentences in which the subject noun is identical to the predicate noun to this special "sentence type".

The intuitive facts just presented can be explained quite naturally in terms of the relative-clause origin of the predicate LF. The nominal predicates in (4.35) do derive from deep-structure relative clause configurations. For example, the deep structure of *On byl čelovekom bezžalostnym* is given in (4.32): $[\textit{čelovekom bezžalostnym}]_{NP2}$ is the result of Relative Clause Reduction, S-Node Deletion, and Case Marking ([+INST]). The feeling that these sentences contain a predicate LF joined to the subject by a "copulative" or "auxiliary" noun, not just a predicate noun with an adjectival modifier, is to be explained by the ease and frequency with which these generic or identical "head" nouns (cf. §4.3.3) are deleted, giving sentences in which the LF becomes the overt nominal predicate (cf. P-marker (4.33)).

Thus while taxonomic grammar expresses the intuitive facts described above by setting up *On byl bezžalostnym* and *On byl čelovekom bezžalostnym* as two different types of sentences, transformational grammar can explain the same facts more simply by relating both sentences by the optional transformation of Antecedent Deletion and a common deep structure. Notice too that a transformational grammar of Russian need not claim that *On byl čelovekom bezžalostnym* and *Puškin byl velikim poètom* are different sentence types.

The free-flowing transformational relationship between sentence pairs related by Antecedent Deletion is illustrated by the following examples:

(4.36) *–Tak vot, logičeski rassuždaja, ty dolžen ujti, potomu čto moja Olja*–devuška skromnaja...
–A raz ona skromnaja, *to mne tem bolee uxodit' ne nado.*
'And so, judging logically, you should leave, because my Olja is a *modest girl...*'
'And if she's *modest* then all the more reason I should not leave.' (Čikar'kov)

(4.37) *Ètot učitel', po slovam Ševčenko, byl* žestokij, *besserdečnyj i grubyj* čelovek. *No on porol učenikov ne tol'ko potomu, čto on byl* žestokij.
'This teacher, in the words of Ševčenko, was a cruel, heartless, and rude *man*. But he thrashed the pupils not only because he was cruel.' (Zoščenko)

(4.38) *Moja mat', rodivšajasja v Sibiri, ne byla takoj* načitannoj, *kak otec, no...*

Kak ja uže skazal vyše, otec moj byl čelovekom načitannym.
'My mother, who was born in Siberia, was not so *well read* as my father, but...'
'As I already said above, my father was a *well-read person.*'
(Evtušenko)

(4.39) *Tol'ko ja ego prosil* tolkovogo čeloveka *prislat'. A pro vas i ne znaju, kakoj vy*–tolkovyj *ili net?*
'Only I asked him to send an *intelligent man.* But about you I don't know–are you *intelligent* or not?' (Kaverin)

(4.40) *No pro vas xoču dumat', čto vy* čelovek porjadočnyj... Porjadočnyj *vy?*
'But I want to think that you are a *decent person*... Are you decent?' (Panova)

4.3.4 EXPRESSION OF TENSE BY THE LF AND SF. Many Russian grammarians feel that the SF somehow expresses tense differently from the LF in the predicate. The most typical formulation of this view was made by V. V. Vinogradov (1947:265), who even claims that this is the most important difference between the predicate LF and SF:

Prinadležnost' kratkix prilagatel'nyx k slovam s formami vremeni *(Zeitwort)* i sostavljaet ix otličitel'nuju grammatičeskuju čertu. Formami vremeni kratkie prilagatel'nye bol'še vsego otličajutsja ot polnyx. ... Formy vremeni kladut rezkuje gran' meždu nimi [short forms] i polnymi prilagatel'nymi, upotreblennymi v toj že funkcii.
[The fact that short adjectives belong to words with tense forms *(Zeitwort)* comprises their distinctive grammatical characteristic. Short adjectives differ most of all from full forms by their tense forms... Tense forms place a sharp boundary between them [short forms] and full adjectives which are used in the same function.]

It is extremely difficult to discuss statements like the above not only because they are vague but also because quite often Russian grammarians fail to maintain the distinction between expression of tense by the LF and the SF and their expression of a "permanent" or "temporal" property (cf. §4.4.1). This type of inconsistency may be illustrated by A. N. Gvozdev's (1955:163) explication of the difference between (4.41a) and (4.41b), both of which may be translated into English as 'She is cheerful'.

(4.41a) *Ona veselaja.*
(4.41b) *Ona vesela.*

Gvozdev claims that the LF denotes a "postojannoe, vnevremennoe kačestvo" 'permanent, atemporal quality' and that the SF denotes a "vremennoe sostojanie" 'a state at a particular time'. Thus the LF, according to Gvozdev, in (4.41a) denotes a permanent character trait and gives no information about the subject's (*ona*) mood at the moment of speech. She may be quite unhappy when (4.41a) is uttered. (4.41b), on the other hand, characterizes the subject at the moment of speech. However, it will be shown that Gvozdev's definition of the difference between the SF and predicate LF is incorrect (cf. §4.4).

In view of the vagueness of the above statements, I will limit myself to only a few general observations about tense and the predicate LF and SF.

Given the deep structures of the predicate LF and SF that have been proposed (cf. §3.9), it is PREDICTABLE that the native speaker should feel, however vaguely, that a sentence containing a predicate LF expresses tense differently from a sentence containing a SF. The surface-structure SF is a deep-structure $\underset{[+\mathrm{ADJ}]}{\mathrm{V}}$ that is the main V of the matrix sentence and undergoes Subject-V Agreement; the surface-structure "copula" that precedes the SF (*byl*, *budet*, etc) is a tense-marker in the deep structure (cf. (3.44), the deep structure of (3.43); (3.47) is its surface structure). The surface-structure predicate LF is a deep-structure $\underset{[+\mathrm{ADJ}]}{\mathrm{V}}$ which is the main V OF A RELATIVE CLAUSE embedded in the predicate of a higher sentence whose main V is *bud-* (cf. (4.32), the deep structure of (4.29); (4.33) is its surface structure). In other words, the surface-structure "copula" that precedes the predicate LF (*byl*, *budet*, etc.) is the main V of the matrix sentence at the level of deep structure, not the tense-marker as it is in the case of the SF. Thus temporal differences between the SF and the predicate LF like those detected by Vinogradov and Gvozdev must be traced back to the difference in deep-structure P-markers, not to the surface-structure SF and predicate LF themselves. Recall that semantic interpretation rests on the deep-structure P-markers, not on the surface structures derived from them.

This is a rather important conclusion, since the major point of this study is that both the LF and SF derive from a deep-structure $\underset{[+\mathrm{ADJ}]}{\mathrm{V}}$. If we were to explain the temporal nuances just discussed in terms of the LF and SF, and not in terms of their underlying P-markers as a whole, we would in effect be claiming that the distinction LF:SF exists at the level of deep structure, since it is at the level of deep structure that the rules of semantic interpretation operate.

4.4 SEMANTIC PROPERTIES. In this section traditional statements about the meaning of the predicate LF and SF will be analyzed. It will be demonstrated that the meaning of the predicate LF can be explained fully in terms of an underlying relative-clause configuration and that the meaning of the SF can be accounted for by the absence of this configuration and by its verbal nature. The fact that the relative-clause origin proposed in §3.9 is able to account for the semantic interpretation of the predicate LF must be considered as further evidence that this derivation is correct.

4.4.1 THE LF DENOTES A POSTOJANNYJ PRIZNAK (PERMANENT PROPERTY). The view held most widely by Russian grammarians is that the predicate LF denotes a permanent property of the subject (*postojannyj priznak*) and the SF denotes a temporary property (*vrémennyj priznak*) (cf. D. È. Rozental', 1967:239; I. A. Kudrjavceva, 1967:131; A. N. Gvozdev, 1955:163). The terms *vnevremennoe kačestvo* (atemporal quality) and *nedlitel'noe sostojanie* (state of short duration) are often used to describe the same phenomenon (cf. §4.3.4).

There are a great many sentences of Russian in which this definition seems to hold:

(4.42a) *Ja zdorovaja, mogu rabotat'.*
'I am (a) healthy (person). I can work.'

(4.42b) *Ja uže zdorova, zavtra pojdu na rabotu.*
'I am well (healthy) again. Tomorrow I'm going to work.'

(4.43) *...on robel ot nežnosti k nej, emu daže stydno bylo dumat' o tom,* krasivaja *ona ili net, potomu čto ona byla prekrasna.*
'...he was shy from tenderness toward her; he was even ashamed to think whether she was *pretty* or not because she was *beautiful*.' (A. Platonov)

(4.44a) *On* spokojnyj, *uravnovešennyj. Mne nravitsja ego xarakter.*
'He is *calm*, well balanced. I like his character.'

(4.44b) *Ja stoju i smotrju. Vsem xorošo. Vse* spokojny. *Značit, i ja* spokojen *tože.*
'I stand and look. Everyone is okay. Everyone is *calm*. So I am *calm*, too.'

(4.45a) *Otec* bol'noj. *On na pensii i ne rabotaet.*
'Father is *sick*. He is on a pension and doesn't work.'

(4.45b) *Otec* bolen *i ne pojdet segodnja na rabotu.*
'Father is *sick* and will not go to work today.'

(4.46a) *Nikolaj* molčalivyj, *bol'še ljubit slušat'.*
'Nikolaj is *quiet*; he prefers to listen.'

(4.46b) *Ves' večer Nikolaj byl* molčaliv, *s neoxotoj otvečal na voprosy.*
'All evening Nikolaj was *quiet*; he answered questions unwillingly.'[1]

This permanent-temporary definition, however, does not account for all sentences containing a predicate adjective. Typical of many grammarians is D. È. Rozental' (1967:239), who, after citing several examples in which this definition holds, adds a list of sentences in which it does not. (4.47) is one of these "counterexamples" along with Rozental''s own comments.

(4.47) *Strana naša bogata, vse u nas est' (kratkaja forma xotja ukazyvaetsja postojannyj priznak).*
'Our country is rich, we have everything.' (SF although a permanent property is indicated.)

There are whole classes of sentences where the permanent-temporary definition proves to be totally inadequate. The most striking case is that of scientific definitions, the paradigm example of "permanency", where the SF is used exclusively.

(4.48a) *Prostranstvo beskonečno.*
'Space is infinite.'
(4.48b) **Prostranstvo beskonečnoe.*
(4.49) *Voda prozračna.*
'Water is transparent.'
(4.50) *Projdennyj put' pri ravnomernom dviženii proporcionalen vremeni.*
'With uniform motion the path traveled is proportional to time.'
(4.51) *Nauka nesoveršenna. Istina–doč' vremeni.*
'Science is not perfect. Truth is the daughter of time.'
(Zoščenko)

[1] Compare (4.42)-(4.46) to the following sentence pairs:

(i a) *Devočka byla bol'naja, slabaja.*
'The girl was sick(ly), weak.'
(i b) *V detsve ona byla bol'noj, slaboj, no potom ej pomogla fizkul'tura.*
'The girl was sick(ly), weak, but then physical exercise helped her.
(ii a) *V molodosti ja byl neprivetlivym, xmurym.*
'In (my) youth I was unfriendly (and) sullen.'
(ii b) *On vsegda byl neprivetlivyj, xmuryj.*
'He was always unfriendly (and) sullen.'

The existence of an entire class of sentences in which the SF denotes a permanent property (space is not infinite at any one particular time (cf. (4.48)) is sufficient reason to reject the notion that the predicate LF invariably denotes a permanent property of the subject and the SF invariably denotes a temporary property or state. Note that the very fact that there exist sentences of Russian in which either the predicate LF or the SF MUST be used, regardless of considerations of permanency, makes it quite clear that the selection of a predicate adjective depends on other factors. In sentences like (4.50) the presence of a complement precludes the appearance of a predicate LF; permanency plays no role. In sentences like (4.48) the exclusive use of a SF is to be explained by the presence of a unique noun as subject. The fact that the TYPE of subject noun directly affects the form of the predicate adjective will prove to be of very great significance (cf. §4.5.3).

4.4.1.1 The fact that the predicate LF in (4.42)-(4.46) and (4.36)-(4.40) is interpreted as denoting a permanent quality or characteristic of the subject can be explained quite simply by the presence of an underlying relative-clause head noun like *čelovek*, which is subsequently deleted (cf. §§4.3.3-4.3.3.1). For instance, the predicate LF in (4.37) (*On byl žestokij*) is felt to denote a permanent quality precisely because it has the same underlying structure as (4.52a), which, as Isačenko points out (cf. quote on p. 186), denotes a permanent, atemporal property.

(4.52a) *On byl čelovek žestokij.*
'He was a cruel person.'

(4.52b) *On byl žestok.*
'He was cruel.'

(4.52b), on the other hand, has no deep-structure relative-clause configuration underlying it and, consequently, is noncommittal with respect to expression or non-expression of permanency. Thus a sentence containing the SF *žestok* may denote a permanent property of the subject IN THE PROPER CONTEXT:[2]

(4.53) *On vsju žizn' byl tak žestok, čto ego nikto nikogda ne poljubil.*
'He was so cruel all his life that no one ever loved him.'

[2] My informants note that *On vsju žizn' byl takim žestokim* [inst.], *čto ego nikto nikogda ne poljubil* has approximately the same meaning as (4.53). Compare these sentences to those in footnote 1, Chapter 4.

Similarly, *molčalivyj* 'quiet, silent' in (4.46a) is felt to express a permanent quality of the subject (*Nikolaj*) because it has the same deep structure, and, consequently, is interpreted in the same way as *čelovek molčalivyj* 'a quiet person'. It is thus no coincidence that (4.54a) and (4.54b) are peculiar in the same way.[3]

(4.54a) (*)*Nikolaj ves' večer byl čelovek molčalivyj.*
'Nikolaj was a quiet person all evening.'
(4.54b) (*)*Nikolaj ves' večer byl molčalivyj.*

As (4.55) clearly demonstrates, the "non-permanent" interpretation of (4.46b) depends on the entire sentence (cf. *ves' večer* 'all evening'), not on the presence of the SF *molčaliv*.

(4.55) –*Otčego on vse molčit?*
–Po nature *on molčaliv.* (Čexov)
–'Why is he always quiet?
–He is quiet by nature.'

Note that the presence of nouns like *person, girl*, etc., in English occasions the same semantic interpretation as does the presence of nouns like *čelovek devuška*, etc., in Russian. While *He is a quiet person* clearly denotes a permanent characteristic of the subject, *He is quiet* is noncommittal with respect to this meaning.

It has been established in this section (§4.4.1.1) that the SF does NOT express a non-permanent property of the subject (cf. (4.48)-(4.51)). The SF is NEUTRAL or noncommittal with respect to "permanency"; whether or not it is felt to denote a permanent property depends on the interpretation of the sentence as a whole.[4] It has also been shown that the LF is felt to express a permanent property or quality only by virtue of the fact

[3] The statements made here about (4.54b) apply only to the literary language, which is the subject of investigation in this dissertation.

[4] The lexical meaning of an adjective may, of course, preclude one or another interpretation. For example, an adjective like *mertv* 'dead' precludes a "temporary" interpretation and an adjective like *gotov* 'ready' precludes a "permanent" interpretation. Thus if the predicate LF were not derived from an underlying relative-clause configuration, we could not account simply for the fact that BOTH the following sentences are incorrect:

(a) **Nikolaj byl gotovyj.*
(b) **Nikolaj byl čelovek gotovyj.*
'Nikolaj was a ready man.'

that at a deeper level it "modifies" a head noun like *čelovek*. Expression of permanency is not an inherent property of the LF itself.[5]

It is extremely important to bear in mind that the semantic interpretations discussed in §§4.4.1-4.4.1.1 (and §4.3.3) have been shown to rest not on the predicate LF or SF themselves, but on the entire deep-structure P-marker of the sentences in which they are contained. This conclusion is crucial for our claim that the surface-structure SF and predicate LF both derive from a deep-structure $\begin{matrix} \text{V} \\ [+\text{ADJ}] \end{matrix}$. In other words, if it were to turn out that the expression of permanency and non-permanency (or any other semantic difference) were INHERENT properties of the predicate LF and SF respectively, we could not claim that the predicate LF and SF were the same category in the deep structure, where the rules of semantic interpretation operate.

4.4.2 EXPRESSION OF ČREZMERNOST'. A number of Russian grammarians claim that the SF may express a property as being "excessive" (*črezmernost'*). This meaning is conveyed in English by *too. Sliškom* 'too' is optional in Russian sentences expressing "excessiveness". As the (a) sentences in the following examples show, sentences containing a predicate LF cannot denote "excessiveness".

(4.56a) *Škaf* vysokij.
'The dresser is (a) high (one).'

(4.56b) *Škaf* vysok, *s nim nel'zja projti v komnatu.*[6]
'The dresser is too high for us to get it into the room.'

(4.57a) *Elka* vysokaja.
'(This) fir is (a) tall (one).'

(4.57b) *Elka* nevysokaja, *no ona vse-taki* vysoka *dlja našej komnaty, pridetsja ee podrubit'.*
'(This) fir isn't (a) tall (one), but it is nevertheless too tall for our room. It has to be shortened.'

(4.58a) *Èti gimnastičeskie upražnenija krasivye, no* trudnye.
'These gymnastic exercises are beautiful but *difficult*.'

[5] Sentences like (4.34), in which the deleted head noun is IDENTICAL to the subject noun, will be discussed in §4.4.3.1.

[6] Gvozdev's (1955: 163) explication of the meaning of *škaf vysok* 'the dresser is too high' is very useful: "...škaf možet byt' i nizkim, no on okazyvaetsja izlišne vysokim, naprimer, dlja togo, čtoby ego pronesti čerez dver' ili pomestit' v izvestnom pomeščenii" [...the dresser may even be low, but it is too high, for example, to be carried through a door or put in a certain place].

(4.58b) *Oni* trudny *dlja načinajuščix sportsmenov, xotja natrenirovannyj sportsmen vypolnit ix legko.*
'They are too difficult for beginning athletes, although the trained athlete can execute them easily.'

(4.58c) *Zadača* prostaja, *no ona* trudna *dlja škol'nika pervogo klassa.*
'The task is *simple*, but it is *too difficult* for a first-grade pupil.'

(4.59a) *Obyčno rukava zimnej odeždy* dlinnye.
'Usually the sleeves of winter clothing are *long*.'

(4.59b) *K sožaleniju, rukava ètogo plašča mne* dlinny.
'Unfortunately the sleeves of this coat are *too long* for me.'

(4.60a) *U Marii dve jubki*: *odna* uzkaja, *drugaja* širokaja.
'Maria has two skirts–one *narrow* and another *wide*.'

(4.60b) *Èta jubka ej* uzka.
'This skirt is *too narrow* for her.'

(4.61a) *Voda* gorjačaja.
'The water is *hot*.'

(4.61b) *Voda* gorjača *dlja kupanija.*
'The water is *too hot* for bathing.'

(4.62a) *On očen* molodoj.
'He is very *young*.'

(4.62b) *On* molod, *čtoby menja učit'.*
'He is *too young* to teach me.'

(4.62c) *On* molod *menja učit'.*
'He is *too young* to teach me.'[7]

The question immediately arises as to whether the meaning of "excessiveness" (*črezmernost'*) is an inherent property of the SF itself, or is a function of the deep-structure P-marker as a whole. If we are correct in asserting that the predicate LF, which does not express "excessiveness" (cf. (4.56)-(4.62)), and the SF are both derived from a deep-structure $\underset{[+\text{ADJ}]}{\text{V}}$,[8]

[7] The sentences in (4.56)-(4.62) leave no doubt that the "permanent-temporal" definition of the difference between the predicate LF and the SF examined in §4.4.1 does not hold up.

[8] Strictly speaking, we are claiming that the LF and the SF derive from the same deep-structure category, $\underset{[+\text{ADJ}]}{\text{V}}$. The surface-structure category SF is a deep-structure $\underset{[+\text{ADJ}]}{\text{V}}$ that has acquired a certain set of features by Subject-V Agreement. The surface-structure category LF is a deep-structure $\underset{[+\text{ADJ}]}{\text{V}}$ that has acquired the same set of features by Subject-V Agreement (= SF) and, in addition, has acquired a case

then it must be demonstrated that "excessiveness" is the property of the deep structure and not $\begin{matrix}V\\ [+ADJ]\end{matrix}$. This is just what was done in §4.4, where we showed that the expression or non-expression of "permanency" is not an inherent property of the predicate LF or SF. In general, if the surface-structure SF and predicate LF both derive transformationally from a deep-structure $\begin{matrix}V\\ [+ADJ]\end{matrix}$, then we should be able to demonstrate that any difference in meaning attributed to them is traceable to a difference in their underlying P-markers, not to the $\begin{matrix}V\\ [+ADJ]\end{matrix}$.

The most conclusive piece of evidence demonstrating that "excessiveness" is not an inherent property of the SF (and of the $\begin{matrix}V\\ [+ADJ]\end{matrix}$) is the fact that SFs which appear in sentences with "excessive" meaning can also be used in sentences without this meaning. This, of course, would not be possible if "excessiveness" were inherent to the SF. In the following examples, the SFs in the (a) sentences do NOT denote "excessiveness"; in the (b) sentences they do.

(4.63a) *Zimnaja noč' tak* dlinna. *A kak* korotok *zimnij den'*.
'The winter night is so *long*. And how *short* is the winter day.'

(4.63b) *Ešče nedavno rukava pal'to byli tebe* dlinny, *a teper'*–korotki.
'Not so long ago the sleeves of this coat were *too long* for you. Now they are *too short* (for you).'

(4.64a) *S severa gory* vysoki *i* nepristupny.
'(These) mountains are *high* and *unapproachable* from the north.'

(4.64b) *Ètot stol* vysok *dlja rebenka.*
'This table is too high for the child.'

(4.65a) *Kitajskij jazyk očen'* truden.
'The Chinese language is very *difficult*.'

(4.65b) *Kitajskij jazyk* truden *dlja škol'nikov pervogo klassa.*
'The Chinese language is *too difficult* for first-year schoolboys.'

(4.66a) *Kakaja noč'*, *kak* tepel *vozdux*, *kak* svetel *mesjac.*
'What a night! How *warm* the air! How *bright* the moon!'

---

feature upon introduction into NP constituency (cf. Chapter 3 for details). We are thus justified in making the pedagogically more useful claim that the LF is derived from the SF, although we are actually employing surface-structure terms in discussing intermediate structures.

(4.66b) *Tvoja odežda* svetla *dlja raboty.*
'Your clothes are *too light-colored* for work.'[9]

Examples (4.63)-(4.66) leave no doubt that the expression of "excessiveness" is not an inherent property of the SF and, therefore, must be explained in terms of other factors in the deep-structure P-marker. It is significant that the majority of sentences with "excessiveness" cited above contain "delimiting" adjectival complements that denote the person or thing with respect to which the subject's "excessiveness" is expressed. For example, in (4.57b) the fir is not a big one as fir trees go (*elka nevysokaja*), but it is nevertheless too big for a particular room ([*vysoka* [*dlja našej komnaty*]$_{PP}$]$_{VP}$). Sentences (4.58c), (4.59b), (4.62b), (4.63b), etc., are further illustrations of this function of the complement.

"Exessive" meaning may, however, also be expressed by sentences containing a SF without an overt complement (cf. (4.56b) and footnote 6). Nevertheless, remarks by native speakers make it seen quite probable that all sentences with an "excessive" meaning contain an adjectival complement at the level of deep structure. In other words, we are claiming that a sentence with a SF must have a "delimiting" complement in its deep structure in order to express "excessiveness". This complement may be deleted by subsequent transformations and not appear in the surface structure. Once we associate expression of "excessiveness" with a deep-structure complement, we automatically explain why the predicate LF cannot express it: only the SF can have a complement (cf. §4.6.3).

Typical of intuitive statements linking the expression of "excessiveness" with a complement, overt or deleted, are those of I. V. Tolstoj and L. Ju. Maksimov. Tolstoj's comments are particularly illuminating:

Ono [značenie črezmernosti] možet ne byt' vyražen nikakimi dopolnitel'nymi sredstvami [complements], no oni (èti sredstva) *vsegda legko vosstanavlivajutsja.* Esli my govorim "zadača trudna", "vorotnik širok", to estestvenno, predpolagaem "komu?", "dlja kogo?", to est' my vosstanavlivaem tak nazyvaemyj kosvennyj ob"ekt, ili dopolnenie, i tem samym obnaruživaem otnositel'nyj xarakter priznaka.
[It [the meaning of excessiveness] may not be expressed by any sort of complements, but they (these means) are *always easily recovered.* If we say "the problem is too hard", "the collar is too wide", then naturally we assume "for whom?", that is, we recover the so-called indirect object, or complement, and by this we reveal the relational nature of the feature.]

[9] As the following sentence clearly shows, *sliškom* conveys the "excessive" meaning: *Ego odežda byla sliškom jarka i smešna* 'His clothing was too bright and funny'.

The same intuitive knowledge is described by Maksimov (1957:16) in his explication of (4.67):

(4.67) *Volja tvoja, opjat' dlinno.–Nataša otošla podal'še, čtob osmotret'sja v trjumo. Plat'e bylo dlinno.*
'"As you please–it's again too long". Nataša went off a bit to look at herself in the mirror. The dress was too long.'
(L. Tolstoj)

Xotja v dannom primere i net dopolnenija v datel'nom padeže, odnako jasno, čto plat'e dlinno Nataše. Pri otsutstvii takoj jasnosti realizacija ètogo značenija nevozmožna.
[Although in this example there is no complement in the dative, it is nevertheless clear that the dress is too long for Nataša. In the absence of such clarity the realization of this meaning is impossible.]

As Maksimov's last remark suggests, if the deep structure of a sentence with a SF does not contain a complement, the sentence is not interpreted as having an "excessive" meaning.

In §4.4.2 it has been demonstrated that the meaning of "excessiveness" (*črezmernost'*) is not an inherent property of the SF or the predicate LF. This meaning must be explained in terms of a deep-structure "delimiting" complement, and not in terms of the deep-structure $\underset{[+\mathrm{ADJ}]}{\mathrm{V}}$ alone (cf. Vinogradov, 1947:403). This conclusion is necessary to our claim that the SF and predicate LF both derive transformationally from a deep-structure $\underset{[+\mathrm{ADJ}]}{\mathrm{V}}$ (cf. §4.4.1.1).

4.4.3 Denotation of an absolute or relative property. Russian grammarians also claim that the predicate LF denotes an absolute property of the subject (*absoljutnyj priznak*) while the SF denotes a relative property (*otnositel'nyj priznak*) (cf. Gvozdev, 1955:163). The traditional view of the difference between the predicate LF and SF analyzed in §4.4.2 is essentially a variant of this relative-absolute distinction, and, therefore, all the examples adduced in §4.4.2 can serve as illustrations for §4.4.3. Thus in (4.56)-(4.62) the adjectives in the (a) sentences are FELT to express an absolute property of the subject (no reference is made to time, place, other objects, etc.); the adjectives in the (b) sentences are felt to express a property of the subject only with reference to a specific time, place, person, etc.

A clear statement of this view can be found in Rozental' (1967:240):

... polnaja forma oboznačaet *absoljutnyj* priznak, ne svjazannyj s konkretnoj obstanovkoj, a kratkaja—*otnositel'nyj* priznak, primenitel'no k opredelennoj situacii.
[...the full form denotes an *absolute* feature, not connected with a concrete situation, and the short form denotes a *relational* feature, with reference to a given situation.]

Rozental' illustrates the above statement by two examples, to which he has added the explanations in parentheses:

(4.68a) *Komnata nizkaja. (priznak voobšče)*
'The room is (a) low (one).' (general property)
(4.68b) *Komnata nizka (dlja vysokoj mebeli).*
'The room is (too) low' (for high furniture).
(4.69a) *Noša tjaželaja (bezotnositel'no k tomu, kto budet ee nesti).*
'The load is (a) heavy (one)' (regardless of who will carry it).
(4.69b) *Noša tjažela (dlja slabogo čeloveka, dlja rebenka).*
'The load is heavy' (for a weak person, for a child).

To the examples already introduced we may add the following:

(4.70a) *Èta kniga dlinnaja i utomitel'naja.*
'This book is long and tiresome.'
(4.70b) *Èta kniga dlinna i utomitelna dlja rebenka.*
'This book is (too) long and tiresome for a child.'
(4.71a) *Èta materija dorogaja.*
'This material is expensive.'
(4.71b) *Èta materija doroga dlja menja.*
'This material is too expensive for me.'
(4.72a) *Letom v Leningrade noči svetlye.*
'In the summer the nights are light in Leningrad.'
(4.72b) *Segodnja noč' neobyknovenno svetla.*
'Today the night is unusually light.' (cf. 4.66))

In (4.69b) the load (*noša*) is characterized as being heavy only with respect (relative) to a particular carrier (*dlja slabogo čeloveka* 'for a weak person'); it may not be heavy for someone else. It is in this sense that the SF is said to denote a relative property of the subject. (4.69a) means that the load is characterized as being heavy without regard to who carries it (it is a heavy one). It is in this sense that the predicate LF is said to express a subject's property without reference to "external circumstances" (time, place, the strength of potential carriers, etc.).

4.4.3.1 However, a careful examination of all the sentences discussed in §4.4 (SEMANTIC PROPERTIES) will make it perfectly clear that the predicate LF does NOT denote an absolute property. On the contrary, the predicate LF's most characteristic feature is precisely the fact that it MUST express a relative property. One may say that it is "marked" for expression of a relative property. The point is that THE PREDICATE LF MUST EXPRESS ITS PROPERTY OR QUALITY RELATIVE TO THE CLASS OF OBJECTS TO WHICH ITS SUBJECT BELONGS. For example, (4.68a) states that the room (*komnata*) is low (*nizkaja*) WITH RESPECT TO ALL OTHER ROOMS: rooms in a given society vary within certain limits, and within this fixed range, the room in question is a low one. Similarly, (4.57a) states that the tree under consideration (*elka*) is a tall tree: it is adjudged tall with reference to the class of possible fir trees, the limits of which are fixed and are not relative to where the tree may be located at a given time. Thus the predicate LF *vysokaja* denotes the property (height) of the fir RELATIVE TO the class of fir trees, and not RELATIVE TO a room in which it may be or a function for which it may be intended.

These relations are particularly clear in (4.57b): *elka nevysokaja* means that the tree is a small tree, i.e. compared to the possible (fixed) range of fir trees, this one is a small one. However, although the tree is small with respect to the class of possible fir trees, it is big with respect to a particular room (*ona vse-taki vysoka dlja našej komnaty*).

Paragraph 4.4.3.1 demonstrates that BOTH THE PREDICATE LF AND SF DENOTE A RELATIVE PROPERTY OR QUALITY. Note, however, that the SF may express relativity only by means of its complement (cf. §4.4.2). For example, in (4.68b) the room is considered low (*nizka*) only with reference to high furniture: the relativity is expressed solely by the complement ([*dlja vysokoj mebeli*]$_{PP}$). Thus expression or non-expression of relativity is not an inherent property of the SF. This room, accordingly, cannot subsequently be characterized as a "low room" (*nizkaja komnata*) on the basis of the predication in (4.68b).

In contrast to the SF, the predicate LF's obligatory reference to the subject's class is not expressed by a deep-structure complement: it is "built into" the predicate LF. The form and the meaning of the predicate LF can be explained quite simply in terms of a deep-structure relative-clause configuration. According to this assumption, (4.73) and (4.74) have the same deep structure and, consequently, receive the same semantic interpretation. (4.74) is "closer" to the deep structure because it has undergone fewer transformations than (4.73) (Relative Clause Reduction, (S-Node Deletion), Case Marking, and Antecedent Deletion). Recall that in §4.3.3 it was noted that Buslaev paraphrases *èti doma novye* 'these houses are new (ones)' as *èti doma sut' doma novye* 'these houses are new houses'.

(4.73) *Èta elka vysokaja.*
'This fir is (a) big (one).'

(4.74) *Èta elka (est') elka, kotoraja vysoka.*[10]
'This fir is (a) fir, which is big.'

The deep structure of (4.73) and (4.74) is (4.75).

(4.75)

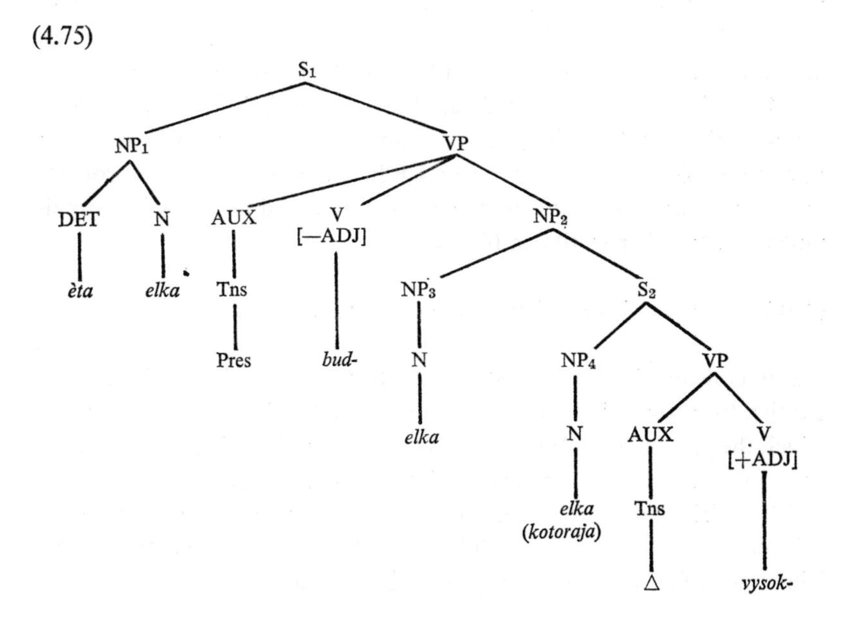

S_1, the "primary predication", states that the subject ([...*elka*]$_{NP1}$) is the member of a class (*èta elka (est') elka*...);[11] S_2, the "secondary predication", defines the place of the subject in this class (*elka (kotoraja) vysoka*).

[10] Sentence (4.74) is fully grammatical, yet it is low on the scale of acceptability. This is due to the fact that the OPTIONAL transformation of Relative Clause Reduction (followed by obligatory S-Node Deletion and Case Marking) almost always is applied in sentences of this type. Predictably, *èta elka (est') elka vysokaja* 'this fir is a big fir', which has the same deep structure as (4.73) and (4.74), is higher on the scale of acceptability than (4.74).

[11] A similar derivation of the predicate LF has been proposed by A. V. Isačenko (1963: 82-85). Sentences like *èta elka (est') elka*... are briefly mentioned in *Grammatika russkogo jazyka AN SSSR* (II, č. 1, 420) and Gvozdev (1961: 64, footnote 1).

It is quite natural that a deep-structure restrictive relative clause should be employed for the purpose of singling out a member from a class of similar objects.

Note once again that the meaning of the predicate LF and SF must be explained in terms of a deep-structure relative-clause configuration and an (optional) deep-structure complement respectively (cf. §4.4.1.1). The predicate LF (*vysokaja* in (4.73)) and the SF (*vysoka* in (4.74); *vysok* in (4.64b); *vysoki* in (4.64a)) both derive from the same deep-structure V [+ADJ] (*vysok-*), which, consequently, cannot explain the difference in meaning between the predicate LF and SF. The predicate LF is, in other words, a headless reduced relative clause and its meaning must always be accounted for in terms of its underlying relative-clause configuration.

4.4.3.2 The fact that the predicate LF contains "a built-in reference to class-membership" enables us to offer an EXPLANATION for why it cannot have a complement. If the predicate LF had a complement, the property or quality expressed by it would be relative to two different points simultaneously. In other words, in (4.76)

(4.76) **Èta elka vysokaja dlja našej komnaty.*

the fir is denoted as being tall relative to the class of possible firs and relative to a particular room simultaneously. The formal mechanism by which the grammar of Russian blocks sentences like (4.76) will be discussed in §4.6.3, where Antecedent Deletion is presented.

4.4.3.3 The notion that the predicate LF involves reference to the subject's "class-membership" while the SF does not is not a new discovery. Vinogradov (1947:263), for instance, observed that:

V suščnosti, pri predikativnom upotreblenii polnyx form imen prilagatel'nyx proisxodit podvedenie tex ili inyx predmetov pod izvestnye kategorii kačestva ili priznaka, kotorymi opredeljajutsja različija rodov i vidov veščej i lic.
[In essence with a predicative use of the full forms of adjectives there occurs a certain categorization of certain objects according to the quality or feature by which the differences in sort or type of things and persons are defined.]

Isačenko (1965:I, 196) is quite emphatic about the predicate LF and class membership:

V predloženii *Kitajskij jazyk očen' trudnyj* utverždaetsja (a) čto suščestvuet klass trudnyx jazykov, i (b) čto imenno kitajskij jazyk vključaetsja govorjaščim v ètot klass, myslitsja im kak èlement dannogo klassa.
[In the sentence *The Chinese language is very difficult*, it is maintained (a) that

there exists a class of difficult languages and (b) that Chinese is included by the speaker in this class, is thought of by him as an element of this class.]

Unfortunately, traditional grammar, due to the vagueness of its formulations, has been unable to elevate this random insight about the predicate LF to the status of a general rule of Russian syntax.

4.4.3.4 In the preceding sections it was demonstrated that traditional Russian grammar was incorrect in claiming that the predicate LF expresses an "absolute property". We may thus state that the predicate LF's most characteristic feature is its obligatory reference to the subject's class and its inability to express an "absolute property". The SF expresses a "relative property" only by virtue of its complement (cf. (4.68) and (4.69)). IT IS ONLY THE SF WITHOUT A DEEP STRUCTURE COMPLEMENT THAT CAN EXPRESS A PROPERTY OR QUALITY ABSOLUTELY, i.e. without reference to either the subject's class or a particular "circumstance" (time, place, person, etc., cf. (4.63)-(4.66)). For example, (4.77a) states that the Chinese language is difficult IN COMPARISON TO OTHER LANGUAGES. (4.77b) states that the Chinese language is difficult FOR A PARTICULAR PERSON. (4.77c) merely states that the Chinese language is difficult WITHOUT SPECIFYING whether it is difficult with respect to the class of human languages or with respect to the particular person trying to master it.

(4.77a) *Kitajskij jazyk (očen') trudnyj.*
'The Chinese language is (very) difficult.'
(4.77b) *Kitajskij jazyk (očen)' truden dlja školnika pervogo klassa.*
'The Chinese language is (very) difficult for a first-grade pupil.'
(4.77c) *Kitajskij jazyk (očen') truden.*
'The Chinese language is (very) difficult.'

(4.78) illustrates the same relationship as (4.77).

(4.78a) *Elka vysokaja.*
'(This) fir is a big one.'
(4.78b) *Elka vysoka dlja našej komnaty.*
'(This) fir is (too) big for our room.' (although it may not be big as firs go)
(4.78c) *Elka vysoka.*
'This fir is big.' (cf. (4.73)-(4.75))

Example (4.79) is a rather nice confirmation of our assumption that the predicate LF and the SF denote a *otnositel'nyj priznak* (relative property) and that it is the SF WITHOUT A COMPLEMENT that expresses a *bezotnositel'nyj* or *absoljutnyj priznak* (absolute property).

(4.79a) **Prostranstvo beskonečnoe.*
(4.79b) **Prostranstvo beskonečno dlja nas.*
(4.79c) *Prostranstvo beskonečno.*
'Space is infinite.'

(4.79a) is impossible because *prostranstvo* 'space' is a "unique" noun, i.e. it does not belong to a class of similar objects. In other words, it forms a class with one member and, consequently, cannot be modified by a restrictive relative clause (cf. §4.5.3). Since there is no class of "spaces" it follows that *prostranstvo* cannot take a predicate LF, which invariably makes reference to the subject's class-membership. Sentence (4.79b) is impossible because space is not infinite with respect to any one person, place, etc. Only (4.79c) is possible because the SF without a complement makes no reference to class-membership or "particular circumstance" (i.e. person, place, time, function, etc.).[12]

The ungrammaticality of sentences like (4.79a) can be predicted and EXPLAINED only in terms of the deep-structure relative-clause origin of the predicate LF that has been proposed in Chapter 4. The traditional Russian treatment, which claims that the predicate LF denotes a "permanent" property of the subject and that the SF denotes a "temporary" or occasional property or state, predicts that (4.79a) should be grammatical and that (4.79c) should be ungrammatical.

4.4.3.5 FURTHER REMARKS ON THE PREDICATE LF AND EXPRESSION OF A *postojannyj priznak* 'PERMANENT PROPERTY' (cf. §4.4.1.1). In §4.4.3.4 it was demonstrated that the predicate LF does not denote an "absolute property"; it obligatorily denotes a property or quality RELATIVE TO THE SUBJECT'S CLASS. The SF is noncommittal with respect to its subject's class and only the SF without a complement can denote a property absolutely. It was also demonstrated that an underlying restrictive relative-clause configuration fully explains the semantic interpretation of the predicate LF.

[12] The ability of the SF without a complement to denote an "absolute property" most likely explains why many Russian grammarians feel that the SF is more "categorical" (*kategoričnyj*) than the predicate LF (cf. G. F. Mjasnikov, 1958: 12; N. Ju. Švedova, 1952: 90; M. Kubik, 1968: 27: "s pomošč'ju kratkoj formy počerkivaetsja kategoričnyj xarakter utverždaemogo priznaka (zemlja prekrasna)" [with the aid of a SF the categorical nature of the feature asserted (the land is beautiful) is emphasized]).

These facts require that we return to §4.4.1.1, where it was established that the ability of the predicate LF to denote a permanent property of the subject can be traced back to an underlying relative-clause configuration with a "generic" noun (cf. §4.3.3) like *čelovek* as its head (cf. (4.29), (4.32), (4.33); (4.52)). However, sentences like (4.56a), (4.57a), (4.68a), (4.69a), (4.77a), etc., are all interpreted as denoting a permanent property of the subject despite the fact that the deep-structure head noun is not a "generic" noun but is in all instances IDENTICAL to the matrix subject (cf. (4.31), the deep structure of *èti doma novye*).

This phenomenon can be explained quite satisfactorily in terms of §4.4.3.1 and §4.4.3.4. More specifically, the predicate LF is interpreted as denoting a permanent property or quality of the subject when the class of objects it makes reference to is a permanent, fixed, "non-linguistic" class (cf. §4.4.3.1). For example, in (4.73) *vysokaja* is interpreted as denoting a permanent property of *elka* because the class of fir trees, with respect to range of height, is fixed and is independent of time and place. Similarly, (4.68a) (*Komnata nizkaja*) is equivalent to *This room is a low one*, and, since the height of rooms varies within a fixed range, *nizkaja* is interpreted as denoting a permanent property of *komnata*. The interpretation of sentences containing a predicate LF that does not make reference to permanent or fixed classes will be discussed in §4.4.4. PREDICTABLY, THESE PREDICATE LFS ARE NOT INTERPRETED AS DENOTING A PERMANENT PROPERTY.

4.4.4 THE PREDICATE LF FULFILLS A RESTRICTIVE FUNCTION. In the preceding section it was shown that a predicate LF which is derived by the deletion of a head noun that is IDENTICAL to the matrix subject (cf. (4.31)) may denote a permanent property of the subject. However, as the following sentences demonstrate, a predicate LF derived by the deletion of a head noun identical to the subject need NOT obligatorily denote a permanent quality as traditional Russian grammar claims it must (cf. §4.4.1).

(4.80a) *Iz dvux protivopoložnyx suždenij vsegda odno istinnoe, drugoe ložnoe.*
'Of two opposing opinions, one is always (the) true (one), and the other (the) false (one).'

(4.80b) *Iz dvux protivopoložnyx suždenij vsegda odno istinno, drugoe ložno.*
'Of two opposing opinions, one is always true, and the other false.'

The primary function of the predicate LF in (4.80a) cannot be denotation of permanency, since the SF in (4.80b) fulfills the same function (cf. §4.4.1).

(4.81a) –*Kotoryj iz ètix primerov* pravil'nyj?
'Which of these (two) examples is (the) correct (one)?'

(4.81b) –*Oba* pravil'ny.
'Both are correct.'
(Izrailevič, 1955:333; Ušakov, 1935, entry for *kotoryj*.)

Once again we see that the predicate LF (4.81a) and the SF (4.81b) do not differ with respect to expression of permanency. The difference between the predicate LF and SF in (4.81) boils down to the following: the predicate LF makes reference to the class of objects to which the subject belongs. In (4.81a) the predicate LF serves to single one out of a class of two (NB: "which one is the correct one"). Since this particular class of two is not a permanent or fixed class (it is created in discourse), the predicate LF is not felt to denote a permanent property of the subject. Any notion of permanency in (4.81) must be explained in terms of the lexical meaning of the adjectives and the broader "semantic context". Since the SF is not derived from an underlying restrictive relative-clause configuration, it does not have this "restrictive" function (cf. (4.80)). The following examples will make this meaning of the predicate LF clearer.

(4.82) *Ja vas tože očen' ljublju, Sonečka....*
Vitja, otčego vy odin grustnyj?
'I love you very much too, Sonečka....
Vitja, why are you the only one sad?' (Aldanov)

In (4.82) there is a group of three (class of three) and Vitja is being singled out as being the only one of the three who is sad. This class of three from which the subject (*Vitja* = *vy*) is singled out is not a fixed class; it has been created in discourse and has no validity beyond this particular situation. It is for this reason that *grustnyj* 'sad' is not interpreted as being a permanent characteristic of Vitja. Thus it is clear that the primary function of the predicate LF is identical to that of a restrictive relative clause: it serves to select one out of a class or set. If the class happens to be a fixed, non-linguistic class (cf. (4.78a)), the predicate LF is felt to denote a permanent property of the subject. If the class happens to be created in discourse (as in (4.82)), the predicate LF is not interpreted as denoting a permanent property of the subject.

(4.83) *Sleduet imet' v vidu, čto, kak bylo skazano vyše, izložennaja zdes' sistema... ne edinstvenno vozmožnaja.*
'One should bear in mind that, as was mentioned above, the system presented here... is not the only possible one.'

(4.84) *V osobennosti u nego ètot god trudnyj. On ved' tol'ko čto dissertaciju zaščiščal.*
'This year has been a particularly difficult one for him. He just defended his dissertation.'

In (4.84) one particular year in a man's life is singled out. Thus the class from which one year is selected is all the past years in the subject's life.

(4.85a) *Èto vino vkusnoe.*
(4.85b) *Èto vino vkusno.*[13]

(4.85b) states that a particular wine is good; it may be translated as 'This wine is good'. No mention is made of whether the subject ever tasted wine before. (4.85a) states that a particular wine is good as wines go, i.e. the speaker compares this wine to other wine he has tasted. Accordingly, (4.85a) can be translated as 'This is a good wine'. Note that both the SF and the predicate LF in (4.85) denote a "permanent property" and can be uttered on the same occasion; the difference is expression of past experience (4.85a) as opposed to non-expression of past experience.

(4.86) *Karta byla* trudnaja, *potomu čto v prežnix kartax mnogoe bylo naputano i teper' vse prixodilos' delat' snačala.*
'(This) map was a difficult one because much was mixed up in the earlier maps and now everything had to be done over.'
(Kaverin)

In (4.86) it is stated that a map (*karta*) is difficult with respect to the class or set of maps done by a particular person. In other words, this map is singled out of the class of maps done by a particular person.

(4.87a) *Obstojatel'stva i pričiny smerti moej ves'ma fotogeničeskoj materi byli dovol'no* original'nye *(piknik, molnija).*
'The circumstances and reasons for the death of my very

[13] This example and its explication were suggested by R. Jakobson (personal communication).

photogenic mother were quite *original* (ones) (a picnic, lightning).' (Nabokov)

(4.87b) *Velikoe proizvedenie iskusstva vsegda* original'no.
'A great work of art is always *original* (*an original one).'

(4.88) –*Vaše podozrenie soveršenno* nepravdopodobnoe.
'Your suspicion is completely *improbable*.'
–*Ja, naprotiv, dumaju, čto ono vpolne* pravdopodobno.
'I, on the contrary, think that it is quite *probable*.'[14]

4.4.4.1 The fact that the predicate LF serves a restrictive function has been recognized by Russian grammarians working in the traditional framework, but the significance of this fact was not fully understood. For example, I. A. Kudrjavceva (1967:133) has noted that:

Polnye formy mogut oboznačat' priznak, vydeljajuščij predmet iz rjada drugix. [Full forms can denote a feature which singles out an object from a series of others.]

[14] The following sentence is another example of the restrictive function of the predicate LF:

Vy verno videli v Luvre poxožee bjuro, prinadležavšee Ljudoviku XV. Razumeetsja, to neizmerimo lučše, no i moe nedurnoe.... (Aldanov)
'You surely saw in the Louvre a similar desk which belonged to Louis XV. Of course, that one is immeasurably better, but mine is not bad.'
(NB: *Golos byl* neduren. '(Her) voice was *not bad*' (cf. Ušakov, 1935))

It has been pointed out in several different places that after the Passive transformation changes a perfective verb from $\underset{[-\mathrm{ADJ}]}{\mathrm{V}}$ to $\underset{[+\mathrm{ADJ}]}{\mathrm{V}}$, there are no transformational rules that are capable of distinguishing a deep-structure $\underset{[+\mathrm{ADJ}]}{\mathrm{V}}$ ("adjective") and a derived $\underset{[+\mathrm{ADJ}]}{\mathrm{V}}$ (past passive participle). If this observation is correct, we would expect to find predicate LFs of the past passive participle with a restrictive meaning. As the following example shows, sentences of this kind are indeed possible in Russian, although they are infrequent:

No čto-to šeptalo ej, čto ona sebja zamarala, čto ona odna zamarannaja *sredi nix, čistyx.*
'But something whispered to her that she had sullied herself, that she was the only sullied one among them, (those) pure ones'. (V. Panova)

The class of people from among whom the subject *ona* is being singled out is the subject's family. The restrictive meaning of the predicate LF is particularly strong in this example.

A. Boguslavskij's (1964:19) comments on the predicate LF's restrictive function are quite interesting.

4.4.4.2 Our examination of the full range of traditional statements concerning the meaning of the SF and the predicate LF allows us to conclude that the primary function of the predicate LF is the same as that of a restrictive relative clause. In other words, the predicate LF serves to single out the subject of the sentence from among a class or set of similar objects. Whether or not the property or quality denoted by the predicate LF is interpreted as being a "permanent property" depends entirely on the lexical items involved and on the "stability" of the class from which the subject is singled out (cf. §4.4.4). As previously noted, both the predicate LF and the SF can denote either a permanent or a non-permanent property of the subject; it is therefore meaningless to claim that the predicate LF's primary function is expression of a permanent property.

This restrictive function of the predicate LF can be most easily explained by our assumption that the predicate LF derives from an underlying restrictive relative-clause configuration ([NP — S]$_{NP}$) and that the surface-structure category known as "predicate LF" is in fact nothing more than a headless reduced relative clause functioning as a "nominal predicate" ([*bud-* — NP]$_{VP}$) (cf. §4.6; H. G. Lunt (1959: §21.3) discusses LF "active participles" in OCS that are equivalent to relative clauses). This explanation accounts explicitly for the predicate LF's semantic interpretation and formal properties (cf. §4.5).

The rather narrow range of semantic interpretation of the predicate LF (in contrast to the SF) is explained by the deep-structure relative-clause configuration which INVARIABLY underlies the predicate LF. The SF's relatively wide range of semantic interpretation is explained by the fact that the SF does NOT derive from a underlying relative clause and, therefore, does not obligatorily make reference to a class of which the subject is a member. In addition, the SF's wide range of semantic interpretation is explained by the SF's ability to take complements and, finally, by the SF's verbal nature. The SF does not express the opposite of the predicate LF's restrictive meaning; it simply leaves reference to the subject's class-membership unspecified or unmentioned.

Speaking in terms proposed by R. Jakobson (1957:5), we can claim that the LF is MARKED for reference to the subject's class and that the SF is UNMARKED, i.e. it is noncommittal with respect to mention of the subject's class. The unmarked term always has a wider range of meaning than the marked term. Since the SF is unmarked, it may replace the predicate

LF when explicit restrictive reference is deemed unnecessary (cf. (4.80) and (4.85)).[15]

4.5 Formal Properties of the Predicate LF.

4.5.1 The following analysis of the formal or syntactic properties of the predicate LF demonstrates that these properties can be EXPLAINED simply and insightfully in terms of a deep-structure relative-clause configuration.

4.5.2 ADJECTIVES LIKE *rad.* It was pointed out in §4.2.2 that JUST THOSE ADJECTIVES (*rad-*, *dolž # n-*, AND *gorazd-*) THAT MUST BE MARKED AS EXCEPTIONS TO THE RELATIVE CLAUSE REDUCTION TRANSFORMATION DO NOT HAVE PREDICATE LFS. For example, *rad-* 'glad' does not have a predicate LF (cf. (4.17)) and (4.89b) must be blocked by marking the lexical item *rad-* an exception to the rule of Relative Clause Reduction.[16]

(4.89a) [*devuška, kotoraja rada vas videt'*]$_{NP}$
('the girl who is glad to see you')

(4.89b) [**devuška, radaja vas videt'*]$_{NP}$

If our grammar of Russian derives the predicate LF from a deep-structure relative-clause configuration contained in a VP ([*bud-* — [NP — S]$_{NP}$]$_{VP}$) by a sequence of transformations that includes Relative Clause Reduction, then it is wholly predictable that just those adjectives that cannot undergo Relative Clause Reduction will not have a predicate LF.

Note also that just those adjectives that must be marked as exceptions to Relative Clause Reduction do not appear in prenominal position (cf. [**radaja vas videt' devuška*]$_{NP}$). If prenominal adjectives are transformationally introduced (by Modifier Shift) into prenominal position from a reduced relative clause, as we have tried to prove in Chapter 1, then the non-occurrence of prenominal **radaja*, **radyj*, etc., can also be explained quite naturally by the fact that *rad-* is an exception to Relative Clause Reduction.

Taxonomic grammars of Russian are unable to explain the fact that the adjectives that are exceptions to Relative Clause Reduction do not occur

[15] Note that the transformational framework provides some insight into the valuable notion of "marked and unmarked grammatical categories": a marked surface-structure category possesses a deep-structure constituent (or, perhaps, feature in the case of verbal aspect) that the unmarked category does not.

[16] This argument, of course, rests on the assumption that a SF in a relative clause becomes a LF after Relative Clause Reducation as the result of S-Node Deletion and Case Marking. We are in effect stating that *rad-* does not have a LF because it is never introduced into the constituency of a NP.

in prenominal position and do not have a predicate LF. A transformational grammar of Russian is able to account for these facts explicitly in terms of a single restriction on Relative Clause Reduction, provided that it derives prenominal adjectives and the predicate LF (which before Antecedent Deletion is really an "attributive adjective") from a deep-structure relative clause.

4.5.3 SUBJECTS THAT PRECLUDE A LF IN THE PREDICATE. In §4.4.3.4 it was pointed out that a LF is not possible as the predicate of a sentence whose subject is a unique noun, i.e. a noun that comprises a class of one and, accordingly, cannot be modified by a restrictive adjunct (cf. (4.48)-(4.51); *voda* {*prozračna* / **prozračnaja*} 'water is transparent'). This syntactic phenomenon can be adequately explained only if our grammar of Russian incorporates the main point of Chapter 4: the predicate LF is derived from an underlying restrictive relative clause configuration.[17] There are, in addition, other types of subjects that preclude a LF in the predicate. These sentences will be discussed in the following section. Note that just those subjects that cannot have a LF as their predicate cannot be modified by a relative clause and cannot take a prenominal adjective.

4.5.3.1 If the subject of a sentence is *èto* 'this, it', *vsë* 'all, everything', *čto* 'that, which', *to* (*čto*...) 'it, what', *ničto* 'nothing', etc., only the SF is possible (cf. *Grammatika russkogo jazyka AN SSSR*, II, *č*. I, 445; Švedova, 1952:97).

(4.90) *On prišel provodit' menja, čto bylo očen'* {**ljubeznoe* / *ljubezno* / **ljubeznym*} s ego *storony*.
'He came to see me off, which was very nice of him.'

(4.91) *Vy xotite ugovorit' ego poexat' s vami? Èto budet* {**trudnym* / *trudno* / **trudnoe*}.
'You want to persuade him to go with you? That will be difficult.'

(4.92) *To, čto on skazal, bylo očen'* {**interesnym* / *interesno* / **interesnoe*}.

[17] Given the fact that a unique noun cannot normally be modified by a restrictive relative clause, it is predictable that a unique noun will not normally have a prenominal adjective, since our grammar derives prenominal adjective from reduced relative clause.

'What he said was very interesting.'

(4.93) *Vsë, čto ona govorila, bylo* {**pravil'nym* / *pravil'no* / **pravil'noe*}.

'All that she was saying was correct.'

(4.94) *Ničto ne novo pod lunoj.*

'Nothing is new under the moon.'

(4.95) *Ja znaju, čto blagorodno i čto čestno.*

'I know what's noble and what's honest.'

If the subject of a sentence is an INFINITIVE, the predicate LF cannot function as the predicate. Surface-structure infinitive subjects derive from deep-structure sentential subjects ($[S]_{NP}$), most often by Equi-NP Deletion.

(4.96) *Kurit' (papirosy)* {*vredno* / **vrednoe*}.

'It is harmful to smoke (cigarettes).'

(4.97) *Rodit'–trudno, naučit čeloveka dobru ešče trudnee.*

'Giving birth is difficult; teaching a person Good is even more difficult.' (Gor'kij)

(4.98a) *Sidet' v temnoj komnate skučno.*

'To sit in a dark room is boring.'

(4.98b) *Skučno sidet' v temnoj komnate.*

'It is boring to sit in a dark room.'[18]

If the subject of a sentence is a true verbal noun (*kurenie* 'smoking', not *proiznošenie* 'pronunciation'), only the SF can appear in the predicate.

(4.99) *Kurenie (papiros)* {*vredno* / **vrednoe*}.

'Smoking (cigarettes) is dangerous.'

[18] Traditional Russian grammar claims that (4.98a) and (4.98b) are synonymous but have different structures: (4.98a) is felt to be a common subject-predicate sentence (*dvusostavnoe predloženie*) with the infinitive phrase as subject; (4.98b) is felt to be an impersonal sentence. It is possible to account for these intuitive statements about (4.98) by deriving both sentences from the same deep structure. (4.98a) is closer to the deep structure ([*sidet' v temnoj komnate*]$_{NP}$[*skučno*]$_{VP}$.) and (4.98b) is derived from the P-marker underlying (4.98a) by Extraposition (note the English gloss of (4.98)). Recall footnote 14, Chapter 3, where it was proposed that the Russian version of Extraposition converts a P-marker like $[[\ S\ ]_{NP} — [\ V\ ]_{VP}\ ]_S$ into $[[\ V — S\ ]_{VP}\ ]_S$ and that an impersonal sentence is to be defined by the (derived) configuration $[\ VP\ ]_S$ (cf. Galkina-Fedoruk, 1957: 138; Dobromyslov and Rozental', 1960: 171).

(4.100) *Kupanie v žarkij den'* {*prijatno* / **prijatnoe*}.
'Swimming on a hot day is pleasant.'
NB: *Kupat'sja v žarkij den' prijatno.*
'It is pleasant to swim on a hot day.'

4.5.3.2 AN IMPORTANT GENERALIZATION ABOUT RUSSIAN THAT WAS MISSED BY TRADITIONAL RUSSIAN GRAMMAR. As the above sentences show, there are several different types of subjects that cannot take a predicate LF.[19] Russian taxonomic grammar merely lists them without attempting to determine why it is precisely these subjects that preclude a predicate LF. In other words, traditional Russian grammar never raised the question of whether those subjects that exclude a predicate LF form a natural class with respect to some semantic or syntactic property (other than preclusion of a predicate LF). Transformational grammar provides a framework in which questions of this kind are raised. An examination of this set of subjects reveals that they DO have at least one syntactic property in common: none of them can be modified by a restrictive relative clause (nor, consequently, can they be modified by a prenominal adjective with a restrictive function (cf. §1.11)). This observation allows us to make an extremely important generalization about modern Russian: A SUBJECT THAT CANNOT BE RELATIVIZED CANNOT TAKE A PREDICATE LF. The fact that unique nouns like *prostranstvo* 'space' (cf. (4.48)) cannot take a predicate LF is thus just a special case of this broader generalization.

This important fact about Russian can be EXPLAINED if our grammar derives a predicate LF from a deep-structure relative clause. The subject NP of a sentence containing a predicate LF is identical to the head NP of the relative clause, i.e. NP_1 is identical to NP_3 in (4.101).

Since NP_1 is identical to NP_3, any restriction that applies to NP_3 will automatically apply to NP_1, the matrix sentence's subject. Thus if NP_3 contains a noun that cannot be relativized, it is predictable that an ungrammatical sentence like (4.48b) will be generated from such a deep

[19] The inventory of subject types in §4.5.3.1 that preclude a predicate LF is not exhaustive. To cite and discuss the additional material would strengthen my arguments but would require excessive space. The relation between subject nouns with modifiers and choice of predicate adjective are of particular interest (cf. Švedova, 1952: 100; *Grammatika russkogo jazyka AN SSSR*, II, č. I: 450; Judina, et al., 1966: 9: "Kratkaja forma objazatel'na, esli pri podležaščem est' soglasovannoe opredelenie." [The SF is obligatory if there is in the subject an agreeing attribute]).

(4.101)

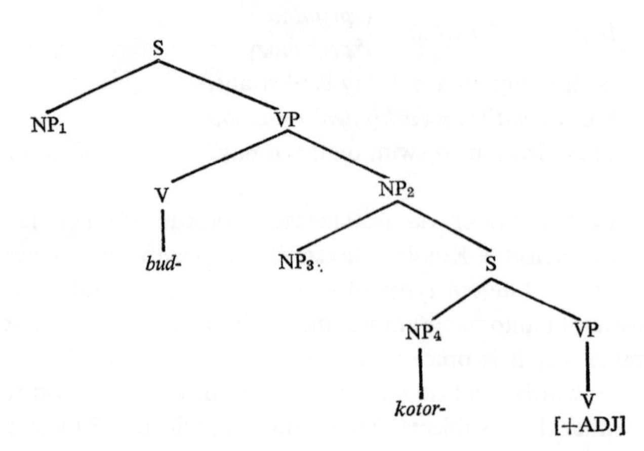

structure. In other words, *[*Prostranstvo*]$_{NP1}$ *beskonečnoe* (approximately *'Space is an infinite one') is ungrammatical because, at a deeper level, [*prostranstvo*]$_{NP3}$ appears in a restrictive relative-clause configuration ([NP_3 + S]$_{NP2}$).[20]

The fact that it is just those subjects which cannot be modified by a restrictive adjunct that cannot take a predicate LF constitutes the strongest single piece of evidence yet offered that the predicate LF derives from a deep-structure relative-clause configuration. If our grammar of Russian did not derive the predicate LF from an underlying relative-clause configuration, the facts presented about Russian in §4.5.3 and §4.5.3.1 could not be explained in a non-ad hoc manner.

Paragraphs 4.5.3 and 4.5.3.1 firmly establish the fact that, speaking in surface-structure terms, IT IS THE SUBJECT OF THE SENTENCE THAT DETERMINES WHETHER OR NOT A LF MAY APPEAR IN THE PREDICATE. This is an empirical fact about Russian, and it must be accounted for by any grammar of Russian, no matter what kind it is.[21] If the relative-clause origin of the predicate LF is not adopted in our grammar of Russian, we will be forced to set up an extremely complex, ad hoc set of "subject-predicate adjective" selectional restrictions in order to account for the non-occurrence of sentences like **Prostranstvo beskonečnoe* and **Kurit' vrednoe*. If, however, the relative-clause origin of the predicate LF is adopted, our grammar will

[20] This same constraint on the relativizability of a unique noun will also account for the ungrammaticality of **(èto) prostranstvo (est') prostranstvo beskonečnoe* *'(this) space is an infinite space'.

[21] To the best of my knowledge, this transformational grammar is the first treatment of Russian to make this important observation.

have no need of selectional restrictions of this kind: NP_1 (cf. (4.101)) is identical to NP_3, and, consequently, the ungrammaticality of sentences like **Prostranstvo beskonečnoe* and **Èto bylo interesnoe* can be accounted for by the more general, independently motivated constraint on relativizability.

4.5.4 The agreement of the predicate with *vy* 'you' when *vy* refers to one person.

4.5.4.1 In all the following sentences *vy* 'you' refers to a single individual (female) and is used to express politeness (*vežlivost'*).

(4.102a) *Vy krasivy.*
'You are pretty.'
(4.102b) *Vy krasivaja.*
'You are (a) pretty (woman).'
(4.102c) **Vy krasivye.*
(4.102d) **Vy krasiva.*
(4.103a) *Vy, Maša, zabyli ob ètom.*
'You, Maša, forgot about that.'
(4.103b) **Vy, Maša, zabyla ob ètom.*
(4.104a) *Vy, Maša, zabyvaete o samom važnom.*
'You, Maša, are forgetting about the most important thing.'
(4.104b) **Vy, Maša, zabyvaeš' o samom važnom.*
(4.105a) *Vy byli krasivy.*
'You were pretty.'
(4.105b) *Vy* byli *krasivaja.*
(4.105c) *Vy* byli *krasivoj.*[22]
(4.105d) **Vy byli krasivye.*
(4.105e) **Vy byli krasivymi.*
(4.105f) **Vy byla* {*krasiva* / *krasivy* / *krasivaja* / *krasivoj*}.
(4.106a) *Vy nasmešnica.*
'You are a scoffer.'
(4.106b) **Vy nasmešnicy.*

[22] (4.105c) is more common than (4.105b). The following is another example of the same phenomenon (cf. *Příruční mluvnice ruštiny*, 1966: 153): *Vy byli takoj grustnoj včera* 'You were so sad yesterday' (cf. footnotes 1 and 2, Chapter 4). The important point here is that *byli* is in the plural and *(takoj) grustnoj* is in the singular, yet both are said to "agree" with the subject *vy*. This phenomenon is, of course, obscured in the present tense, since the copula is realized as zero. Unfortunately, Russian grammars usually discuss predicate "agreement" with *vy* in the present tense.

Russian grammars state merely that when the subject of a sentence is *vy* and refers to one person, the SF must be in the PLURAL (4.102a) and the predicate LF must be in the SINGULAR (4.102b). It is also noted that the LF agrees with *vy* in case (the nominative; cf. (4.102b) and (4.105b)).

Taxonomic Russian grammar regards this kind of agreement as irregular or anomalous when compared to subject-predicate agreement not involving the subject *vy* (cf. Gvozdev, 1961: II, 77. Gvozdev includes his remarks on agreement with *vy* under the heading "*Narušenie i otsutstvie soglasovanija*" [Violation and absence of agreement]). On the other hand, a transformational grammar of Russian that incorporates the derivations of the SF and predicate LF proposed in the preceding chapters can demonstrate that the agreement phenomena involving *vy* in (4.102)-(4.106) all reflect DEEPER REGULARITIES and are wholly predictable. In other words, it can be demonstrated that predicate agreement with *vy* is not anomalous.

The relative-clause origin of the predicate LF was proposed to account for semantic and syntactic phenomena that have nothing to do with sentences containing *vy* as subject (cf. §3.9 and §4.1-§4.5.3). The fact that it also enables our grammar to capture previously unobserved regularities about agreement of *vy* with its predicate must be considered a very strong piece of evidence supporting the relative-clause origin of the predicate LF.

4.5.4.2 An examination of the data presented in (4.102)-(4.106) reveals that the agreement of the SF with *vy* is identical to the agreement of a verb with *vy* (cf. (4.103)): both agree only in number (Russian does not distinguish gender in the plural). The fact that both a verb and SF have the same kind of agreement with *vy* can be accounted for by the fact that the SF is itself a verb (i.e. a $\underset{[+\text{ADJ}]}{\text{V}}$; cf. Chapter 2): both a verb ($\underset{[-\text{ADJ}]}{\text{V}}$) and a SF undergo Subject-V Agreement (cf. (4.107)).

(4.107) THE SUBJECT-V AGREEMENT TRANSFORMATION.[23]

$$\begin{array}{llllll} \text{SD:} & \text{X} & - \ \text{NP} & - \ \text{V} & - \ \text{X} & \\ & 1 & 2 & 3 & 4 & \Longrightarrow \\ & & \begin{bmatrix}\text{NUMB}\\ \text{GEND}\\ \text{PERS}\end{bmatrix} & & & \\ \text{SC:} & 1 & 2 & 3 & 4 & \\ & & & \begin{bmatrix}\text{NUMB}\\ \text{GEND}\\ \text{PERS}\end{bmatrix} & & \end{array}$$

[23] It seems at this point in the transformational investigation of Russian syntax that

Thus the behavior of a SF when the subject is *vy* is entirely regular once it is recognized that the SF is a V (note that the SD of (4.107) does not specify the feature [+ADJ] or [—ADJ] on the V).

4.5.4.3 Most Russian grammarians consider predicate agreement with *vy* (referring to one person) anomalous because: (i) while the SF must be in the PLURAL, the LF (nominative or instrumental) must be in the SINGULAR (cf. (4.102)); (ii) while LF must be in the SINGULAR, the copula must be in the plural (cf. (4.105) and footnote 22, Chapter 4), yet both are said to agree with *vy*. From the point of view of a taxonomic grammar, these facts certainly do seem to constitute anomalous subject-predicate agreement.

However, an examination of the data presented in (4.102)-(4.106) allows us to educe an extremely important fact. The predicate LF behaves just like a predicate noun with respect to agreement with *vy*: both must be in the singular (cf. (4.106); §3.9: (3.171)-(3.172); §3.10.2).[24] The noun-like behavior of the predicate LF manifests itself in the following three ways when *vy* is the subject: (a) both the noun and the LF must be in the SINGULAR (cf. (4.102) and (4.106)); (b) the copula must be in the PLURAL (cf. (4.105), *Vy byli durak(-om)* 'You were a fool'); (c) both the predicate LF and predicate noun may be in the instrumental singular (cf. (4.105c) and footnote 22).

Given the relative-clause origin of the predicate LF proposed in §3.9, it is entirely predictable that a predicate LF and predicate noun behave identically in "agreement" with *vy*: they are both predicate nominals with essentially the same surface structures. The deep structure of any predicate nominal in Russian may be abstractly represented by (4.108).

Any surface-structure constituent of NP_2 may be termed a predicate nominal (LF, N, N + LF, LF + N, N + relative clause, etc.).

Accordingly, the deep structure of *Vy byli durakom* 'You were a fool' is (4.109).

---

the feature [animate] must be also copied by the Subject-V Agreement transformation in order to generate sentences like *Ja znaju umnogo professora* 'I know a smart professor' and block sentences like **Ja znaju umnyj professora*, since it is the feature complex $\begin{bmatrix} +\text{ANIM} \\ +\text{ACC} \\ +\text{MASC} \\ +\text{SING} \end{bmatrix}$ that is realized in the surface structure in a form that coincides with the genitive (*-ogo*).

[24] The fact that the SF (and past passive participle) behave like a verb and the predicate LF behaves like a predicate noun in agreement with *vy* was observed in some traditional grammars (cf. V. V. Vinogradov, 1947: 266).

(4.108)

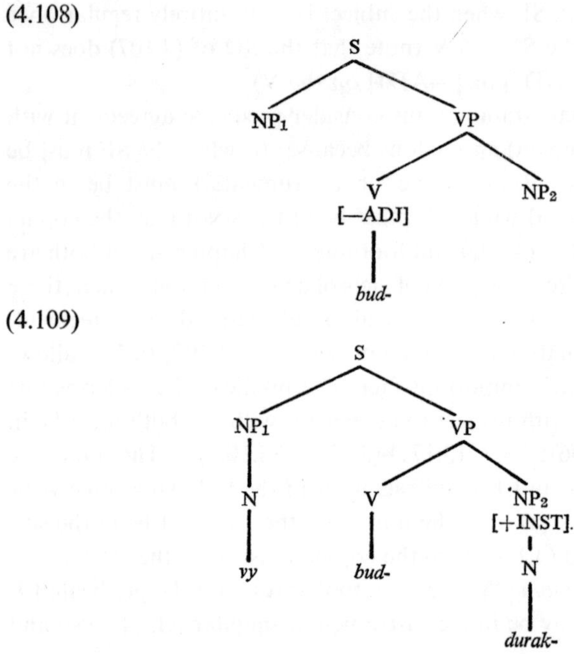

(4.109)

NP₂ has the case feature [instrumental] as a result of "government" by the V *bud-*. *Durak-* is marked [+INST] (*durakom*) by the Case Marking rule (3.24). The Subject-V Agreement transformation (4.107) copies the features of the subject *vy* ([+PLUR], [+II]) onto the main V *bud-*. These transformations convert (4.109) into (4.110), the surface structure of *Vy byli durakom.*

(4.110)

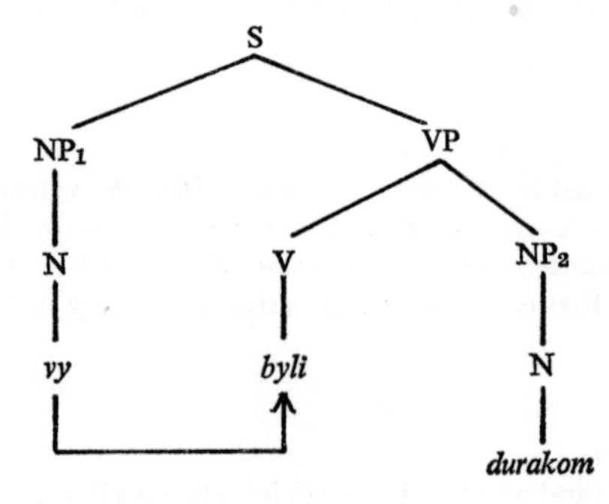

Note that *bud-* is in the plural as a result of Subject-V Agreement. There is no transfer of syntactic features (i.e. agreement (see arrow in (4.110))) between $[vy]_{NP1}$ and $[durakom]_{NP2}$.

The deep structure of (4.105c) is (4.111); irrelevant details have been omitted.[25]

(4.111)

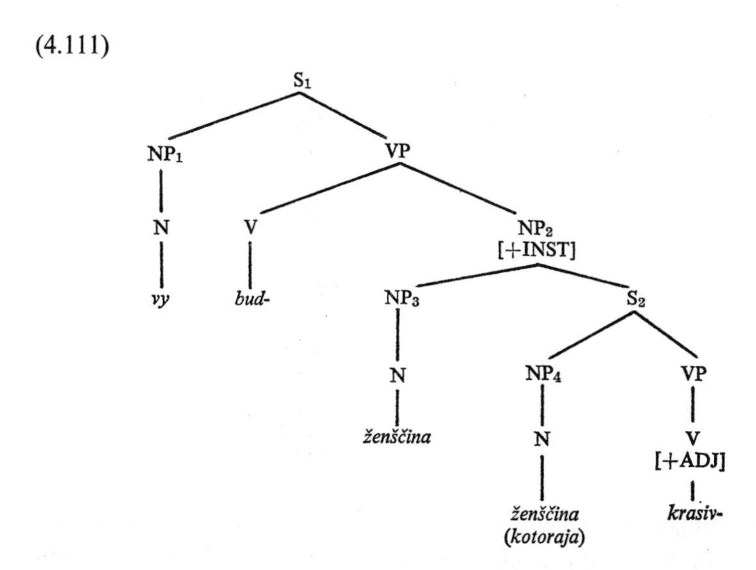

On the first cycle, Subject-V Agreement will copy the syntactic features from $[\textit{ženščina}]_{NP4}$ onto *krasiv-*. Relative Clause Formation then changes the subject of S_2 $[\textit{ženščina}]_{NP4}$ to *kotoraja* 'which'. On the last cycle (S_1), Relative Clause Reduction, S-Node Deletion, Case Marking, and Antecedent Deletion (NP_3) produce the intermediate derived P-marker (4.112).

The Case Marking transformation copies the case feature from NP_2, which is "governed" by the V *bud-*, onto *krasiv-*. Notice that the predicate LF is derived from what would emerge as a SF by the acquisition of a case feature. Notice too that traditional Russian grammarians are right when they claim that the predicate LF is marked for case, but they are wrong when they claim that the predicate LF agrees in case with the subject: the case feature comes from NP_2, not $[vy]_{NP1}$. In other words, neither *krasivoj* in (4.105c) nor *krasivaja* in (4.105b) agrees with *vy* in case.

[25] The deep structure of (4.105c) should most likely be more abstract: instead of a noun like *ženščina* 'woman', it should contain the more abstract N [+PRO] [+ANIM] [+FEM]. Similarly, *čelovek* should be merely a feature bundle at the level of deep structure.

(4.112)

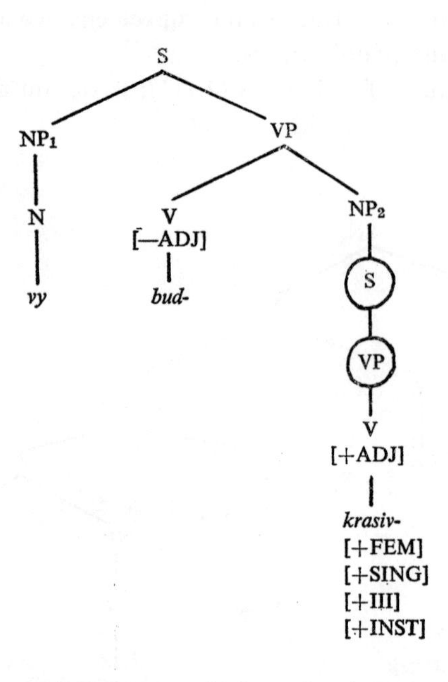

Finally, Subject-V Agreement, which copies the syntactic features from *vy* onto *bud-*, will map the intermediate P-marker (4.112) into the final derived P-marker (4.113).

Note that *krasiv-* [+FEM] [+SING] [+III] [+INST] is realized as *krasivoj.*

(4.113)

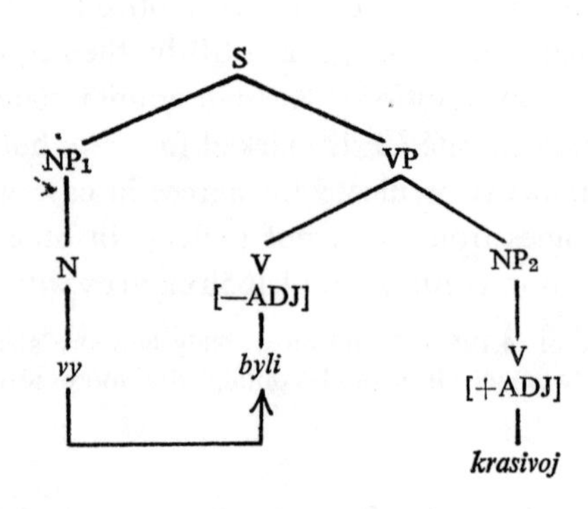

Observe that (4.113), the surface structure of (4.105c), is essentially the same as (4.110).

The derivation of (4.105c) ((4.111)-(4.113)) clearly demonstrates that if the relative-clause origin of the predicate LF is adopted, the fact that the surface-structure predicate LF must be in the singular (when *vy* refers to a single individual) is wholly regular (i.e. predictable) and not at all anomalous: the predicate LF does NOT agree with the matrix subject ($[vy]_{NP1}$) in number, gender, person, or case, as traditional grammar claims it does, and, therefore, no anomaly in agreement occurs. The gender and number of the predicate LF (*krasivoj*) are received from the subject (NP_4 in (4.111)) of the relative clause by Subject-V Agreement (before Relative Clause Formation and Relative Clause Reduction). The predicate LF's case is received from the NP governed by *bud-* (NP_2), not from the matrix subject (NP_1). Only *bud-* agrees with *vy* by means of Subject-V Agreement in the matrix sentence (on the last cycle). There is no "subject-predicate nominal (cf. (4.108)) agreement" in Russian.

Thus our proposal that the SF is a deep-structure V and that the predicate LF is a deep-structure relative-clause, besides explaining a wide range of other phenomena (cf. Chapters 3 and 4), actually explains a syntactic phenomenon that has long perplexed Russian grammarians: *vy* IN EVERY GRAMMATICAL SENTENCE IN (4.102)-(4.106) AGREES WITH THE MAIN V OF THE MATRIX SENTENCE (*bud-* OR SF) IN THE PLURAL. In the present tense, the V *bud-* is realized phonetically as zero, so that this regularity in agreement is not manifest in sentences like (4.102b). The predicate nominals (predicate LF and predicate noun (4.106)) do not agree with *vy* in any sentence in (4.102)-(4.106). Accordingly, all the agreement phenomena in (4.102)-(4.106) are perfectly regular.

Our claim that the predicate LF in the above examples does not agree with *vy* in gender, person, number, or case has much wider implications. We are in effect claiming that THE PREDICATE LF (AND N) DOES NOT AGREE WITH THE SUBJECT OF THE SENTENCE NO MATTER WHAT IT IS. Traditional grammars state that a predicate LF agrees with the subject in gender, number, and case (Kubik, 1968:67). However, the fact that the predicate LF (and predicate N) may be in the instrumental shows that there is no agreement in case (cf. footnotes 1 and 2, Chapter 4, for examples). The above sentences with *vy* show that there is no agreement in gender and number. The following sentences show that there is also no subject agreement in gender, number, person, or case with predicate nouns.

(4.114a) *Ee doč' prelestnaja devuška.*
'Her daughter is a charming girl.'

(4.114b) *Ee doč' byla prelestnoj devuškoj.* (Case)
'Her daughter was a charming girl.'

(4.114c) *Ee doč' prelestnyj rebenok.* (Gender)
'Her daughter is a charming child.'

(4.114d) *Ee doč' prelestnoe suščestvo.* (Gender)
'Her daughter is a charming creature.'

(4.114e) *Lisy–zver' umnyj.* (Number)
'Foxes are a clever beast.'

(4.114f) *Studenty–narod veselyj.* (Number; cf. *Grammatika russkogo jazyka AN SSSR*, II, *č.* I, 516)
'Students are a gay people.'

There is no agreement transformation that copies the features of the subject onto a predicate nominal ([*bud-* — NP]$_{VP}$). What most Russian grammarians take for "agreement" is merely a high probability of COINCIDENCE in number, gender, and case. This fact was recognized by E. M. Galkina-Fedoruk (1958:187):

Imennaja časť skazuemogo ... možet sovpast' v rode, čisle i padeže s podležaščim, no možet i ne sovpast' ni v odnoj forme. Takoe sovpadenie nel'zja nazyvat' soglasovaniem, ...
[The nominal part of the predicate... may coincide in gender, number, and case with the subject, but it may also not agree in any form. *Such a coincidence cannot be called agreement*....]

4.5.4.4 The syntactic phenomena discussed in §4.5.4 once again makes it clear that Russian requires only two transformations in order to account for AGREEMENT (this same point was made in another context in §3.10.2): (a) Subject-V Agreement, which copies inherent syntactic features from the subject of a sentence onto the main V; (b) Case Marking, which copies a case feature from a NP onto every markable constituent of that NP. Speaking metaphorically, we can say that case features are never copied "horizontally" (by Subject-V Agreement); they are only copied "vertically" (by Case Marking (cf. 3.24)).

The agreement phenomena analyzed in §4.5.4 can be summarized by schematic diagrams (4.115) and (4.116).

The enclosed portion of (4.116) is deleted by transformations (Relative Clause Reduction, S-Node Deletion, and Antecedent Deletion).

The kind of agreement represented in (4.117) ("subject-predicate nominal agreement") is impossible in Russian.

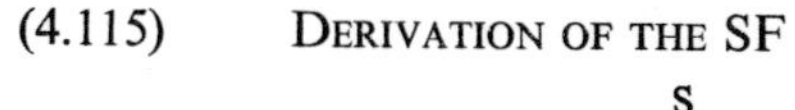

(4.115) DERIVATION OF THE SF

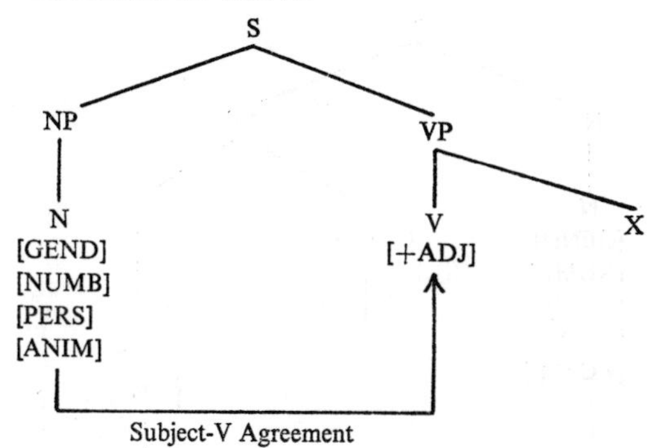

(4.116) DERIVATION OF THE PREDICATE LF

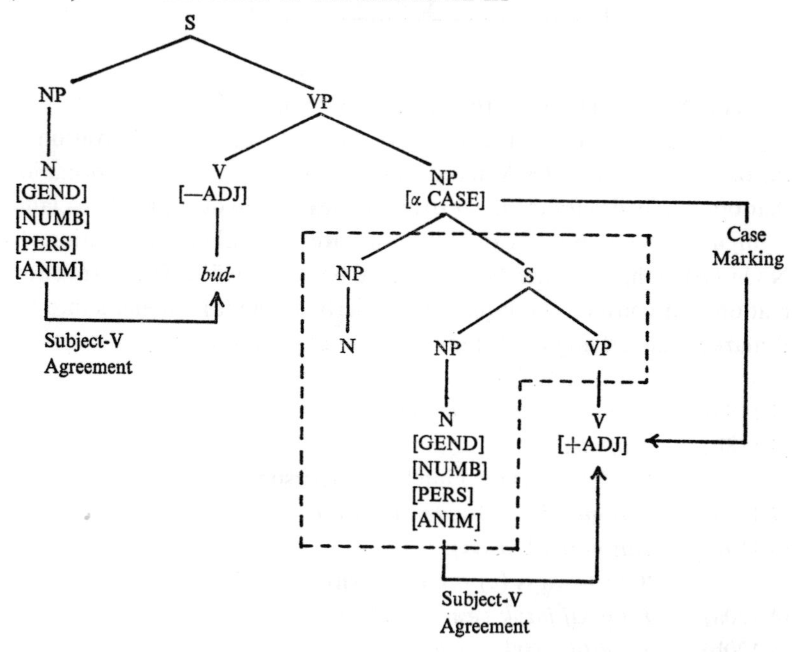

4.5.4.5 In §3.3.0 it was proposed that the surface-structure copula (*byl*, *budet*, etc.) derives from two distinct deep-structure sources (a tense-marker or a full verb (*bud-*)). In §3.3.1-§3.3.4 several syntactic phenomena supporting the dual origin of the copula were discussed. The insight our transformational grammar has provided into the agreement of *vy* with the SF and predicate LF may be offered as further evidence that our analysis of the copula in §3.3.0 is essentially correct.

(4.117)

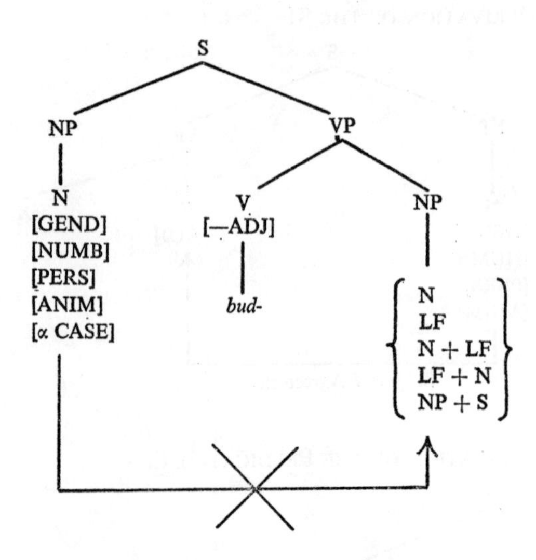

4.6 THE ANTECEDENT DELETION TRANSFORMATION.

4.6.1 The sequence of transformations employed in the derivation of the predicate LF includes Antecedent Deletion (cf. §3.9), a transformation that optionally deletes the deep-structure head noun of the relative-clause configuration (cf. NP_3 in (4.111)) after Relative Clause Reduction, S-Node Deletion, and Case Marking have been applied. It is this transformation that converts the P-markers underlying the (a) sentences into the P-markers underlying the (b) sentences in (4.118)-(4.120).

(4.118a) *Moj otec čelovek umnyj.*
(4.118b) *Moj otec umnyj.*
'My father is (an) intelligent (person).'
(4.119a) *Naš gorod (est') gorod krasivyj.*
(4.119b) *Naš gorod krasivyj.*
'Our town is (a) pretty (town).'
(4.120a) *Kitajskij jazyk (est') jazyk trudnyj.*
(4.120b) *Kitajskij jazyk trudnyj.*
'The Chinese language is (a) difficult (language).'

The other transformations involved in the derivation of the predicate LF (Relative Clause Formation, Relative Clause Reduction, S-Node Deletion, and Case Marking) have been widely discussed in recent literature on transformational grammar and are fairly well understood. Antecedent Deletion, however, has not, to the best of my knowledge, ever been discussed in the literature. I will therefore devote §4.6 to this transformation. Antecedent Deletion must occupy a central position in the syntax of Russian adjectives because it provides us with the formal mechanism for blocking the derivation of sentences containing a predicate LF with a complement (cf. (4.1), (4.7), (4.8)).

4.6.2 The deep structure of (4.29), *On byl bezžalostnym* 'He was (a) pitiless (man)', is (4.32) (cf. Peškovskij, 1938:226). Subject-V Agreement (first cycle), Relative Clause Formation ($[$*čelovek*$]_{NP4}$ → *kotoryj*), Relative Clause Reduction (*kotoryj* + Tns → Ø), S-Node Deletion, Case Marking, and Subject-V Agreement (second cycle, between *on* and *bud-*) map (4.32) into the derived P-marker (4.121).

(4.121)

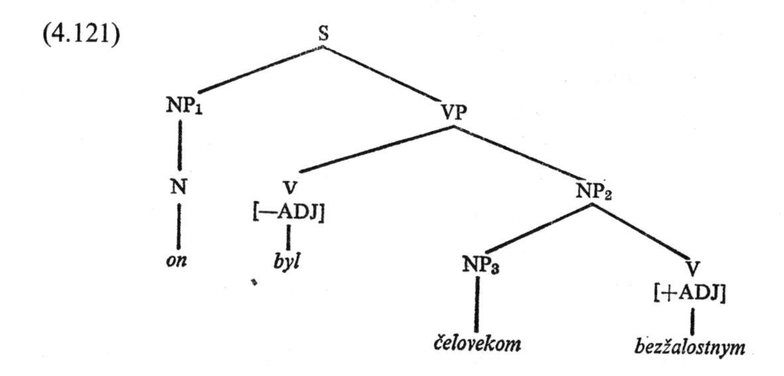

Note that (4.121) is the final derived P-marker of (4.122).

(4.122) *On byl čelovekom bezžalostnym.*
'He was a pitiless man.'

However, the optional transformation of Antecedent Deletion may operate on P-marker (4.121), producing (4.33), the final derived P-marker of (4.29), by deleting $[$*čelovekom*$]_{NP3}$.

As was noted in §4.3.3.1, head nouns like *čelovek* are so easily deleted that Russian grammarians feel that they are not head nouns modified by adjectives, but "connectives" or "copulas" that join the subject to a predicate LF. If the head noun is not a generic noun like *čelovek, ženščina*, etc., but is identical to the matrix subject (cf. (4.31), the deep structure of *Éti doma novye*), then its deletion seems to be even more frequent. In other words, Antecedent Deletion will operate if the head noun of the predicate relative clause is easily recoverable (cf. §4.3.3.1). Accordingly, Antecedent Deletion will not operate on a sentence like *Moj otec soldat xrabryj* 'My father is a brave soldier' to produce a sentence like *Moj otec xrabryj* 'My father is (a) brave (soldier)' unless the immediate context permits the easy recoverability of *soldat*. Details of the operation of Antecedent Deletion in sentences like this have not yet been elaborated.

4.6.3 Notice, however, that the rule of Antecedent Deletion must not be allowed to operate freely, since there would be nothing to prevent this transformation from converting the P-markers underlying the (a) sentences in (4.123)-(4.124) into the P-markers underlying the ungrammatical (b) sentences.

(4.123a) *On* čelovek *dostojnyj velikoj ljubvi.*
'He is a *man* worthy of great love.'

(4.123b) **On dostojnyj velikoj ljubvi.*

(4.123c) *On* dostoin *velikoj ljubvi.*

(4.124a) *Nado pomnit', čto Glinka byl* čelovekom *očen* dalekim ot *voprosov izobretatel'stva i texniki.*
'One must remember that Glinka was a man very far from questions of invention and technology.' (N. E. Kočin)

(4.124b) **Nado pomnit', čto Glinka byl očen* dalekim ot *voprosov izobretatel'stva i texniki.*

(4.124c) *Glinka byl očen* dalek ot *voprosov....* (cf. §3.3.3)

Sentence pairs like (4.123) and (4.124) illustrate that the unconstrained operation of Antecedent Deletion will freely derive ungrammatical sentences containing predicate LFs with complements.

Antecedent Deletion can be prevented from producing surface structures containing a predicate LF with a complement by providing the rule with a condition stipulating that the head noun cannot be deleted if the deep structure $\underset{[+ADJ]}{V}$ is TRANSITIVE ($\underset{[+ADJ]}{V} + \begin{Bmatrix} NP \\ PP \end{Bmatrix}$).[26] This condition or constraint can be built right into the SC of Antecedent Deletion.

[26] This constraint does not operate in substandard Russian, where sentences like *On byl nedovol'nyj svoim vystupleniem* 'He was dissatisfied with his speech' are possible (cf. V. A. Livšic, 1964: 83); in literary and colloquial Russian only *On byl nedovolen svoim vystupleniem* is possible. Further discussion on the behavior of the SF and predicate LF in non-literary codes of Russian can be found in I. V. Tolstoj, 1966, and G. F. Mjasnikov, 1958.

In §3.8.6.3 we introduced a constraint that strongly resembles the one just mentioned in §4.6.3. In both instances a transformation does or does not operate on a NP (deletes it in §4.6.3, "raises" it in §3.8.6.3) depending specifically on whether the $\underset{[+ADJ]}{V}$ is TRANSITIVE. It is still too early to tell whether these two constraints are realizations of the same more general constraint or not.

We need only specify that $\underset{[+\mathrm{ADJ}]}{\mathrm{V}}$ is the last constituent of the VP of the deep-structure relative clause. Accordingly, the derived configuration permitting Antecedent Deletion may be schematically represented by (4.125).

(4.125)

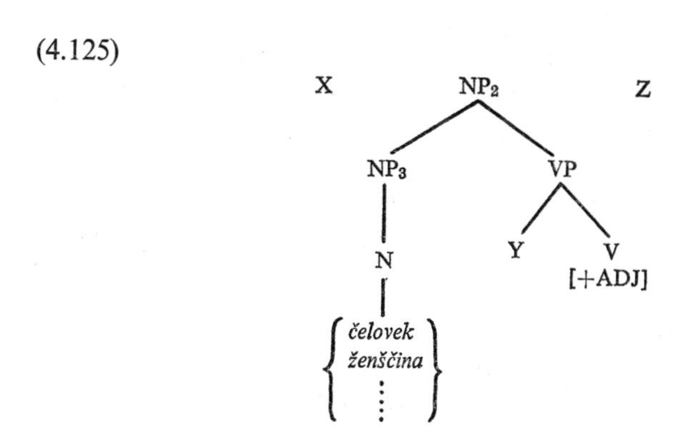

Anything to the right of $\underset{[+\mathrm{ADJ}]}{\mathrm{V}}$ dominated by the VP will prevent the P-marker from meeting the SC for Antecedent Deletion. (4.126) is the schematic representation of a derived configuration that will NOT meet the SD of Antecedent Deletion.[27]

(4.126)

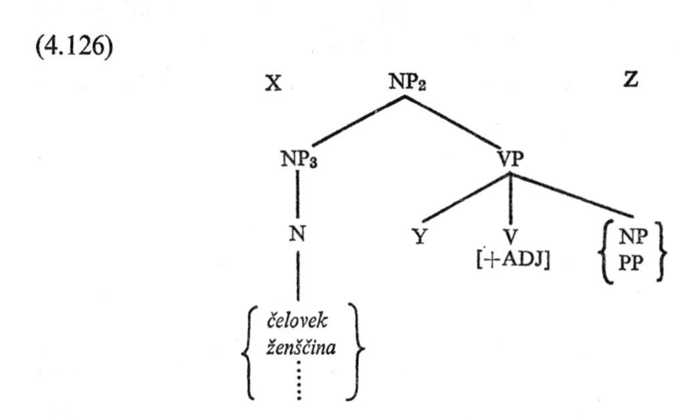

Thus in the derivation of (4.29) (Antecedent Deletion was able to apply because the derived P-marker (4.121) meets the SD given in (4.125): *bezžalostnym* is the last constituent in the VP. (4.125) will prevent the

[27] G. Lakoff (1965: A-13) utilizes a similar constraint on the SD of the Modifier Shift transformation in English.

derivation of the (b) sentences in (4.123) and (4.124) because the derived P-markers on which Antecedent Deletion should operate contain configurations like the one in (4.126).[28]

The constraint represented in (4.125) enables our grammar to explain quite naturally why adjectives like *gotov-* 'ready' and *nameren-* 'intend', which allow Relative Clause Reduction, do not normally have predicate LFs: JUST THOSE ADJECTIVES THAT ARE STRONGLY TRANSITIVE (i.e. do not permit Object Deletion) WILL NOT MEET THE SD OF ANTECEDENT DELETION, since the complement will be present when Antecedent Deletion applies (cf. (4.125)).

4.6.4 Having established the need for the constraint introduced in §4.6.3, we may proceed to a first approximation of the Antecedent Deletion transformation:

(4.127) ANTECEDENT DELETION.

SD: X [*bud-* [N [$Y_{\overset{V}{[+ADJ]}}$]$_{VP}$]$_{NP}$]$_{VP}$ Z optional

	1	2	3	4	5	6 ⇒
SC:	1	2	Ø	4	5	6

CONDITION: term 3 is easily recoverable (cf. §4.3.3).

P-marker (4.121) meets the SD of (4.127), producing (4.29), *On byl bezžalostnym*. The P-marker underlying (4.123a) does NOT meet the SD of rule (4.127) (*dostojnyj* is not the last constituent of the deeper VP, its complement [*velikoj ljubvi*]$_{NP}$ is) and, consequently, the ungrammaticality of (4.123b) is accounted for as a violation of (4.127) (cf. (4.126)).

4.6.5 A MORE GENERAL VERSION OF ANTECEDENT DELETION. As it stands, (4.127) is a rather specialized rule, since it requires that Antecedent Deletion operate only on structures dominated by a higher VP, i.e. it stipulates that the antecedent of a reduced relative clause may be deleted only if the relative clause is a predicate nominal (cf. (4.108)). However,

[28] In §2.12 it was pointed out that the LF is the "active participle" of the SF, i.e. active participles and LFs are surface-structure categories derived by the same transformations from underlying Vs ($\overset{V}{[-ADJ]}$ and $\overset{V}{[+ADJ]}$). Active participles and LFs therefore display the same syntactic behavior; and this holds true for the predicate LF as well. This explains Peškovskij's observation (1938: 223) that *On byl znajuščij* 'He was knowing' is grammatical, while **On byl znajuščij èto* '*He was knowing this' is not. The latter sentence is ungrammatical for the same reason that (4.123b) and (4.124b) are: they violate the constraint given in (4.125).

Note that it is only the assumption of a deep-structure relative clause underlying the predicate LF that allows us to relate these syntactic phenomena.

an antecedent may be deleted even if its (reduced) relative clause is not a predicate nominal. In all the following sentences the LFs (adjectives and active participles) are derived from deep-structure relative clause configurations that are subjects ($[[NP — S]_{NP}\ VP]_S$) or objects ($[NP — [V — [NP — S]_{NP}]_{VP}]_S$) of the matrix sentence.

(4.128a) {*Te* / *Ljudi*}, *kotorye* sčastlivy, *ne nabljudajut vremja.*

(4.128b) Sčastlivye *ne nabljudajut vremja.*
'{People / Those} who are *happy* do not watch the time.'

(4.129) Smelye *ne bojatsja opasnosti.*
'Those who are *brave* do not fear danger.'

(4.130a) *To, čto* prekrasno, *ne umiraet.*
'That which (= what) is *beautiful* does not die.'

(4.130b) Prekrasnoe *ne umiraet.*
'The *beautiful* does not die.'

(4.131) Progressivnoe *toržestvuet nad* ustarevšim.
'The *progressive* triumphs over the *obsolete.*'

(4.132a) *To, čto ja pročital, nadolgo soxranilos' v moej pamjati.*
'What I have read was kept in my memory for a long time.'

(4.132b) Pročitannoe *mnoju nadolgo soxranilos' v moej pamjati.* (cf. Kubik, 1968:123)

(4.133a) *Tem, kto želaet bolee osnovatel'no poznakomit'sja s ètim voprosom, prednaznačen naučnyj doklad.*
'The scientific report is intended for one who wishes to acquaint himself more thoroughly with this question.'

(4.133b) Želajuščim *bolee osnovatel'no poznakomit'sja s ètim voprosom prednaznačen naučnyj doklad.*

(4.134) *Partija nikomu ne daet uspokaivat'sja na* dostignutom.
'The party does not let anyone rest content with what has been achieved.'

(4.135a) *Narjadu s vzgljadom, kotoryj izložen zdes', est' i dva inyx vzgljada.*
'Along with the view which is set forth here there are two other views.'

(4.135b) *Narjadu s* izložennym *zdes' est' i dva inyx vzgljada.* (Peškovskij, 1938:249)

(4.136) *A mne kto-to skazal, čto nado pojti na to mesto, gde čto-to zabyto, i togda možno vspomnit' èto* zabytoe.

'But someone told me you must go to the place where something was forgotten and then you can remember what was forgotten.' (Zoščenko)

(4.137) *On možet... ne imet' v vidu vosproizvedenija uže* govorivšegosja.
'He may not... have in mind the reproduction of what has already been said.'

Dostignutom in (4.134) is derived from a deep-structure relative-clause configuration that is the "object of a preposition" ($[P - [NP - S]_{NP}]_{PP}$).

Sentences (4.128)-(4.137) demonstrate that the sequence of transformations employed in the derivation of the predicate LF (Relative Clause Reduction, S-Node Deletion, Case Marking, and Antecedent Deletion) has a much broader function in a transformational grammar of Russian; it is precisely this sequence of transformations that is involved in the process known in traditional Russian grammar as the "substantivization of adjectives (and participles)".[29] Thus THE SUBSTANTIVIZED ADJECTIVES (AND PARTICIPLES) IN (4.128)-(4.137) AND THE PREDICATE LF ARE BOTH MERELY HEADLESS REDUCED RELATIVE CLAUSES (cf. §4.3.2.2, where it is pointed out that not all substantivized adjectives are headless reduced relative clauses).

If the rule of Antecedent Deletion as stated in (4.127) is retained, another rule almost identical to (4.127) must be posited to account for sentences like those in (4.128)-(4.137). But one of the main advantages of of deriving the predicate LF from an underlying relative clause is that the "attributive adjective" (cf. §2.12) is derived in the same way, i.e. no new transformations were required. It therefore is quite natural that Antecedent Deletion, too, not be a rule restricted to the derivation of only the predicate LF, but that it be general enough to account for any headless LF derived from a relative-clause configuration. A single Antecedent Deletion transformation permits us to capture an important generalization that (4.127) fails to capture: LFs that are derived from underlying

[29] Words like *stolovaja* 'dining room', *nasekomoe* 'insect', *soglasnyj* 'consonant', and even *prójdennoe* 'school material that has already been covered' (cf. *Slovar' russkogo jazyka AN SSSR*, 1959) must be considered NOUNS (N) in the lexicon of modern Russian. A "substantivized" adjective (*smelye* 'the brave') or participle (*govorivšijsja, pročitannoe*) is DERIVED by rules of the syntactic component from a deep-structure V ($\overset{V}{[+ADJ]}$ or $\overset{V}{[-ADJ]}$) and, consequently, is NOT dominated by a N. Since a LF in modern Russian invariably has acquired a case feature, a substantivized adjective is always dominated by a NP.

relative clauses[30] are all derived by the same set of transformations, without regard to what dominates the upper NP (NP_X) in the relative-clause configuration ($[NP_Y — S]_{NPX}$). In other words, a "predicate LF" (cf. (4.116)) is derived by the same sequence of transformations that is employed in the derivation of the "subject LF" (cf. (4.138); (4.129)) and the "object LF" (cf. (4.139): *Sytyj golodnogo ne razumeet* 'The full do not understand the hungry').

(4.138) "SUBJECT LF"

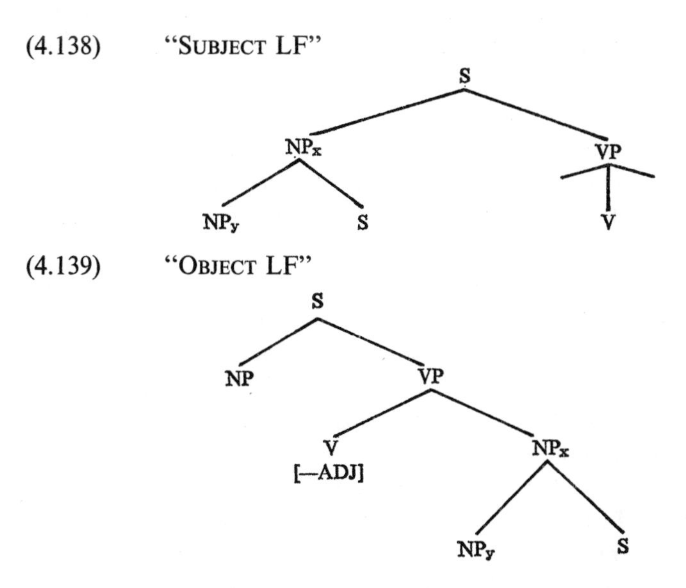

(4.139) "OBJECT LF"

It is only the LF's SYNTACTIC FUNCTION that is determined by NP_X's position in the deep structure P-marker.

Thus (4.140) is the more general form of the rule of Antecedent Deletion.

(4.140) ANTECEDENT DELETION

$$\text{SD: } X — [N — [Y — \underset{[+ADJ]}{V}]_{VP}]_{NP} — Z$$

optional

$$\begin{array}{lccccc} & 1 & 2 & 3 & 4 & 5 \Rightarrow \\ \text{SC:} & 1 & \varnothing & 3 & 4 & 5 \end{array}$$

CONDITION: term 2 is easily recoverable.

[30] Recall that Chapter 3 was devoted to a syntactic analysis of surface-structure LFs derived from deep-structure $\underset{[+ADJ]}{V}$ s that were NOT the main Vs of relative clauses: *pravymi in* (3.2), *Oni sčitali sebja pravymi*, does not derive from the predicate of an underlying relative clause.

The Antecedent Deletion transformation is obligatory when the antecedent of the reduced relative clause is the pronoun *tot*.

(4.141a) *Partija nikomu ne daet uspokaivat'sja na* [*tom, čto dostignuto*]$_{NP}$.
'The party does not let anyone rest content with what has been achieved.'

(4.141b) **Partija nikomu ne daet uspokaivat'sja na* [*tom dostignutom*]$_{NP}$.

(4.141c) *Partija nikomu ne daet uspokaivat'sja na* [*dostignutom*]$_{NP}$.

Note that (4.140) is contained in (4.127): to account for the sentences in (4.128)-(4.137) we have merely removed the restriction that a higher VP must be mentioned in the rule's SD. (4.140) will perform the same operation as (4.127), but it is not restricted by anything outside the relative-clause configuration.

4.6.6 ANTECEDENT DELETION IN ENGLISH. The demonstration that Antecedent Deletion's function is not exclusively to derive predicate LFs may serve as evidence that it is not an ad hoc transformation. The assumption that Antecedent Deletion is not ad hoc is further strengthened by the fact that what is essentially the same transformation has been posited for English by Z. Vendler (1967:56).

Vendler claims that the definitite article THE always presupposes a restrictive clause. In order to explain a sentence like *None but the brave deserves the fair*, Vendler suggests the paraphrase *None but the* [*man who is*] *brave deserves the* [*woman who is*] *fair*. This derivation, according to Vendler, follows the "deletion pattern" *the N wh... is A* → *the A*. Vendler's "deletion pattern" deletes an entire "redundant clause" by one transformation. We have accomplished the same thing with TWO transformations (Relative Clause Reduction and Antecedent Deletion) in order to account for intermediate structures. Vendler, who does not operate with the notion of underlying structures and surface structures, is not concerned with these intermediate structures. What is important, however, is the fact that English needs a transformation (or transformations) that deletes the antecedent of a reduced relative clause and that this antecedent must be "redundant" and "easily recoverable". The fact that a transformation equivalent to the Russian rule of Antecedent Deletion is needed in a language other that Russian must be considered evidence that some version of Antecedent Deletion is a candidate for inclusion among the set of language-independent transformations.

SUMMARY OF CHAPTER 4.

All the arguments presented in Chapter 4 taken together constitute very strong evidence that the predicate LF is derived from a deep-structure relative-clause configuration and, therefore, is derived from a deep-structure $\underset{[+ADJ]}{V}$ which has undergone Subject-V Agreement (as main V of the relative clause) and Case Marking after introduction into the constituency of the relative-clause configuration's upper NP (NP_X in $[NP_Y$ — — $S]_{NP_X}$) as the result of Relative Clause Reduction and S-Node Deletion. Thus Chapter 4 has provided us with further evidence that the LF is basically a SF ($\underset{[+ADJ]}{V}$ + Subject-V Agreement only) that has acquired a case feature.

APPENDIX

TRANSFORMATIONAL RULES

ANTECEDENT DELETION.

$X — [N — [Y — \underset{[+ADJ]}{V} \quad]_{VP}]_{NP} — Z$

optional

SD: 1 2 3 4 5 ⇒

SC: 1 Ø 3 4 5

CONDITION: term 2 is easily recoverable.

byt'-DELETION.

$X — [V —$ *byt'* $— Y]_{VP} — Z$

SD: 1 2 3 4 5 ⇒

obligatory

SC: 1 2 Ø 4 5

CONDITION: 2 is marked for *byt'*-Deletion.

CASE MARKING.

$[X — Y — Z — [CASE_j]]_{NP_i}$

obligatory

SD: 1 2 3 4 ⇒

SC: 1 2 3 4

$[CASE_j]$

CONDITION: it is not the case that $NP_i > S_k$ and $S_k > Y$.

EQUI-NP DELETION.

$X — [NP — Y]_S — Z$

obligatory

SD: 1 2 3 4 ⇒

SC: 1 Ø 3 4

CONDITION: 2 is identical to the nearest NP in the S being processed.

EXTRAPOSITION.

$X — [S]_{NP} — VP — Y$

optional

SD:	1	2	3	4	⇒
SC:	1	Ø	3+2	4	

CONDITION: 2 and 3 are in the same simple S.

INFINITIVE FORMATION.

$X — [Tns — V — Y]_{VP} — Z$

obligatory

SD:	1	2	3	4	5	⇒
SC:	1	Ø	3 [infin]	4	5	

CONDITION: 2 is in the same simple S as a higher tense-marker (tns).

MODIFIER SHIFT.

$X — [(DET) — N — VP]_{NP} — Y$

optional

SD:	1	2	3	4	5	⇒
SC:	1	2 4	3	Ø	5	

CONDITION: 3 is not a pronoun.

OBLIGATORY INSTRUMENTAL RULE.

X — [*byt'* — V [+ADJ] [αCASE] — $Y]_{NPi}$ — Z

obligatory

SD:	1	2	3	4	5	⇒
SC:	1	2	3 [+INST]	4	5	

CONDITION: term 3 is a constituent of NP_i.

PREPOSITION DELETION.

$X — [P — S]_{PP} — Y$

obligatory

SD:	1	2	3	4	⇒
SC:	1	Ø	3	4	

REFLEXIVIZATION.

X — NP — Y — NP — Z

obligatory

SD: 1 2 3 4 5 ⇒

SC: 1 2 3 4 5

[reflex]

CONDITION: (a) 2 = 4 and (b) 2 and 4 are in the same simple S.

RELATIVE CLAUSE FORMATION.

W — [NP — [X — NP — Y]$_S$]$_{NP}$ — Z

obligatory

SD: 1 2 3 4 5 6 ⇒

SC: 1 2 4 3 Ø 5 6

[*kotor-*]

CONDITION: 2 = 4

RELATIVE CLAUSE REDUCTION.

X — [NP — [NP — Tns — Y]$_S$]$_{NP}$ — Z

[*kotor-*]

optional

SD: 1 2 3 4 5 ⇒

SC: 1 2 Ø 4 5

SUBJECT RAISING.

X — [NP_2 — VP_2]$_{NP_1}$ — Y — VP_1 — Z

optional

SD: 1 2 3 4 5 6 ⇒

SC: (a) adjoin 2 to the node dominating NP_1.

(b) adjoin 3 to the end of 5.

CONDITION: VP_1 and NP_1 are in the same simple sentence.

SUBJECT-V AGREEMENT.

X — NP — V — Y

obligatory

SD: 1 2 3 4 ⇒

[NUMB]
[GEND]
[PERS]

SC: 1 2 3 4

[NUMB]
[GEND]
[PERS]

BIBLIOGRAPHY

Babby, L. [1973] "The Deep Structure of Adjectives and Participles in Russian", *Language* 49.

Bach, E. [1965] "On Some Recurrent Types of Transformations", *Report to the Sixteenth Annual Round Table Meeting on Linguistics and Language Studies* (= *Monograph Series on Languages and Linguistics* 18), 3-18.

Bauer, J., R. Mrázek, and S. Žaža [1966] *Príruční Mluvnice Ruštiny Pro Čechy*, II (Skladba) (Praha).

Belevickaja-Xalizeva, V. S., et al., *Sbornik upražnenij po sintaksisu russkogo jazyka: složnoe predloženie* (Moskva).

Boguslavskij, A. [1964] "O kratkix i polnyx formax prilagatel'nogo v skazuemom", *Russkij jazyk v škole* 1, 14-19.

Bolinger D. [1967] "Adjectives in English: Attribution and Predication", *Lingua* 18: 1, 1-34.

Bowers, J. [to appear] *Grammatical Relations*, M.I.T. Press (Cambridge, Mass.).

Brecht, R. [1972] "Problems of Deixis and Hypotaxis: Towards a Theory of Complementation", Unpublished doctoral dissertation, Harvard (Cambridge, Mass.).

——, [to appear] "Deictic Reference".

Bulaxovskij, L. A. [1949] *Kurs russkogo literaturnogo jazyka* (Kiev).

Buslaev, F. I. [1868] *Istoričeskaja grammatika russkogo jazyka* (Moskva).

Channon, R. [1968] "On Passivization in Russian", *Studies Presented to Professor Roman Jokobson* (ed. C. Gribble) (Cambridge, Mass.).

Chomsky, N. [1965] *Aspects of the Theory of Syntax* (Cambridge, Mass.).

Chvany, C. [1970] "Deep Structures with *Dolžen* and *Moč*", unpublished doctoral dissertation, Harvard (Cambridge, Mass.).

——, [to appear] *On the Syntax of be-Sentences in Russian* (Preliminary version of forthcoming monograph).

Dmitriev, B. A. [1964] "K voprosu o složom skazuemom", *Russkij jazyk v škole* 2, 10-15.

Dobromyslov, V. A. and D. È. Rozental', [1960] *Trudnye voprosy grammatiki i pravopisanija* (Moskva).

Dudnikov, A. V. [1958] *Punktuacija složnogo predloženija* (Moskva).

Emonds, J. [1970] "Root and Structure-Preserving Transformations", M.I.T. dissertation, reproduced by the Indiana University Linguistics Club.

Evseeva, L. P. [1964] "Upravlenie pri imenax prilagatel'nyx v zavisimosti ot ix roli v predloženii", *Russkij jazyk v škole* 2, 6-10.

Galkina-Fedoruk, E. M. (ed.) [1957] *Sovremennyj russkij jazyk–Sintaksis* (Moskva).

——, (ed.) [1964] *Sovremennyj russkij jazyk* II (Moskva).

Georgieva, V. L. [1968] *Istorija sintaksičeskix javlenij russkogo jazyka* (Moskva).

Grammatika russkogo jazyka AN SSSR (V. V. Vinogradov, ed.) [1960] (Moskva).

Gvozdev, A. N. [1961] *Sovremennyj literaturnyj russkij jazyk* II (Sintaksis) (Moskva).

——, [1955] *Očerki po stilistike russkogo jazyka* (Moskva).

Ickovič, V. A. [1968] *Jazykovaja norma* (Moskva).

Isačenko, A. V. [1963] "Transformacionnyj analiz kratkix i polnyx prilagatel'nyx", *Issledovanija po strukturnoj tipologii*, (Moskva) 61-93.

——, [1965] *Grammatičeskij stroj russkogo jazyka v sopostavlenii s slovackim* I (Bratislava).

Izrailevič, E. E. and K. N. Kačalova, [1955] *Praktičeskaja grammatika anglijskogo jazyka* (Moskva).

Jakobson, R. [1948] "Russian Conjugation", *Word*, 155-167.

——, [1957] *Shifters, Verbal Categories, and the Russian Verb* (Russian Language Project, Department of Slavic Languages and Literatures, Harvard University).

Jakubinskij, L. P. [1953] *Istorija drevnerusskogo jazyka* (Moskva).

Jespersen, O. [1958] *The Philosophy of Grammar* (London).

Judina, L. P., G. A. Bitextina and I. P. Slesareva, [1966] *Upražnenija na upotreblenie kratkoj i polnoj formy prilagatel'nyx* (Moskva).

Kamynina, A. A. [1958] "Upotreblenie vtorogo imenitel'nogo imen suščestvitel'nyx v sovremennom russkom jazyke", *Russkij jazyk v škole* 2, 23-28.

Kiparsky, P. and C. Kiparsky, [1968] "Fact", to appear in Bierwisch and Heidolph (eds.), *Recent Advances in Linguistics* (Mouton).

Kržižkova, E. [1968] "Predikativnaja funkcija prilagatel'nyx i suščestvitel'nyx i struktura predloženija", *Československá Rusistika* 4, 210-219.

Kubik, M., et al. [1968] *Lekcii po sintaksisu russkogo jazyka* (Praha).

Kudrjavceva, I. A. [1967] "Imennoe sostavnoe skazuemoe v sovremennom russkom jazyke", *Učenye zapiski MGPI imeni Lenina* 264, 129-141.

Lakoff, G. [1965] *On the Nature of Syntactic Irregularity* (= *Report No. NSF-16 to the National Science Foundation, The Computation Laboratory, Harvard University*) (Cambridge, Mass.).

—— [1966] "Stative Adjectives and Verbs in English" in *Mathematical Linguistics and Automatic Translation* (= *Report No. NSF-17 to the National Science Foundation, the Computation Laboratory, Harvard University*) (Cambridge, Mas.).

Livšic, V. A. [1964] *Praktičeskaja stilistika russkogo jazyka* (Moskva).

Lunt, H. G. [1959] *Old Church Slavonic Grammar* (The Hague).

Lyons, J. [1968] *Introduction to Theoretical Linguistics* (Cambridge).

Maksimov, L. Ju. [1957] "Častica 'ne' i pristavka 'ne' s kratkimi prilagatel'nymi", *Russkij jazyk v škole* 2, 7-17.

Meščaninov, I. I. [1945] *Členy predloženija i časti reči* (Moskva-Leningrad).

Mjasnikov, G. F. [1958] "Stilističeskoe ispol'zovanie kratkix i polnyx prilagatel'nyx v sostave skazuemogo", *Russkij jazyk v kšole* 1, 12-15.

Ovsjaniko-Kulikovskij, D. N. [1912] *Sintaksis russkogo jazyka* (S.-Petersburg).

Panov, B. T. [1967] *Rabota po stilistike pri izučenii sintaksisa* (Moskva).

Papp, F. (ed.) [1968] *Kurs sovremennogo russkogo jazyka.* (Budapest).

Pavlov, V. M. [1960] "O razrjadax imen prilagatel'nyx v russkom jazyke", *Voprosy jazykoznaija* 2, 65-70.

Peškovskij, A. M. [1938] *Russkij sintaksis v naučnom osveščenii* (Moskva).

Rosenbaum, P. [1967] *The Grammar of English Predicate Complement Constructions* (Cambridge, Mass.).

Ross, J. [1967] "Constraints on Variables in Syntax", unpublished doctoral dissertation, MIT (Cambridge, Mass.).

Ross, J. [1969] "A Proposed Rule of Tree-Pruning", in D. Reibel and S. Schane (eds.), *Modern Studies in English (Readings in Transformational Grammar)* (Englewood Cliffs, New Jersey), 288-299.

——, [1969] "Adjectives as Noun Phrases", in D. Reibel and S. Schane (eds), *Modern Studies in English* (= *Readings in Transformational Grammar*) (Englewood Cliffs, New Jersey), 352-360.

Rothstein, R. [1966] "Predicate Complementation in Contemporary Polish", unpublished doctoral dissertation, Harvard University (Cambridge, Mass).

——, [1970] "Reflexive 'Reflexive Verbs' in Polish", *SEEJ* 2

Rozental', D. È. [1965] *Praktičeskaja stilistika russkogo jazyka* (Moskva).

——, [1967] *Spravočnik po pravopisaniju i literaturnoj pravke* (Moskva)

Slovar' russkogo jazyka AN SSSR (in four volumes) [1957-1961] (Moskva).

Smirnickij, A. I. [1956] *Leksikologija anglijskogo jazyka.* (Moskva).

——, [1957] *Sintaksis anglijskogo jazyka* (Moskva).

Sprinčak, Ja. A. [1960] *Očerk russkogo istoričeskogo sintaksisa (prostoe predloženie)* (Kiev).

Šaxmatov, A. A. [1941] *Sintaksis russkogo jazyka* (Leningrad).

Švedova, N. Ju. [1952] "Polnye i kratkie formy imen prilagatel'nyx v sostave skazuemogo v sovremennom russkom literaturnom jazyke", *Učenye zapiski MGU* 150, Russkij jazyk, 73-132.

Tolstoj, I. V. [1966] "Leksiko-grammatičeskie i stilističeskie osobennosti polnyx i kratkix prilagatel'nyx v funkcii imennogo sostavnogo skazuemogo", in V. P. Vomperskij (ed.) *Voprosy stilistiki* (Moskva).

Ušakov, D. N. (ed) [1935-1940] *Tolkovyj slovar' russkogo jazyka* (Moskva).

Vendler, Z. [1967] *Linguistics in Philosophy* (Ithaca, New York).

Vinogradov, V. V. [1938] *Sovremennyj russkij jazyk* II (Moskva).

——, [1947] *Russkij jazyk* (Moskva-Leningrad).

—— and N. Ju. Švedova, (eds.) [1964] *Očerki po istoričeskoj grammatike russkogo literaturnogo jazyka XIX veka*, III: *Izmenenija v sisteme prostogo i osložnennogo predloženija v russkom literaturnom jazyke XIX veka* (Moskva).

Zaliznjak, A A [1967] *Russkoe imennoe slovoizmenenie* (Moskva).

INDEX